MANAGING
CONFLICT
AT WORK

MANAGING CONFLICT AT WORK

UNDERSTANDING AND RESOLVING CONFLICT FOR PRODUCTIVE WORKING RELATIONSHIPS

CLIVE JOHNSON & JACKIE KEDDY

KoganPage

LONDON PHILADELPHIA NEW DELHI

Publisher's note

Every possible effort has been made to ensure that the information contained in this book is accurate at the time of going to press, and the publishers and authors cannot accept responsibility for any errors or omissions, however caused. No responsibility for loss or damage occasioned to any person acting, or refraining from action, as a result of the material in this publication can be accepted by the editor, the publisher or any of the authors.

First published in Great Britain and the United States in 2010 by Kogan Page Limited

120 Pentonville Road	525 South 4th Street, #241	4737/23 Ansari Road
London N1 9JN	Philadelphia PA 19147	Daryaganj
United Kingdom	USA	New Delhi 110002
www.koganpage.com		India

ISBN   978 0 7494 5952 9
E-ISBN   978 0 7494 5953 6

British Library Cataloguing-in-Publication Data

A CIP record for this book is available from the British Library.

Library of Congress Cataloging-in-Publication Data

Johnson, Clive, 1962-
    Managing conflict at work : understanding and resolving conflict for productive working relationships / Clive Johnson, Jackie Keddy.
        p. cm.
    Includes bibliographical references and index.
    ISBN 978-0-7494-5952-9 -- ISBN 978-0-7494-5953-6 (ebook) 1. Conflict management. 2. Interpersonal communication. 3. Interpersonal relations. 4. Conflict management--Case studies. I. Keddy, Jackie II. Title.
    HD42.J643 2010
    658.4'053--dc22

2010014011

Typeset by Jean Cussons Typesetting Ltd, Diss, Norfolk
Printed and bound in India by Replika Press Pvt Ltd

Contents

Acknowledgements

Working on this book has been a pleasure and an education thanks to the warm support, wise words and keen observation of a host of wonderful people. My special thanks are due to the fine team at Kogan Page, to David and Sue – the most exceptional hosts at Hale Farm, my regular retreat for research, reflecting and writing – and of course to my inspiring and ever-encouraging co-writer, business partner and dear friend, Jackie. Never a cross word has been shared between us.

Clive Johnson

It has been an absolute joy working on this book, a wonderful creative journey that has touched my heart. Many thanks to the switched-on crew at Kogan Page, Hannah for her faith, and as always to my Denis for his never-ending love and support. Our thanks to Chris Hanney for his contribution to 'RESOLVE'. A special thanks to Denisé and Adam and my fantastic, gorgeous family, of whom I'm so very proud. To Adriana and Sitka, my lovely friends. To Liz and Mags for all their encouragement, and without a doubt to Clive, my co-writer, dear friend, business partner and ally (my complete dichotomy opposite and with truly never a cross word between us!).

Jackie Keddy

Praise for *Managing Conflict at Work*

"This new book embodies a grounded and practice-rich perspective on workplace conflict. It deploys an excellent set of practical tools and techniques, surveys the theories and main schools of thought, and leaves the reader feeling enriched and engaged with this often prickly subject. With an abundance of useful models and metaphors Johnson and Keddy bring the world of workplace conflict management alive for every audience. Overall an excellent treatment of a subject all too readily sensationalized or written from a victim perspective. This grown up grounded approach will help all practitioners in the field."
Dr John McGurk, Adviser: Learning and Talent Development, HR: Practice Development Team, Chartered Institute of Personnel and Development

"This book 'gets it' – it articulates basic truths and insights into human nature and behaviour which those involved in workplace disputes have observed all too often. Best of all, it is full of practical ideas and 'top tips' on how to nip problems in the bud and explains how communication and mediation can resolve seemingly intractable problems. My only worry is that the authors will put employment lawyers out of business!"
Gary Freer, Partner in Employment Law, McGrigors LLP

"This useful book draws together the most current thinking in communication and provides straightforward models for those dealing with complex and difficult negotiations."
Richard Mullender, Communications Trainer and former Hostage Negotiator with the Metropolitan Police

"The authors make the claim that they intend to cover a lot of ground – and they do. What stands out is the integration of theory and practice and an insightful balance between the positive and negative effects of conflict. Together their combined 'EQ' has produced a rigorous and beautifully balanced text; it is a must read that should be included as essential reading for students and practitioners of HRM; mediators, conflict coaches and above all leaders at all levels who are ultimately the 'custodians' of organizational cultures in which the human spirit either thrives or dies."
Margaret A Chapman, Chartered and Registered Psychologist, Coach, Supervisor, Accredited Mediator (ADR) and Author of *The Emotional Intelligence ('EQ') Pocketbook*

1

The nature of conflict

THE TRUE COST OF NOT MANAGING CONFLICT

Conflict is everywhere. Even at a time when the number of global armed and political conflicts has actually fallen (Human Security Center, 2005; Ignacio, 2004), old enemies have agreed to share power in the interest of peace, and politicians in many countries are increasingly talking about the need for bipartisan cooperation to see us through 'difficult times', it's virtually impossible to turn on the TV news or browse the pages of a broadsheet without stories of war and violence stealing the headlines. Many bitter disputes endure, the number of intra-state conflicts remains high (Uppsala University, 2004), and in the past 10 years, the world has woken up to fighting a new kind of enemy – the war against a 'virtual state' terrorist network.

Conflicts play out on any scale: between blocs of trading nations, local communities and neighbours separated by just a garden wall; they can be multinational, intra-societal or inter-personal, and concern ideological, cultural or economic differences, amongst others. But it's not just on the global stage that conflict abounds. Bitter battles flourish in the boardroom, divorce courts, between businesses and their suppliers and over service commitments.

Whilst set in different contexts, the lessons and insights that can be learnt by studying conflicts of any kind are invaluable for understanding how to confront disputes in the workplace. We'll therefore borrow from the wide base of knowledge built up from the experience of resolving conflicts in general, not confining ourselves to lessons learnt about conflicts at work.

In the workplace, the time, energy and resources spent resolving conflicts is staggering. Recent research suggests that conflict resolution costs UK businesses nearly £40 billion each year (CEDR, 2006), not to mention the adverse publicity, unproductively channelled energy and additional pressures that ineffectively managed conflicts can produce, often leading to work-driven sickness for the aggrieved and 'accused' alike. Litigation alone costs US businesses hundreds of millions of dollars annually, easily reaching close to $100,000 a case when an employer is found liable and so required to pay a plaintiff's legal fees and compensation, quite apart from the cost of continuing to comply with a court's decision (Barnaba, 2009).

Were this not bad enough, legal costs are soaring, with the annual cost of civil litigation related to employment disputes now approaching $300 billion in the United States (AAA, 2006). A survey of corporate legal departments by international law firm Fulbright & Jaworski LLP revealed that larger US organizations typically witness 50 new cases crossing their desks annually, including a growing number of employment disputes (*Indus Business Journal,* 2009). Indeed, 54 per cent of the in-house lawyers surveyed claimed that employment disputes ranked amongst their top three listed concerns (*Business Wire,* 2006).

It's then little surprise that a desire to reduce the volume of conflict-based cases reaching the courts, often without any attempt at earlier resolution, was an important motivation for the recommendations made in the 2007 Gibbons report on employment dispute resolution, commissioned by the UK government in 2006 (Gibbons, 2007). In the United States too, the American Arbitration Association (AAA) states that the rising cost and resource commitment needed to bring employment conflicts to court has been a spur for increasing interest in Alternative Dispute Resolution (ADR). Its extensive consultation with more than 250 legal counsels, representing organizations across different industry sectors and of varying sizes, confirmed a perception that 'a stream of evidence has long suggested that there is real business value to the rapid, comparatively inexpensive, and easily-accessed alternative to the judicial system' (AAA, 2006).

Meanwhile, in a survey of 1,200 UK organizations, the Chartered Institute of Personnel and Development (CIPD) found that respondents spent almost 450 days per year on average on activities relating to grievance, disciplinary hearings and employment tribunals. The survey found that the task of just preparing for tribunal hearings consumed an average 12.8 person-days of effort, considering the input required from line managers, HR and legal specialists (Haslam and Willmott, 2004).

Quite apart from the monetary costs involved, employee disputes consume management time, take staff away from productive tasks and may foster ill-feeling and resentment amongst more than those who bring their complaints to their organization's notice, as illustrated in Figure 1.1.

Figure 1.1   Left unchecked, conflict involves people, ever-increasing time, and money

WHAT THIS BOOK IS ABOUT AND HOW IT'S ORGANIZED

This book is about conflict in the workplace – the type that creates divisions between people and workgroups, managers and their teams, and between managers and other managers. We'll look at the dynamics of unhealthy disputes, how to resolve them and contain their fall-out, but also give attention to those conflicts that are actually positive, such as those that encourage constructive debate, a willingness to air ideas and healthy competition.

'Managing conflict' is broader than what most people understand as 'mediation', which we might paraphrase as: 'an intervention between disagreeing parties involving a third party, aimed at bringing the dispute to a conclusion that both can accept'. It is a responsibility that needs to be shared by the whole management team of any organization as much as with those who might often be thought of as 'the conflict specialists':

- Front-line managers can play a vital role in recognizing the early stages of potentially unproductive conflict, step in and stop many disputes from developing further, as well as helping to minimize or prevent conflict from happening in the first place.
- HR managers are often the first point of contact for escalated disputes, though members of the HR team (as well as other managers with the right personal qualities, will and proper training) can play the role of mediator in formal disputes.
- Leaders have a key role to play in modelling desired behaviours, ensuring that conflict management strategy is given prominence and adequate resourcing, and in supporting a drive toward building a 'happy company'.

The benefits of managing conflict effectively should be easy to identify for each of these, not to mention for those who find themselves embroiled in disputes. Crucially, time can be saved managing unproductive and unnecessary activities, energy can be better channelled into outputs that focus on business need rather than 'people problems', and incidences of stress-related sickness, discontented staff lapsing in motivation and commitment, and precious HR, management and organizational time and reputations being kept under wraps.

So, we'll cover a lot of ground, considering the perspectives and needs of these different groups, and how these differing interests may be satisfied. To this end, the book is structured as follows:

- This chapter considers the relevance of conflict management in organizations, setting the scene for understanding where to start the task of reducing and better managing unhealthy disputes.
- Chapters 2 and 3 expand on how to diagnose conflict and outline a range of approaches for resolving disputes that have reached a different stage in their lifecycle.
- Chapter 4 offers a powerful model for conducting both informal and formal mediation.
- Chapters 5 and 6 consider the role that a front-line manager can play in stemming and preventing unproductive conflict, as well as in channelling constructive conflict.
- Chapters 7 and 8 focus on the tasks of formal mediation of escalated disputes, offering approaches for tackling the wide range of challenges and complexities that often get in the way of finding a 'lasting peace'.

- Chapters 9, 10 and 11 consider how organizations can implement or build upon their existing approaches for minimizing and managing conflict, concluding with a powerful technique for assessing the impacts of such strategies.
- Appendix 1 provides an easy reference to what we have termed 'micro-tools' – question structures and techniques that might be used in many formal and informal conflict scenarios, whilst Appendix 2 offers a range of templates referred to in the text. Appendix 3 lists a wide range of online resources that aim to support the conflict manager.

The book is supported by its own website, giving access for downloading a wide range of the templates and tools that we refer to in the following chapters as PDF files, as well as including additional information and resources and regular updates. To access the site, please visit www.managingconflictatwork.com.

Before settling into the practicality of how to manage conflict, we should say a word or two about *why* conflicts often take on an unproductive character, and look at what typically happens when they're allowed to take on a life of their own.

WHAT CAUSES CONFLICT?

What might appear to be a simple question – what causes conflict? – is far less easy to answer and may well be amongst the most difficult questions that need to be addressed during a conflict resolution process. However, some of the more common explanations can go some way to providing an answer. Three 'big ideas' will give a flavour of these:

Big Idea 1: Humankind is naturally predisposed to engage in conflict.
Big Idea 2: The 'maturity-immaturity' dilemma.
Big Idea 3: The 'four worlds' model of perception and behaviour.

Big Idea 1: Humankind is naturally predisposed to engage in conflict

Some biologists have argued that conflict is in our genes, though curiously this appears to be a relatively recent development in the human genome (McAuliffe, 2009). To survive, our Neolithic ancestors needed the protection of their tribe and a readiness and skill to fight. Capture by another tribe represented an every-day threat, whilst strength in the group made it easier to protect territory and the resources it provided for survival.

In our predatory relationship with other animals too, early man's trump cards were his cunning and intellect. A need to survive encouraged the development of highly accomplished abilities to ensnare and kill prey, driven by a belief that it is necessary to fight or die. However, within their own groups, whenever hunter-gatherers faced a conflict, the fight tended to be short-lived, with one party quickly backing down. The energy expended on local quarrels was just not worth the effort. Today, this principle is well illustrated by the approach for resolving conflict taken by a small ethnic group from the island of Sumbawa in Indonesia, the Dou Donggo (Monaghan and Just, 2000).

Rapid dispute resolution – the way of the Dou Donggo

One night in the village of Doro Ntika, a relative of a young woman named ina Mone burst into the home of a friend, claiming that his sister-in-law had been assaulted. Rushing to her house to offer help, it seemed clear to the friend that ina Mone was in distress, her shirt torn and her face daubed with a medicinal paint where she said she had been beaten.

An elder of the village was called, and a court was convened the next day to hear the case. ina Mone's evidence was presented, but the accused admitted to no more than having had a disagreement with her. His later confession resulted in a speedy judgement: to pay a minor fine, offer an apology, and receive a slap to the face from ina Mone.

What was not mentioned in the exchange was that there was more to the case than might have been obvious to the casual observer: most individuals in the village knew that ina Mone's daughter had spurned a romantic approach by la Ninde, the accused, since she had been betrothed to another man. ina Mone had sought to ward off la Ninde's advances by complaining to his mother, enraging la Ninde and prompting him to shout and argue with ina Mone. It was common knowledge that ina Mone had torn her clothes and daubed her face to make it appear as though she had suffered an attack. ina Mone's real motivation in claiming assault was to protect the sanctity of her daughter's promised marriage, and this was widely known in the village and to the elder who passed judgement.

Once the court was discharged, the matter was put to rest. It was generally accepted by the Dou Donggo that closed cases should no longer be discussed. Within 24 hours, an angry dispute had been resolved and the real underlying cause of the conflict had been acknowledged, if only in silence.

Reflecting on this breathtakingly fast conclusion to what at first seemed a very serious allegation, anthropologist Peter Just, who witnessed the events at first-hand, commented that 'dispute settlement, like law in many small-scale societies, stresses consensus and the restoration of ruptured social relationships rather than a winner-take-all decision of guilt or innocence' (Monaghan and Just, 2000, pp 14–19).

For such societies, allowing deep divisions to grow and prolonging the valuable time and energy they consume can be destructive for the whole community. Ia Ninde's 'confession' was a humbling act to save the village from the prospect of focusing its energies on survival, and one that undoubtedly earned him the respect of many.

For most of humankind, things have changed in our more recent history. Research by geneticists in California suggests that as many as 40 per cent of the neurotransmitters in the brain have been naturally selected in the past 10,000 years (Wang *et al*, 2006). One of the scientists leading the research, Robert Moyzis of the University of California at Irvine, explains the significance:

with the establishment of the first farming communities, we put down roots – 'you can't just walk away' – a fact that would have created selective pressure to revise the mechanisms regulating aggression, such as the glutamate pathways involved in arousal. (McAuliffe, 2009)

However, echoes of the same tribal instincts that enabled our ancestors to survive are still seen today amongst supporters of football teams and in the pride individuals often take in their national identity. As for the notion of survival of the fittest, humans are of course past masters at gaining 'one over' each other, albeit some more forcefully than others. A 'dog eat dog' philosophy rules in many boardrooms and one-upmanship is a preoccupation for many.

Instinctive or biological factors may seem relevant when considering the history of inter-societal conflicts, but what about the day-to-day disputes that emerge in the workplace today? Unfortunately, the personal qualities that are often upheld as being ones to admire at work are ones that can lead to expectations of personal rights and a need to stand against perceived aggressors. These include common beliefs that:

- arrogance or at least strong self-assurance is good;
- successful negotiation always requires tough talking and bringing the opposing party's offer down;
- the sensitivities and conduct appropriate in personal life rarely have any place at work;
- game playing is acceptable; and
- encouraging competitiveness between staff drives high performance.

Big Idea 2: The 'maturity-immaturity' dilemma

Writers such as Abraham Maslow (1943), Argyris (1957), and McGregor (1960) have suggested that once their more basic needs have been satisfied, humans seek fulfilment or to achieve 'self-actualization' through spiritual, intellectual or physical achievement or other means. This quest usually requires increasing opportunity, discretion and responsibility. For many, the workplace is the main environment for finding such openings, driving aggressive action to help advance a career.

However, for many, the workplace stifles rather than offers such opportunities; their subordination and occasional exposure to bullying or disrespectful treatment by senior managers can ultimately blow over into resentment and complaint, whilst the possibility of changing employers is not an option that all feel is available to them or that they seriously want to explore. And for those who do make some progress up a corporate hierarchy, there's normally a price to be paid in sacrificing individuality for allegiance to the organization (Maslow, 1943).

Faced with the frustration to satisfy a basic need, Richard Arvid Johnson suggests that employees may:

> respond to organizational pressures and threats by defensive reactions such as aggression against their supervisors and co-workers, fixated behaviour or apathy, compromise and gamesmanship, or psychological withdrawal and daydreaming. All of these defence mechanisms reduce a person's potential for creative, constructive activity on the job. (Johnson, 1978)

In other words, the theory suggests that there is an inherent contradiction built into the way many modern organizations are organized, which directly encourages the conditions for conflict. The implication for developing a people strategy is that attention needs to be given to motivating employees in addressing conflict management strategically – in short, HR policy-makers need to get back to the basics of motivational theory and find how best to accommodate the interests of human need.

Big Idea 3: The 'four worlds' model of perception and behaviour

Dennis Sandole, a leading academic in the field of conflict resolution and international relations, presents a way of understanding how individuals come to perceive matters in the way they do (Sandole, 1980). Sandole's model can be broken down into three main processes:

1. we absorb information from one of two external 'worlds' (natural or manmade);

2. we then process this via our biological/physiological world (the physical act of passing information from neuron to neuron);
3. then in our mental world, our cognitive processes, core beliefs and ideas come into action to decode the incoming message. This requires four further sub-processes:
   - bare sensation: a vague sense of what may be in the field of perception (Y);
   - recognizing and identifying: a clear definition of what is in the field of perception;
   - analysing and explaining: a theory of why what is in the perceptual field might exist (X);
   - interpreting: forming an explanation for the 'what' – 'why' relationship (Y–X) and exploring possible alternative explanations.

This is illustrated in Figure 1.2.

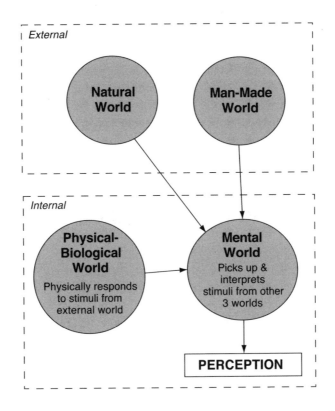

Figure 1.2 The 'four worlds' model (adapted from Sandole, 1987)

According to Sandole, an understanding of what is happening in each of these four worlds is crucial for understanding why individuals perceive themselves to be under threat, discriminated against or have some other basis for grievance. Having an appreciation of what prompts belief and action in a person (his or her mental world) can help identify the likely nature of what Sandole calls the 'discharge potential' of stimuli in the two external worlds.

In this model, an individual's root beliefs and internalized paradigms accentuate his or her sensitivity. An individual's conditioning, sources of identity, purpose and core beliefs all play their part in defining what the especially sensitive stimuli might be. For example, a personal assistant who is a capable professional may be especially sensitive to the demands of a boss who expects that he or she serves coffee and washes the cups every day. The unthinking demands of a boss indicate subservience, although this may not be their intention. Worryingly, Sandole points out that 'identities based on different paradigms – different worldviews – inclusive of different ethnicities, religions, different ethnocentrisms, and the like, are, by definition, in conflict with each other' (Sandole, 2002).

The model has been extended by Thurston to also consider how the influence of power structures and the different ways individuals respond in different situations may give rise to conflict (Thurston, 2008). These may include factors such as the fear of the consequences of complaining (eg, being fired may be a bigger worry if an individual fears being unable to find an alternative job) and the influence of any powerful support that the individual may be able to call upon if needed.

COMMON TRIGGERS FOR CONFLICT IN THE WORKPLACE

The underlying reasons for workplace conflicts arising are often difficult to diagnose, but several common triggers can help kindle the fire. Amongst these are:

- individual suspicion and conspiracy theories become an individual's reality;
- genuine but unrecognized psychological disorders, such as obsessions and paranoia, do not allow a grievance to go away;
- organizations or HR advisers adopt an unwritten policy of protecting themselves above the interests of employees, for example driven by a desire to avoid setting precedents, such as payments made with compromise agreements;

- organizations concern themselves with following the letter of the law, rather than the spirit of what's right for each party;
- lobbying from third-party advisers, colleagues, family and friends encourages complainants to 'take their employer to the cleaners';
- lack of relevant training for managers in managing conflict, or a lack of skill and awareness to spot the early signs of dispute (see the example below);
- a fear amongst complainants that once a dispute has reached a certain point, there can be no return without risking later, if covert, sanctions by their employer;
- fear and anxiety resulting from uncertainty (such as expected job losses).

Case study: The hesitant boss

Phil, a newly appointed Finance Manager working for a Harley Street cosmetic surgery clinic, struggled to know how to deal with a persistent reluctance of a new member in the team to follow procedures for reconciling the cash account of the clinic each day.

The individual concerned, Mick, adopted his own system of working, refusing to change to fit in with new processes Phil wanted to implement. Mick's claim was that he 'didn't need to be told how to do his job', seeming unconcerned about ignoring the boss (having survived the coming and going of several previous managers). Mick's indifference wasn't helped by the fact that he was soon approaching an age when he could retire, and having worked for the company for more than 20 years, he felt secure in his position.

Not knowing how to address the obstinate way his requests were dealt with and lacking personal authority, Phil retreated from pressing the matter further, trying as best he could to deal with the daily in-flows of cash to the clinic.

Further requests by the manager were met with a cold shoulder by his bullish assistant. Being popular with several directors in the company and well liked by others in the team for being 'a funny guy', Mick seemed to actually enjoy provoking his timid superior.

Some months later, a £20,000 gap appeared when Phil attempted to reconcile the monthly income account with the sales register. A frantic investigation revealed that customers paying by cheque or 'on account' couldn't be accounted for – the missing revenue had to be made up by the handful or so who preferred to pay by cash.

Responsibility for keeping the cashbooks and arranging for payments into the bank rested with Mick, and was one of the procedures that he insisted on carrying out his way. Faced with the prospect of explaining the loss at the approaching board meeting, Phil finally decided that it was time to confront Mick.

The ensuing meeting, facilitated by the part-time HR consultant who had been engaged by Phil, did not go well: Phil claimed that Mick had failed to take on the new process, which should have prevented the loss being unnoticed over several weeks; Mick claimed that Phil hadn't made clear what the boundaries of his role were and had been content to allow him to work with a system that had always worked in the past.

Mick's command of the meeting was impressive. He repeatedly pressed Phil to say whether he was making an accusation of incompetence or theft. He demanded to know why Phil thought that he alone was to blame (the suggestion that a colleague who usually deposited the money in the bank might be to blame hadn't been investigated), and took the opportunity to criticize Phil's ineffective style of management.

The exchange became increasingly aggressive, although it was Mick's voice that dominated and Mick's anger that showed through most obviously. Without proof of what had happened and facing the reality that Mick's performance hadn't been properly addressed earlier, Phil felt unable to offer any reasonable answer to Mick's powerful challenges.

Feeling helpless and defeated, Phil decided that he would need to take the blame when he faced the board. His relationship with Mick worsened to the point that conversation between the two was almost non-existent. Mick's arrogance and intransigence grew, whilst Phil knew that he had lost virtually all respect of someone who (he thought) by rights should acknowledge who was the boss.

Following an embarrassed board meeting in which Phil took full responsibility for the loss, Phil increasingly realized that his position had become untenable. Racked with humiliation, isolated from a key team member and others, it wasn't long before the finance department was again recruiting for a new manager.

This is not an unusual scenario: a new manager finds him or herself unable to cope with a strong personality in the team. A lack of adequate management training, or promotion on the basis of technical ability or professional qualification might compound the difficulty, but so too might an opportunity to sound out how to handle a growing concern with a trusted colleague. Informal manager networks across departments and even organizations, may help fill this gap, although ultimately managers who can't take on responsibility for confronting hard conversations before they become unavoidable and who can't point to clear examples to explain their concern when they do, may themselves need some strong management or training.

In this example, Mick is clearly a difficult individual to manage, but he might also hide deeper motivations that others rarely see. For example, Mick may resent being managed by someone who is much younger than him, or bear a grudge that he wasn't invited to apply for the manager's role. Mick's friendship with the directors and general popularity may strengthen his sense of security, whilst his long-standing service may make him believe that he has a right to stand his ground.

Ultimately, it is what he sees as a direct personal attack that tipped the balance for Mick. Strong emotions become inflamed and his intellectual energy is directed to undermining Phil's attack. The calm, if difficult, discussion that Phil had hoped would take place had little chance of ever reaching a satisfactory conclusion.

There's another unhappy reality that can prompt disputes to quickly escalate: contrary to what might be claimed, many organizations aren't totally fair. Careers may be protected by a powerful sponsor for reasons other than nurturing talent. In the survival game, the tribal instincts mentioned earlier can quickly kick in, as groups or cliques bond and act in their own interests. The stage is then set for inter-team disputes, heads of department show-downs and the isolation of non-conformists and those who lack the favour of friends in high places.

Those on the periphery are especially vulnerable to being hung out to dry, especially if they cannot survive without the support of others. It's perhaps not surprising that those who are the last to complain are often those who succumb to mental illness. In his book, *Depressive Illness: The curse of the strong,* consultant psychiatrist Tim Cantopher explains that a high percentage of patients who are admitted to his clinics at The Priory Hospital following a psychological crisis at work are conscientious, tolerant and the least likely to complain (Cantopher, 2003).

Lone-operators are quickly isolated, often members of minority groups such as ethnic groups, lesbian, bisexual, gay and transgendered (LBGT) people and those having an autistic spectrum condition. Policies of positive discrimination may themselves provoke anger amongst others who perceive that an organization isn't pursuing a just policy, even sparking industrial disputes, at the extreme.

HOW CONFLICTS OFTEN DEVELOP

If it's frequently clear what the seeds of conflict are, how does conflict often develop? Unfortunately small differences have a bad habit of escalating into major disputes that have little connection to where they started from, taking on lives of their own. Several theories attempt to explain how conflict develops. Whilst not contradictory, two of these offer quite different perspectives on how conflict can quickly take hold: the 'pinch-crunch' conflict cycle and the conflict lifecycle.

1. The 'pinch-crunch' cycle

Sherwood and Glidewell (1973) and more recently Lapid-Bogda (2004) have sought to explain the progression of disputes by examining the effects of relationships and behavioural type. Their 'Pinch-crunch conflict cycle' model (see Figure 1.3) describes the following main stages:

a.   hope;
b.   grace;
c.   pinch; and
d.   conflict.

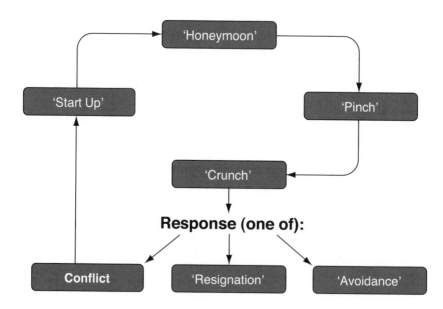

Figure 1.3   The 'pinch-crunch' cycle

a. The starting-up period ('hope')

Most new relationships normally start well and with a degree of optimism about the future. For example, after leaping from an unhappy past job into the promise of a fresh start with a new organization, a future line manager may seem to be perfectly polite during a recruitment or induction day, only later showing his or her true colours as a tyrant or a bully.

Time is usually taken to build a relationship and find common ground, whilst having had only limited time to get acquainted with each other means that there's likely to be little to irritate or dislike about another person initially. Conflicting ways of working, unguarded personalities and displays of 'foolish mistakes' or other *faux pas* usually need more than a few days to set in as recognized differences and potential touch-points for future friction.

b. The honeymoon period ('grace')

The first hundred days in a new relationship tend to be a period of tolerance. Alliances with colleagues may only just be forming, whilst the firm perceptions of 'what's wrong with this place', which might preoccupy the minds of some longer serving employees, are unlikely to have taken hold. Small mistakes may be overlooked as being inevitable during a period of learning, whilst minor differences in style are unlikely to have built up into entrenched irritations. Of course there are exceptions that don't follow the rule. Nevertheless, this is also a period in which personal styles, ways of working and bugbears are made known, and one in which what may be initially negligible differences and irritations can build into ones that shape an individual's enduring perception.

c. Irritation ('pinch')

This is the moment when one person's tolerance boundary is violated, for example, a core value is compromised or an unwanted criticism comes across as a deliberate attack. Examples of such triggers include offensive language, anti-social behaviour and a failure to acknowledge a favour. The trigger may generate strong emotion such as anger, resentment or panic.

With the emotion comes a negative thought, often a judgement. Cognitive therapists and other adherents of cognitive behavioural therapy, which is a means for treating anxiety disorders and depression[1], categorize such thoughts as one of a number of 'thinking styles'. For example 'black and white thinking' refers to a tendency to interpret a situation in a very stark, uncompromising way, whilst someone who is inclined toward 'prophetic' thinking has a tendency to predict what will happen or be said, often inaccurately.

Left unresolved, such thoughts can form part of an individual's internalized system for evaluating the amiability of a relationship, and so set the direction for future interaction. 'Pinches' can have a powerful influence because the impressions and associations they create settle into memory, ready to fire again when the triggering irritation is repeated.

d. Conflict ('crunch')

The 'crunch' usually comes after several 'pinches', though sometimes this may only take one. The 'crunch' is the point where individuals feel they cannot just keep suppressing their emotion, that action is needed. This might include sounding out a colleague, considering the prospect of resigning, or directly challenging the aggressor. It may also result in an unguarded outburst, so further alienating the relationship.

Start-over ('hostility')

Following the 'crunch', a relationship may never be the same. Individuals may find it hard to face each other and unable to work effectively with each other. Earlier openness, empathy and mutual respect may be replaced with ill-feeling; the positive inter-personal life of the relationship may seem to be over. Yet this is also a point where one final attempt might be made to break through the emotional deadlock – where resolving the conflict may offer a chance for starting afresh.

We could possibly add another dimension to this view of how conflict develops: the influence of allegiances. Even in what are apparently impartial hearings, subconscious associations with one or other disputing party can be made that may influence an observer's tendency to believe one person's account over the other's. For example, the calm, articulate and empathetic tone used by one individual may carry greater credibility than the frantic, angry criticism offered by another, so more readily persuading others to the first person's version of the dispute. Stronger allegiances may in turn help perpetuate one party's belief that they are right, quite apart from possibly also having an influence on those who are meant to be helping to bring the dispute to an end.

2. The conflict lifecycle

Traditional studies of political and ideological conflict have often referred to a lifecycle pattern of conflict. The origin of this depiction of a conflict's typical stages isn't known, but it is widely used in analysing intra-' or international conflicts and is equally applicable when considering employment contexts. The version we present below is widely known, although several variations may be encountered.

This model of conflict development, shown in Figure 1.4, breaks down into five main stages:

a. emergence;
b. escalation;
c. entrapment;
d. de-escalation;
e. termination.

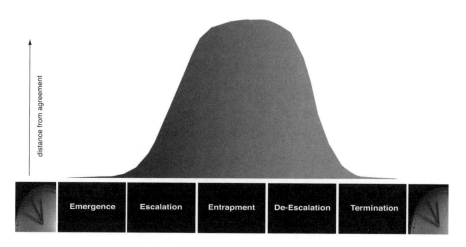

Figure 1.4 Conflict lifecycle

a. Emergenc

Differences may start to appear, but be overlooked or treated as relatively insignificant matters by one or both parties. A wish to protect the *status quo* in a relationship usually prevails over a drive to confront the cause of disagreement, and any broaching of the difference is likely to be made courteously and respectfully, if assertively and directly. An ability to listen and consider the other party's perspective is usually still present.

Note: This stage may occasionally be missed altogether, for example when a major cause for grievance suddenly erupts or when one party is faced with a situation that he or she cannot accept.

b. Escalation

During this stage, one or both parties' interests become more important than trying to find an amicable, informal way out of the disagreement. In the minds of each individual, the validity of their case strengthens and becomes all the more important to drive home to the 'opponent'.

A period of exchanging explanations, allegations and pleading for the other side to 'see sense' may culminate in frustration and heavily polarized views. An attempt may be made by one or both parties to withdraw from what they see as a mounting confrontation, but rarely until they feel they have made their points.

Simple triggers such as one party's attempt to gain ground with the arguments or a provocative action like involving third-party advisers can cause the perceptions of difference to escalate, that is if a single explosive event hasn't already led to a grave fracture in the relationship. Unfortunately, tit-for-tat actions may become increasingly provocative in response to hostile moves by the other party, encouraging a rapid escalation in the conflict's intensity.

c. Entrapment

Reaching what may be seen as a stalemate, each party realizes that the prospect of converting the views of the other, or at least reaching a compromise, seems hopeless. Strong emotion and narrow, deeply critical perspectives of each other may set in. Any attempt at a constructive dialogue to remove the impasse will have ended. Energy is now directed toward taking action to criticize, crush or resist the opposition.

A lack of clear thinking is often shown during this stage, whilst the ability to even contemplate the opposing party's perspective is likely to become a distant memory.

d. De-escalation

A cooling-off in the seemingly hopeless situation may only be possible with the help of a third party. Physical and emotional exhaustion might prompt consideration of this option, especially if the dispute seems set to only become resolved after a costly and possibly hard-to-win legal battle. Third-party advisers may counsel that minimizing potential risk or cutting losses may be preferred, and so the prospect of re-engaging dialogue on more constructive terms may return.

It's during this stage that a mediator or arbitrator may be called upon to help move the warring sides out of deadlock toward a way forward that both can accept. Once each can see some positive progress toward this goal, a rapid de-escalation in the intensity of the conflict may be achieved. A level of compromise and humility by one party may allow the other side to feel able to let down his or her guard without losing face.

e. Termination

The conclusion to a dispute may happen quickly, but even when both parties accept a final proposal to end the disagreement, the conflict may take some time to be fully resolved. A level of suspicion and private disappointment with the outcome may simmer away for many months, only ultimately being quashed when both parties have demonstrated their total commitment to both the spirit and the words of their agreement.

Considering this not untypical progression from what often may be quite a simple beginning, we can quite easily see that, ideally, any difference that does start to emerge would never progress into the 'escalation' stage. The focus on stemming the growth of a conflict is an important principle in conflict management and conflict prevention, as we'll see later.

However, we might consider the consequences if de-escalation doesn't occur during the cycle described above. In such cases, the absence of a mediator to intervene during the 'entrapment' stage, or a lack of willingness of either party to cooperate in a fresh attempt at constructive dialogue might often be apparent.

Case study: Missing the point

Barbara had been teased ever since she had started working for the plastic mouldings company on the industrial estate near her home. Being conscientious and always concerned to play by the rules, Barbara took her work seriously, never returning to her bench late from lunch and preferring not to engage in idle conversation. This wasn't the way of the day shift: gossip and charge-hand dodging were the stock in trade of the factory crowd. Barbara's shyness and reluctance to join her colleagues at lunchtime further isolated her from the others. As she became more remote, the teasing continued.

But the teasing wasn't intended in spite: gentle ribbing was the norm around the factory. No one was spared from an occasional tease, chargehands and supervisors being amongst the first to be the butt of someone's joke. Jovial ribbing, if occasionally a little crude, was all a part of life in the factory.

Barbara didn't see things this way. Afraid to speak up, she quietly took the teasing without a word, even usually breaking a small smile as if to gesture acceptance that she was happy to be ribbed. Privately, she felt alienated and disliked. Facing her colleagues' banter every working day began to become a living hell, and at home she ruminated about the cruel way she was always made into a figure of fun.

Barbara's outburst came unexpectedly. Molly, one of the more vocal of her fellow workers, had likened Barbara's new T-shirt to a tea shop tablecloth. Inevitable ripples of laughter and further attempts at witty observations from the rest of the line followed, but Barbara had stopped working and was crying. The tears came in a flood and she was inconsolable. An attempt by her charge-hand to calm her fell on deaf ears. Even a sincerely-meant apology from Molly had no effect – for Barbara, it wasn't good enough to be told that 'we didn't mean any harm'.

Following several days' sickness, Barbara was called over to the office block by the personnel department and asked to open up about her many experiences of being the butt of others' jokes. Her doctor's certificate indicated that the repeated headaches and panic she had suffered during recent weeks were undoubtedly due to her treatment at work. The personnel manager explained that he had no option but to follow procedure: Barbara's grievance needed to be fully investigated. Relationships and morale in the factory were never going to be the same again.

A need to enact a formal grievance process is always regrettable in situations where earlier informal intervention might have been possible. In the example we've just described, this might have been the case had Barbara known that she could talk confidentially with her personnel manager, who might have been able to suggest a different way of dealing with her colleagues, or had her charge-hand been more alert to the unease that Barbara felt, stepping in to deflect the usual barrage of teasing when it next came.

An alternative ending

Theoretically, a deadlock may last indefinitely, but in practice, this is rarely satisfactory for either party. Unless one party leaves the stage (eg, when an aggrieved employee resigns), personalities or circumstances radically change, or a trusted adviser encourages a dignified backing down, uncomfortable relationships are best not left to fester.

If de-escalation or procrastination doesn't follow, there's just one logical way forward: protracted conflict. The lifecycle of the conflict will then take a different course (see Figure 1.5), usually involving three further stages:

f.   further escalation;
g.   judgement;
h.   the aftermath.

f. Further escalation

Escalation at this point is inevitably directed toward an authority that can make an ultimate decision on the points of contention and – usually – enforce sanctions. This may be an independent arbitrator, a judge or tribunal. For individuals

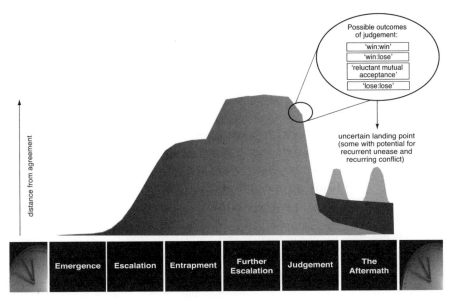

Figure 1.5 Conflict lifecycle (alternative ending)

who are convinced that their argument is irrefutable, who are set on achieving the ultimate victory over their opponent and for whom objective argument has passed by, this usually means that the scene is set for litigation.

g. Judgement

Ultimately, unless a final out-of-court settlement is agreed, both parties will face the judgement of an appointed authority. The judgement may force both to a compromise or commitments to uphold in future, or it may find in favour of one party. Depending on which party is deemed to be at fault, this may involve imposing a penalty if the organization has failed to demonstrate a reasonable attempt to resolve the dispute.

h. The aftermath

Judgements might bring an end to the back-and-forth dialogue of a dispute between two parties, but rarely bring about an easy closure. One or both parties are likely to feel compelled to commit to an unsatisfactory agreement they didn't anticipate; for the vanquished, the outcome may leave a sense of humiliation and anger, quite apart from potentially being financially very costly. This is the consequence of taking a bitter argument to its ultimate conclusion: the ending may be devastating.

Even for the victor, the outcome may often be less than satisfying: a realization of achieving what is ultimately a shallow victory after an exhausting process may set in, whilst for some, a judgement may only have been made in their favour because there was insufficient evidence to convict wrong-doing on a point of law. Even by winning the argument, the financial cost of doing so might not be repaid by any compensation the other is expected to give up. Employers and the business-focused professionals representing them are not immune from such effects themselves.

If both individuals still need to face each other even if only occasionally, their psychological and emotional relationship may never be the same again. Compromise agreements in which both parties are required to make concessions to work together – or keep apart – and possibly with each sharing some degree of blame may provide a way forward, but still require genuine cooperation to overcome an old enemy. A landing point that leaves one person still feeling aggrieved also offers the potential for future friction and conflict: the impact of one unresolved dispute may be to sow the seeds for future conflicts, with all the expense of effort, energy and time that they involve. The aftermath to a judgement is rarely an easy path.

Recognizing that a large number of conflicts tend to follow or at least approximate to a similar pattern can help a mediator determine which stage a conflict has reached in its lifecycle, and so know how best to help guide the continuing process. Whilst, as we've seen, a mediator may normally be called upon during the 'entrapment' or deadlock stage in the dispute, this is by no means always the case. In practice, a mediator might be called upon at any stage in a conflict's lifecycle.

Variations on the model lifecycle pattern should be expected. Stages may be passed over or occur in a brief interval of time (for example, 'entrapment' may sometimes last for no more than a few days before a litigation process is set in motion). A conflict may begin to defuse and then re-escalate following some future trigger; personalities representing an organization may change, allowing for the possibility of an impasse being broken.

Case study: A jibe too far

A hard working member of staff did not drink alcohol or go to bars for religious reasons. Consequently, he passed over invitations to join colleagues for after-work drinks each Friday, but felt more and more ostracized from the team for not 'joining in'.

The manager chose to ignore the ripples of discontent, and refused to entertain alternative suggestions made for Friday evening socializing such as taking in a local coffee bar or booking a few lanes at the nearby bowling alley. Instead, light-hearted banter was tolerated, with jibes like

'No point inviting you, eh?' and, 'How can you not drink?' becoming commonplace.

The seeds for conflict were sown, with the unhappy individual feeling evermore isolated and victimized. Eventually, he initiated a grievance for racial discrimination, resulting in the team being badly affected. The manager was aware and knew that it was their responsibility to ensure fair treatment for all staff in the team; however, they chose to ignore the rumblings of discontent during an extended 'Golden Hour' (the opportunity for early, informal mediation), to the organization's peril: a clear case of a manager being at fault.

CALL IN THE LAWYERS

Developing societies created rules to protect their members. As early as 18th century BC, the first written codes began to appear, for example those proclaimed by Hammurabi, the first king of the Babylonian Empire. Taking their lead from the Romans' sophisticated approach to justice, western societies later evolved ways of resolving disputes, from travelling magistrates determining judgements and in time pronouncing common law, through to electing politicians to be the new law makers.

Happily, we've come some distance from reaching judgements based on whether an accused person floats or sinks to the bottom of a pond. But the notion of how best to achieve justice still heavily favours looking up to the occupier of a high bench in the expectation of achieving justice, protecting individual rights, leaving open the option of following an appeal process or applying to some higher court if 'justice' isn't achieved at the first attempt.

The law is often seen as the only outlet aggrieved employees may feel they can turn to if they've lost faith in their own organization to uphold their interests. Courts and tribunals offer structure, objectivity and a clear benchmark to measure claimed wrong-doing against and assess reparations – or so it seems. However, what the law states and what an individual believes is morally right do not always coincide. Many who've rushed blindly into litigation without fully appreciating the very specific issues that their case might actually be reduced to have learnt the hard way that the just and fair outcome they expected the law to provide is often less than what they had hoped for.

Some savvy employees are also waking up to the free legal advice that is often provided as part of a general insurance policy or to privileged bank account holders. For them, the temptation to line up an external ambassador who they believe might at least scare an employer into taking their grievance seriously must be great. High-profile cases in which large payments have been made in settlement of a dispute do not help to discourage the appetite for litigation. Unfortunately, it seems likely that stories of large pay-outs will continue to hit the headlines for a while to come.

SHOULD WE BE WORRIED?

A major argument presented in this book is that it should be in every employer's interest to take the business of conflict seriously – not just the approach they take for resolving conflicts, but how they manage and prevent conflicts taking hold in the first place. We've already presented some recent data about what conflict is known to cost. As we've seen, the scale of these costs is staggering. Nevertheless, letting a dispute take its natural course might still seem to be the simplest option and a preferred strategy for some.

Some might argue that the current recession will reduce the likelihood of disputes taking hold – employees will be too concerned about keeping their jobs to risk antagonizing their employer. Others may say that the ultimate penalties they might face if a court or tribunal finds against them on some disputes aren't really offset by the cost of attempting mediation – especially if they expect a dispute to escalate into the public domain anyway.

Such suggestions ignore the powerful influence of anger and mis-channelled energy, the negative impacts of conflict that might not be seen, the effect on reputations and grist for the workplace rumour-mill. Such arguments also ignore the determination and frequent irrational thinking of individuals whose basic instinct and core values make them ready to fight for what they see as achieving 'justice' – if not as extreme, at least with the same conviction that drives political prisoners to stand up for their beliefs and with the same mentality of many debt-laden consumers who believe that it remains their right to have access to credit. All-in-all, in virtually every sphere of life, the need for mediation is on the rise. Legislative changes in many countries are further strengthening the incentive for both employers and employees to allow mediation a chance to work before rushing to litigation.

Employers who need to reduce head-count can't expect that all will go quietly, especially if some suspect that they've been unfairly treated or smell an opportunity to take their old bosses to task. The potential touch-points are mounting: wage disputes, concern over lower payment for reduced hours, stalled salary increases at a time when some economies might be facing a new period of inflation, a fall-off in final salary pension schemes, and revised contracts relating to bonus payments are becoming a reality.

For example, many sales people, consultants and others whose success or otherwise is likely to be recession-sensitive and who suddenly find themselves the subject of a tough 'performance improvement plan' are likely to harbour feelings of resentment for being made the victim of a situation they see as being outside their control – feelings that may sow the seeds of future conflict. What's more, the critics' arguments ignore the fact that as pressures on individuals mount, they may become more likely to go for broke, not less. Fear of losing a job or benefits may encourage a strengthening of trade union membership and influence, bringing with it a powerful threat of sanction and specialist support for any members who find themselves in an apparently legitimate dispute with an employer.

Already, moves favouring employee's rights to join trade unions or increasing the rights of members are looming in several countries. In China, large multinational and previously union-free organizations such as McDonald's and Wal-Mart have struck deals with the All-China Federation of Trade Unions (*Business Wire,* 2006), whilst in the United States, President Barack Obama has declared that he believes that 'the basic principle of making it easier and fairer for workers who want to join a union… is important' (*The Washington Post,* 15 January 2009). Obama voted in favour of the new Employee Free Choice Act (EFCA), which aims to:

> amend the National Labor Relations Act to establish an efficient system to enable employees to form, join, or assist labor organizations, to provide for mandatory injunctions for unfair labor practices during organizing efforts, and for other purposes (Open Congress, 2009).

Companies operating in the European Union that employ more than 1,000 staff (and where at least 150 of whom must be employed in two or more Member States) will be required to comply with an amendment to the Works Councils Directive (94/45/EC) (*Europa,* 2009), which comes into force in 2011. Amongst other matters, this will recognize the role of trade unions within works councils as 'expert advisers' and increase the power of works council members who wish to assert their legal rights.

Individuals who succeed in winning an argument with an employer can set a precedent for others, especially if they have exposed a potentially wide fault-line of discrimination or other injustice, or received a generous pay-out in compensation. High-profile cases can only serve to accelerate this trend, whilst the possible alleged bases for such claims are increasing.

For example, in the UK, anti-ageist discrimination has been added to the scope of legislation protecting employees, which already includes discrimination on the grounds of sex, physical disability, religious belief and sexual orientation. Meanwhile, the EU's Equal Treatment Directive (2000/78/EC) (*Europa,* 2000) now makes employers vicariously liable for discrimination by one employee against another, whether or not the allegation at the time of an alleged practice was known or not.

The potential damage from public awareness of individual cases shouldn't be under-estimated either. High-profile allegations, whether they are valid or not, can galvanize feelings and cause lasting damage for the reputation of the supposed offending organizations. Alienated customers may switch their loyalties, charities and other not-for-profit organizations may lose funding, and public sector organizations may find themselves fighting an expensive PR battle against mistrust and suspicion. It's not an exaggeration to say that an inability to prevent conflict spilling over into the public domain can ultimately affect the mood and collective perception of society at large: conflict management is a matter for corporate responsibility.

Left unmanaged, the causes of conflict will fester and generate a relentless chain of events. Where several causes combine, the force of such impacts can build into a near-stoppable momentum. Consider the example impacts depicted in Figure 1.6. (Note the diagram shows several possible starting points that can combine into a single chain).

Here, as many as seven separate origins may trigger reactions or set the conditions for a conflict to develop. Suspicion, fear or paranoia[2] (Freeman and Freeman, 2008) may be amongst the starting points for generating false beliefs and rumour. Combined with pre-existing beliefs, an irritation ('pinch') or dislike of a person or organization and the encouragement of colleagues, family, friends and others, most individuals will have sufficient confidence in their conviction to pursue their case with gusto. The consequence of under-estimating the cost of conflict may prove to be disastrous.

The benefits of trying to resolve conflict the alternative way

As we've already noted, we live in litigious times. 'You'll hear from my solicitor,' 'I have rights' and 'You've not heard the last about this' are all too familiar cries. The enforcers of law are seen as being true and fair by many, the ultimate arbiter to turn to when all else fails. The law will defend the rights of the underdog, the worthy and the true victim, and a good advocate will provide a suitable match for any employer's defence, or so it may be thought. Once a supporter is engaged – such as an employment lawyer who sees that there may be a claim worth pursuing – the path to litigation is usually a foregone certainty.

The concept that warring factions might be able to not only resolve a dispute without the judgement of a judge or tribunal but actually reach a better settlement is a mystery for many, and the burgeoning practice of Alternative Dispute Resolution (ADR), or even taking a case into public through popular TV

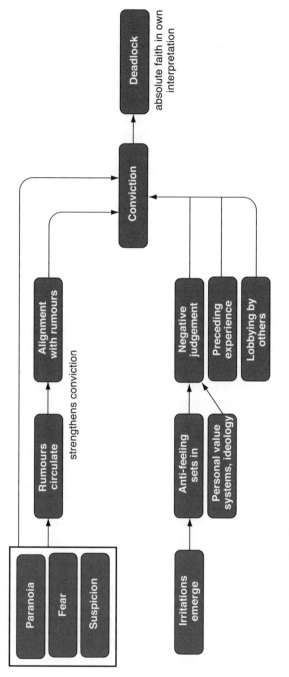

Figure 1.6 Typical impact chain

reality shows such as 'Judge Judy' are still relatively new. The ADR cases we hear about are mainly restricted to divorce settlements amongst the famous, payments for defamation and resolution of large company commercial disputes. Of course occasional high-profile employment disputes that have been settled out of court do hit the headlines but, protected by non-disclosure agreements, the details of most never reach the public domain.

The spirit of agreement, readiness to compromise, honest treatment of underlying issues, even concern for morality rather than the technicalities of law and allowing time for reflection and external counsel may all have a greater chance of succeeding in the field of ADR than under the scrutiny of law. Whether in an employment dispute or not, a 'benefit of doubt', learning and action planning, apologies and appeasement might more typically be agreed through ADR than within the strict boundaries of a legal process. So too may a broader focus be given to what is really at issue rather than being concerned with proving an argument on quite specific points of law. The Dou Donggo people might have more than a few useful lessons to teach about the benefits of resolving disputes their way.

Summary

Human beings may well be predisposed to conflict, whether coming to blows on an international, inter-organizational or interpersonal level. The conditions that often give rise to conflict and the path that a dispute often takes once it becomes entrenched are similar in each of these different contexts, whilst ineffectively managed conflict in the workplace costs many organizations dearly, not to mention also having destructive effects for the individuals who find themselves in dispute.

Conflict management embraces the tasks of minimizing, resolving and managing the aftermath of disputes, as well as knowing when and how to channel constructive conflict. It should be a strategic concern for every organization.

Notes

1. Cognitive behavioral therapy combines cognitive and behavioral therapies to help treat a range of psychological disorders. For further information see, for example, Greenberger, D and Padesky, C (1995) *Mind Over Mood: Change how you feel by changing the way you think,* The Guilford Press.
2. We use this term advisedly: paranoia is increasing in western societies and is perhaps more prevalent in the workplace than many believe.

2

Deciphering conflict management

WHAT IS CONFLICT MANAGEMENT?

We turn now to consider some basic principles for managing conflict. We start by defining what conflict management is, as well as what it isn't.

Mention of the term 'conflict management' (or 'CM' as we prefer to abbreviate it throughout the text) may suggest that we're only concerned with disputes that have already taken hold, whether they've developed into full-blown arguments or are still at an early stage. Of course we are concerned with how to deal with live disputes; however, we take a broader view of the subject, both as a management discipline and as a vital concern for any organization.

Rather than just being about resolving the existing disputes, we suggest that a challenge for managers is to create the conditions that will minimize the risk of unhelpful conflict occurring in the first place. This requires an ability to recognize and quickly defuse potential triggers for dispute when they first arise. Preventing conflict from arising in the first place may not always be possible: however, in many cases, painful and prolonged disputes can be avoided.

To manage conflict effectively means being not only able to limit or remove altogether potential triggers for dispute, but also quickly recognizing when an individual or group of individuals show possible signs of a disagreement. The task of managing conflict is therefore closely integrated with managing people in a more general sense, for example in the way they are motivated and the style of leadership being used. The scope of conflict management is shown in Figure 2.1.

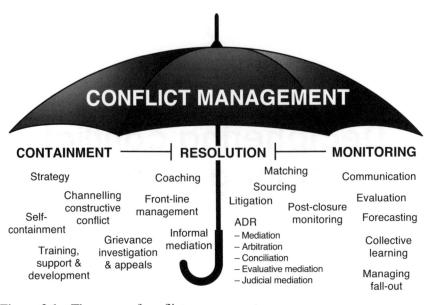

Figure 2.1   The scope of conflict management

However, the scope of CM shouldn't stop here. Many conflicts between individuals and teams aren't only healthy but may be valuable – for example in deciding how to resolve a problem, tackle a project task or simply when sounding out ideas. To be able to exploit this type of *constructive* conflict requires that it can first be identified and then channelled appropriately. Conversely, a failure to harness constructive disagreement may inadvertently generate an avoidable and unhelpful conflict of its own.

Organizations have a role in helping to limit the prospect of unhealthy conflict. HR policy clearly has an important part to play, as do the attitude of leaders and the diverse mix of ingredients in the 'cultural recipe'.[1] Similarly, the way in which information is communicated to staff and the level of access they feel they have to make known their emerging concerns without fear of reprisal require a determined commitment from senior management. This means not just speaking about having strong corporate values, but living them!

A simple definition of conflict management that we can use is therefore:

A learnt and ongoing discipline, focused on preventing or minimizing unproductive or harmful disagreements from arising, and quickly and resource-efficiently bringing any which do to an enduring conclusion that the disagreeing parties can both accept.

This is distinct from the idea of conflict resolution (or CR), for which we offer the following definition:

> A positive intervention with disagreeing parties, aimed at concluding or directing their disagreement in an advantageous way that both can accept.

Conflict resolution may fall under the umbrella of CM, but since it includes the task of channelling both unhealthy and constructive conflict, it embraces a further practice of its own – dispute resolution (DR), or:

> A positive intervention with disagreeing parties, aimed at bringing their dispute to a conclusion that both can accept.

Whilst we are considering definitions, we might want to pin down meanings for some of the more common terms in the 'conflict lexicon'. The box below provides a brief summary of these. Others may beg to differ with some of these definitions; our aim here is simply to be clear about our intended meaning when using these terms.

Alternative dispute resolution (ADR): 'A formal process for settling a dispute adopted as an alternative to litigation.'

ADR may involve one or more of the interventions listed below. A dispute may progress to litigation if it remains unsettled at the end of ADR, or prior agreement between the parties or the nature of the intervention used may preclude this.

Arbitration: 'A process for settling a dispute facilitated by an independent individual or body that is empowered to reach a judgement to reach closure.'

Conflict coaching: 'An application of coaching to help individuals gain awareness of the true nature of the dispute, acknowledge emotions, clarify their own and understand others' perspectives, and recognize the possible outcomes that may be achieved. Coaching may be offered on an individual basis to either party involved in the dispute, or on a group basis for both parties.'

Grievance procedure (or 'Fairness at work' process): 'A formal, defined process accessible to all employees for considering a grievance or complaint brought by an employee against the organization, an individual or group of individuals. Usually involves an investigation to isolate facts and obtain witness testimony.'

Mediation: 'An intervention between disagreeing parties involving a third party, aimed at bringing the dispute to a conclusion that both can accept.'

> Mediation may be *informal* (involving a front-line manager or other third party as an intermediary), or *formal* (resulting from escalation via a formal process). The concept of 'mediation' has different meanings for different people, and its application is necessarily context-specific. We use the term throughout in a broad sense to apply to a 'helpful intermediary', although make clear when a more specific interpretation is intended.
>
> Similarly, our use of the term 'mediator' extends to any informal or formal intervention where a third party becomes involved in the task of attempting to help others find a resolution to their dispute, in contrast to an 'arbiter', who is empowered to reach a judgement on a dispute, and a 'conflict coach', who works with one individual and whose intervention is restricted to *coaching* (usually to help an individual gain insight into his or her situation and make sense of the options that are available for moving forward).
>
> Both conflict coaching and mediation may involve joint or *tandem* working, involving more than one coach or mediator. Both require neutrality, equality, honesty and a commitment amongst participants to reflect, reflect and reflect!

Except when exploring specific types of mediation (and when we do, we will make this clear), to avoid what might otherwise become an unwieldy writing style, in this text we use the terms 'mediation' and 'mediator' interchangeably with 'intermediary', 'broker', 'arbitration', 'conflict coaching' and 'ADR' – in other words, as generics for these various different types of intervention. Similarly, we use the term 'mediator' in both formal and informal contexts – the former being more the domain of highly trained specialists engaged to intervene in formally escalated disputes, and the latter being more typically the domain of the front-line manager. On another point of style, we regularly use the term 'disputing parties' or just simply 'parties' as a general label for the individuals, groups and organizations that are in conflict in a particular dispute.

To attempt CR doesn't require an assumption that a perfect solution will be found for the disputing parties. By their very nature, brokering activities such as arbitration and mediation often involve compromise. Resolution may be reached when one or both parties recognize that continuing to pursue a disagreement doesn't best serve either's interests. In some cases, this may mean accepting what might seem like an apparent injustice or offering to stand down from proving what is believed to be right.

As we'll see later, conflict management is also about learning. Helpful insights might be drawn from every experience of dispute management. However, to be usefully applied, the lessons learnt need to be recorded and communicated.

WHAT CONFLICT MANAGEMENT ISN'T

We should also be clear about what conflict management isn't, or rather consider definitions that are either too narrow or too broad for our intended purpose.

Interpretations that are too narrow include referring to conflicts solely in the context of formal disputes, or those that have reached a point where continuing escalation seems inevitable unless a third party is able to broker a satisfactory resolution. This of course includes employee disputes that appear set on a track toward litigation. However, we want to limit our discussion to conflicts that occur in the workplace. This isn't to deny that the seeds for conflict may often exist externally, nor that conflict is prevalent in many different contexts.

Generally speaking, we don't distinguish between individual and group conflict in the following chapters. In particular, we don't specifically consider industrial disputes or inter-organization commercial disputes. However, we'll draw on the lessons and insights offered by those who have practised conflict resolution in other fields, such as in the geopolitical sphere, and the principles that underpin much of our discussion are relevant for dealing with conflict in these and other contexts (including personal matters).

AN ANATOMY OF CONFLICT MANAGEMENT

We might consider the various aspects of managing conflict as being analogous to the workings of a living organism. This seems to us to be a very appropriate metaphor, drawing attention to the fact that the conditions in which conflict emerges and develops are often complex, driven by a number of semi-autonomous functions (with the 'heart', 'liver', 'kidney', etc), and going beyond merely skin deep.

This approach is relevant both for diagnosing and informing how to manage the resolution of a single dispute, as well as for monitoring and developing a cross-organization strategy for CM. This is by no means the only way we might choose to break down a study of conflict, but it's one we'll consider in more detail below.

A typically highly colourful diagram of a human (or other animal) body reveals a complex web of veins and arteries, each spreading out into different parts of the body, but ultimately being connected as part of the same system. So too, as we begin to peel away the detail of each area of interest in CM, we quickly find a large number of sub-categories branching out from these and with many inter-connections between them. For example, a breakdown of the category 'resourcing' might involve questioning:

- what cost, risk and reward is acceptable for bounding the time, resource and energy invested in resolving a conflict;
- whether to outsource or undertake DR in-house;
- whether and when to mediate, arbitrate or coach;
- what venue to use for convening a dialogue;
- what skills and personal attributes are needed for the individuals who become involved in DR activities;
- what cost is involved in not training and developing individuals to manage conflict.

Of course, this list can be continued, and many other levels of breakdown might be revealed. For example, a consideration of skills and attributes might open up a more detailed review of the demands and needs of negotiation, uncovering reality, self-management and the ability to manage emotional outbursts, amongst others.

Just as diagnosing illness in a living body may need to call upon the skills of a range of specialists, so too may quite large numbers of specialisms be relevant throughout the course of the diagnosis and treatment of a dispute (coaching, mediation and local management amongst them). For our purposes, a top-level anatomy of conflict might contain the various elements shown in Figure 2.2.

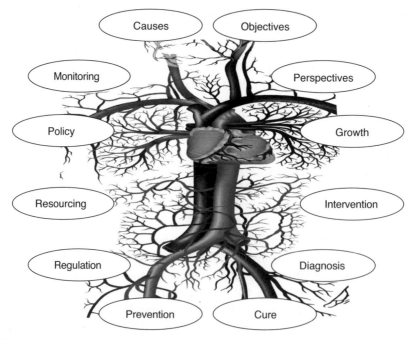

Figure 2.2 An anatomy of conflict

Causes

The focus of this element is self-explanatory. The emphasis is on uncovering the underlying causes of a dispute, or (in a broader context) identifying the conditions that often result in conflict arising and developing.

We've already explored some of the more common seeds of conflict, making the point that the real causes may often not be obvious even to those who are embroiled in a dispute. It may not be necessary, appropriate or even possible to identify causes, but a skilled coach or mediator should at least be able to probe whether the explanation given by an individual or the origin of a dispute is always what it seems, going below the skin to diagnose a root cause.

Objectives

An individual's objectives for pursuing a dispute may not always be what they seem. Perhaps more so than in seeking an understanding of what has caused a dispute, a serious search for the true objectives and expectations of the DR process must be high on the list of priorities for a conflict manager.

Even where objectives aren't explicitly stated, an intermediary must keep in mind the possibility that covert objectives may be at play, and to have an appreciation of the possible intentions that these may cover. As with a root cause, the true motivation for pursuing a dispute may not be clear to any of the parties involved.

This element also prompts consideration of the objectives of different interested parties. These of course include achieving a common agreement on what should reasonably be expected at each stage in a CM process (for example, identifying the best and least outcomes from mediation). Some question structures and techniques for clarifying objectives and achieving consensus are presented in later chapters, as well as being amongst the 'micro-tools' listed in Appendix 1.

Perspectives

The focus here is less on specific objectives and more on appreciating what each individual's view of the dispute is, and why they've formed this view. This includes understanding the range of factors that have or may influence their perspective, as well as seeking to understand how they process the information available to them.

This doesn't imply a need for psychoanalysing each individual, but it does involve attempting to understand what makes people think the way that they do.

Growth

Growth draws attention to the role of a conflict manager in defusing an emerging conflict, as well as containing any negative fallout from a conflict that has matured into a full-blown furore. It encompasses a knowledge base of the dynamics that allow a conflict to escalate, and the technique to prevent or limit this; much as an experienced fire-fighter knows how a fire takes hold and is able quickly to determine appropriate strategies to ring-fence the hazard. As such, growth is closely aligned to an understanding of the causes of conflict, as well as informing policy, prevention and cure.

Intervention

Intervention focuses attention on the parts played by individuals other than those who are directly involved in the dispute. These include any intermediaries – line managers, mediators, arbitrators, coaches or any other third party engaged to help find a resolution – and considers which type of intervention (arbitration, coaching, mediation, etc) is relevant for the stage the dispute has reached.

Diagnosis

Diagnosis is of course an activity in its own right, embracing the knowledge, techniques and approaches used for analysing the causes, objectives and perspectives underpinning a dispute.

Cure

As you may expect, *cure* concerns finding an effective resolution to an ongoing dispute, as well as being an element in the prevention mix (for example, something learnt from a closed dispute that may inform policies to help prevent a similar dispute from arising in future).

This embraces the approaches, styles and mix of interventions used to help bring a dispute to a close, but crucially also considers the provisions that must be made to ensure that a dispute is truly put to bed, with little or no prospect of it recurring in future.

Prevention

Prevention concerns the policies, management practices and other factors that can help to minimize or stop disputes from emerging. It focuses attention on what can be done to help limit the incidence of conflict, as well as how to bring a dispute that has already emerged to a satisfactory conclusion as quickly as possible. This includes providing appropriate training for managers, influencing organizational attitudes (to encourage cooperation and non-aggressive relationships), and attending to the continuous professional development needs of those who take on intermediary roles.

It's unlikely that any strategy will be able to prevent conflict from ever occurring, but much may be done to limit the prospect of disputes emerging and to restrict the damaging effects of untamed conflict. Furthermore, significant benefit can be gained by actively seeking to apply what has been learnt from each dispute case. An organization's appreciation and response to conflict prevention is therefore an ongoing or living activity, and one in which all leaders and managers have a vital part to play.

Regulation

Regulation serves as a reminder that in dealing with employee disputes, organizations have legal obligations as well as a duty of care. This definition might also be extended to refer to an organization's core values and ethical code, as well as to acknowledge the *spirit* of regulation, not just the letter of the law.

Resourcing

Resourcing applies the principles of good project management to ensure that the most appropriate people are engaged in the conflict management process at the right time, according to the financial and scheduling constraints that may exist.

Ultimately, this element forces a consideration of the balance of time, resource and cost relative to the benefits and disadvantages of achieving a resolution. A risk-reward analogy isn't entirely appropriate, however isn't dissimilar to the balanced decision making that must be made.

Adopted policies may also direct the type of activity and interventions that may be involved. The potential negative consequences of not following through with a thorough DR process may also need to be considered; for example, the potential penalties an organization may face if found liable in a tribunal (and without being seen to have reasonably attempted mediation ahead of the dispute being brought to court), damaged reputation or poorly impacted staff motivation.

Resourcing decisions of course apply on a dispute-by-dispute basis, but guidelines may be appropriate when considering an organization strategy for dispute resolution.

Policy

For the organization, this element focuses attention on what policies, procedures and guidelines should be put in place for managing conflict. These may integrate or complement existing policies, for example in connection with how grievances are currently handled.

Where specific disputes are concerned, *policy* concerns both the ground rules and the strategy agreed for handling a dispute. Optionally, this may include time-bounding activities and resources dedicated to finding a satisfactory resolution.

It may also include consideration of which interventions may be called upon to help bring this about.

Monitoring

Monitoring includes ensuring that the way conflict is being managed continues to be appropriate and effective. As with other elements, this applies at both an organizational policy level and at the level of individual disputes. In the latter case, attention is focused on ensuring that the policy adopted for resolving a particular dispute remains appropriate, that the dispute doesn't creep beyond the objectives or time, resource and cost boundaries previously set, and that a 'helicopter vision' (or objective view) is maintained on the progress of the conflict dialogue.

Monitoring may be needed following an agreed settlement of a dispute to ensure that all parties involved meet their part of the bargain. This might include ensuring that there is no recrimination or discrimination against an individual who initiated a disagreement against another person, or ensuring that an individual who has agreed to refrain from continuing to express his or her point of view on an alleged injustice remains true to their word. Responsibility for such monitoring may be passed to a front-line manager, may involve a pre-planned review appointment some months after the resolution agreement, or may depend on voluntary escalation by any of the individuals involved if they perceive a breach of agreement.

Monitoring also embraces the essential but often overlooked parts of evaluating the effectiveness of an existing CM policy, which may additionally include an assessment of the impacts and return on investment arising from the application of the policy. We'll consider this critical task in detail in Chapter 11.

Inter-workings of the elements

Healthy management of conflict within a well functioning and growing organization might be thought of as being akin to good physical and mental health in a living being.

Policy, for example, might be likened to a heart, pumping the blood around the veins. *Perspectives* and *Objectives* could be likened to the process of breathing – providing the continued supply of oxygen needed to keep a conflict alive. And the mechanisms designed to prevent or limit conflict might be compared with the body's integumentary system, including the skin, hair and nails, whose role is to protect the body's inner organs from raw exposure to the physical environment.

Each part of the body doesn't function in isolation from all others. It's therefore vital for a conflict manager to recognize how the various interdependencies in the conflict anatomy work; for example to consider:

■ the influence of *policy* on *prevention*;
■ the dictates or guidance offered by *regulation* on *policy*;
■ the closely aligned influence of *perspectives* on *objectives*; and
■ the clear sequential link between *diagnosis* and *cure*.

Disciplinary procedure, organizational learning and HR strategy may be closely aligned with the elements of a CM anatomy, although normally these might be considered to be broader than a conflict anatomy *per se*. Similarly, related concerns that may need to be taken account of in developing a conflict management strategy as well as potentially being influenced by it include approaches toward staff engagement, core values promotion, diversity training and supplier engagement (external mediator/other intermediary sourcing).

RELATIONSHIPS BETWEEN DISPUTING PARTIES AND THEIR PERSPECTIVES

We now turn our attention to examining the differing perspectives which each group or individual who is affected by a dispute may take on it, as well as considering the roles that may be taken in different DR approaches. Armed with an understanding of stakeholders' likely perspectives, any intermediary should be better equipped to anticipate the likely sensitivities and relationship dynamics of the conflicting parties, as well as being better informed when proposing an approaches for moving discussions forward.

We might look at the more common roles played in DR in a number of ways:

■ the relationship between the parties;
■ the function played by the parties and intermediaries; and
■ the relationship of each individual to the organization (for example, considering the perceived power dynamic between an employee and an HR officer).

The following are amongst the more common relationship types that might exist between disagreeing parties.

Peer to peer (in the same team or across a virtual team)

Example: Two team leaders denying to their project manager that they were responsible for organizing a back-up plan following a failure of shared computer systems.

Possible perspectives: Self-justification, misunderstood perception of the other's role, fear (desire to avoid being reprimanded in front of a peer).

Subordinate to manager

Example: A long-serving employee who feels he or she is being constantly overlooked for promotion, whilst a manager shows favour toward others.

Possible perspectives: Suspicion, mistrust, poor self-awareness (appreciation of their own performance), desperation.

Team (or a mix of several individuals) to manager

Example: Representation to complain that a promised change to shift patterns would be fair for all staff hasn't been followed through.

Possible perspectives: Perception of bias or management weakness, suspicion, detachment, strength in solidarity, harassment from group confrontation.

Peer to peer (who may be a more senior colleague) in different teams

Example: A PA in a marketing team alleges being shouted at and verbally abused when asking for an operations manager's up-to-date sales figures.

Possible perspectives: Fear, generalized characterization, dismissiveness, widely differing perceptions of the significance of the request.

Manager to manager (across teams)

Example: Conflicting beliefs on who has first call on resources in a matrix team.

Possible perspectives: political manoeuvring, single-mindedness, inflated perception of the importance of own needs, competitive machismo.

Team member (or members) to 'the organization'

Example: HR refuses to allow flexible shift arrangements for working parents based in a contact centre; but are accommodating of the family needs of individuals working in other departments.

Possible perspectives: Misunderstood rationale for restricting flexible working in some areas, bias, rank-led policy favouring more senior staff, detachment.

Manager to executive or more senior manager

Example: Line manager left out of the loop on a direct instruction given to a member of his or her team by a director.

Possible perspectives: Being deliberately ignored, down- and up-line loyalties, insecurity.

Inter-team

Example: Different perspectives on who should host a visiting government official.

Possible perspectives: Political manoeuvring, inflated view of self-importance, pride, competitiveness, fear of being regarded as unimportant (which may be prompted by underlying insecurity).

Cross-organization

Examples: Denial of responsibility for causing a client to be left without a jointly-developed product, supplier consultant alleges verbal abuse from a member of the customer's staff.

Possible perspectives: Differing interpretations of an ambiguously worded contract, fear (loss of image with client, delayed revenue, need to explain failing to own organization), misaligned values.

These are by no means the only relationship types that might be encountered. Some involve the roles of an accuser (or 'originator' of a complaint) and being a 'subject'; some arise from friction between two parties who perceive the other as the 'subject'; whilst others manifest without either party acknowledging that they are in dispute. What's more, the possible perspectives we've suggested aren't intended as comprehensive lists and may be under-pinned by deeper, root perceptions (for example, a view that a manager always favours a colleague's opinions may result from a desire to be liked or to feel secure).

Upward conflict

Notably, many of the relationships mentioned above affect individuals of different rank, including line relationships and differences involving individuals who may be in a position to influence the other's career course or level of empowerment. Intermediaries acting in a dispute and managers of a conflicting party too may find themselves needing to mediate with individuals who hold positions of power within the organization.

Managing upward conflict often presents special challenges, not least where a more junior party fears the consequences of continuing to work for a person with authority whose path he or she has crossed – to be isolated, passed over for promotion or treated with suspicion for ever more.

Given that this is a common fear, the perceived stakes for subordinates who are complaining are high: their discontentment may have built up over quite a long period as they hesitated about making their concern known, whilst at the same time, generalized perceptions of the subject of their dispute may have become strongly entrenched.

DR involving upward conflict typically requires intervention from a third party. This may be a manager who fits within the line between the two individuals in dispute, and so may have mixed or one-sided allegiances. Occasionally, a senior party who is a target of an allegation might be a normally trusted 'third party' or have responsibility for a company's DR policy. For example, we encountered a situation where an HR director in a large multinational organization, who also had broader divisional responsibilities, had been accused of harassing a newly recruited graduate, some four levels down the line hierarchy; an investigation of the alleged abuse had proved inconclusive, but the originator of the complaint remained unmoved in their testimony of what had happened.

Downward conflict

As with upward and peer-level conflict, the perspectives of those involved in downward conflict may not be what is often assumed. For example, a subordinate may have no concern about launching into an argument with a person in authority, either by virtue of his or her personality type or because he or she feels protected by others with power, is preparing to resign or some other unknown motivation. A senior manager may by contrast fear that his or her perceived popular reputation with 'the troops' may be damaged by an allegation of wrong-doing, and may defer to a subordinate role when feeling challenged (or to use the terminology of transactional analysis[2], take on the role of an 'adaptive child').

MODELS FOR APPROACHING CONFLICT MANAGEMENT

Models for mediating in conflict

Approaches to resolving conflicts of all kinds – from interpersonal quarrels to major international stand-offs – may usefully be applied to resolving conflict at work.

The Thomas-Kilmann Conflict Mode Instrument (TKI) (Thomas and Kilmann, 1974–2009) is perhaps the best known model used in workplace DR. This distinguishes five styles for working with conflict, set out according to whether an individual is ready to cooperate in a DR process and their tendency to be passive or assertive:

1. Competing – strongly assertive and not inclined to cooperation, an individual whose natural style is 'competing' is likely to be uncompromising, a poor or reluctant listener, single-minded and aggressive.

2. Collaborating – a collaborator will not be shy to express his or her views, but be far more ready than someone whose usual style is *competing* to consider the perspectives of others.
3. Accommodating – displayed by passive individuals who are also ready to compromise.
4. Avoiding – typical of those who put off facing a problem.
5. Compromising – shown by those who differ in their readiness to cooperate and who may be active or passive at different times or when facing different circumstances.

A variety of other models present similar inventories of conflict styles, such as Ronald Kraybill's Conflict Style Inventory (Kraybill, 2009) and the earlier Mouton-Blake Managerial Grid model (which uses task-focus and people-focus as its axes for categorization), (Blake and Mouton, 1964).

Such models aren't without criticism, for example for their tendency to put a negative slant on conflict and suffering from the inherent weakness of trying to box or label people.[3] However, being able to recognize which style an individual adopts is an important part of stakeholder analysis (which we'll discuss in Chapter 7), making it easier for an intermediary to assess what style of language, method for unravelling a dispute and which style of intervention may best engage each party, not to mention helping to identify potential triggers that may act as red flags. Judgements on individuals' style may also help inform choices about which DR approach may be most likely to succeed.

INTRODUCING 'RESOLVE'

Ultimately, which approach or mix of approaches a mediator adopts is very much a matter for personal choice, although mediators need to be sufficiently flexible to accommodate the preferences of the individuals who are sitting on opposite sides of the table.

Nevertheless, a simple model that attempts to synthesize many of the attractive elements in the approaches we've described should be useful to call upon. Our chosen model adopts the rather appropriate mnemonic 'RESOLVE', which we'll develop in detail in Chapter 4. This incorporates the following elements:

R – Review, Rules and Roles: The '3 Rs' cover the ongoing task of reviewing what is said to establish answers, setting and referring to ground-rules when appropriate and making clear the role of mediation and mediator.

E – Emotions: Acknowledges the fact that there are emotions involved at the outset and points out that it's often unproductive to allow these to encroach when searching for a mutually agreeable outcome.

S – Summarize: Mediators need to routinely summarize what they've heard to ensure they have a thorough understanding of all the relevant points in the issue. Both parties can correct the summary so that the final summary is satisfactory to both sides.

O – Outcome: Agrees a mutually acceptable outcome, identifying the existing common ground on both sides as a starting point for finding a suitable ending.

L – Learning: Learning from the experience of a dispute can be gained for all parties involved, not to mention helping to inform changes individuals and the organization as a whole can make to enhance preventive CM and improve the effectiveness of DR in future. So too, learning and insights gained for individuals as the penny drops during the resolution of their particular dispute shouldn't be allowed to get lost after further discussion.

V – Value: Once an outcome has been agreed, a mediator should thank and affirm all those involved for their efforts, emphasizing what they've achieved.

E – Engage: Invites all parties to engage with each other to continue going forward in a positive way and to help prevent similar occurrences in the future.

The model was developed by Jackie and Chris Hanney, a fellow colleague at the London Metropolitan Police. It applies a number of principles that they had recognized as underpinning successful DR and borrows learning gained from their policing work in facing danger and frequent confrontation on the streets of London.

Summary

A conflict might be likened to a living organism, having a life of its own. Both inter-related and autonomous variables are usually at play in giving life to a dispute, and the task of diagnosing these might be likened to the process of anatomizing the human body.

The nature of the working relationships between disputing parties might normally point to likely perspectives that each might hold in the dispute, though mediators and managers should be wary about rushing to assumptions. Nevertheless, models and theories can be useful when seeking to understand individuals' conflicting styles and choosing a mediation approach that is most likely to be appropriate when working with them.

Notes

1. The term 'cultural recipe' was coined by Gerry Johnson and Kevan Scholes in their book *Exploring Corporate Strategy*. They suggest that the recipe (or mix of influences that create organizational culture) incorporates a mix of both formal regulatory mechanisms (eg, role profiles) and informal ingredients (eg, attitudes).

2. Transactional Analysis (TA) explores the different internal 'ego states' we display at different times, such as 'parent', 'adult' and 'child'. It examines how these affect individual relationships with others and what can be controlled to improve interpersonal 'transactions'. The concept was originated by Eric Berne; see Berne, E (1996) *Games People Play: The basic handbook of transactional analysis*, Ballantine Books.

3. See for example, the following critiques: Wilson, C (October 2009) 'Tools of the trade', *Training Journal*, and Berens, L V (2001) *Understanding Yourself and Others®: An introduction to interaction styles*, Telos Publications. Berens' typology of initiating and responding roles and directing and informing communications includes a mapping to Myers Briggs Type Indicator (MBTI Schema) codes, The Five Temperaments theory, DiSC and other well-known ways for describing personality types.

3

Options for resolving conflict

TAKING STOCK OF THE OPTIONS

When a dispute takes hold, several alternative approaches might be taken for reaching a satisfactory conclusion. These include:

- attempting to resolve the matter on a one-to-one basis;
- taking a direct approach (bashing heads together);
- engaging a conflict coach to work with each party;
- engaging one or more third parties to help broker a way forward;
- engaging a collaborative legal process;
- moving swiftly to litigation;
- engaging an arbitrator or tribunal panel to hear and reach a judgement;
- letting a line manager play the role of arbitrator;
- letting the dispute run its course, potentially never reaching a definite conclusion.

Factors such as the stage a dispute has reached, the readiness of the disagreeing parties to participate in a dialogue, and the desire or need to reach a speedy conclusion may influence the choice of approaches.

In some countries, organizations may be influenced by a desire to demonstrate that they had undertaken appropriate steps to attempt DR before a dispute reached court. In the UK for example, to comply with legislation (the Employment Act 2008), this means being sure that the ACAS Code of Practice for dispute resolution had been followed.

Attempting to resolve the matter on a one-to-one basis

In most cases, some attempt is made to resolve a dispute locally. This may take the form of a private, frank discussion between the two parties, or it may involve an aggrieved party discussing the issue with (for example) his or her line manager. Any dispute that hasn't reached an impasse may be suitable for one-to-one treatment. Indeed, this might normally be one of the first options to be tried. However, the need to engage a more formal process or to involve a third party becomes more likely as a dispute develops.

Taking a direct approach

Sometimes, a third party can play an altogether different role from the normal concept of mediation: 'bashing heads together', or getting both parties to wake up to the senselessness of pursuing their argument, to make amends and move on. In terms of a *transactional* relationship, the mediator plays the role of 'critical parent' in a situation where the other parties are locked in a child-to-child dispute. This is of course a risky strategy, but one which, when used appropriately, can quickly bring a dispute to a definite end, whilst also challenging both parties to quickly set aside their differences and defuse their feelings of animosity.

This very direct way of dealing with conflict doesn't have to be taken by a more senior colleague, but it does require the involvement of someone who has the respect of both parties, and who is well positioned to properly appreciate what the dispute is about. A calm, level-headed peer may be able to play this role if they are available and willing to do so. However, uncovering the real issues underpinning a dispute is often not straightforward. An informal approach, when put into the wrong hands, can not only fail to resolve a dispute and so increase the likelihood that it will re-emerge in future, but may also open up resentment toward the mediator and potentially (and sometimes justifiably) form the basis for complaint, for example, if apparent insensitivity toward a grievance has been shown.

This said, in close working teams in which individuals are familiar with taking criticism, there are many situations where such direct intervention may be appropriate. In our experience, a common example is when what appears to be a genuinely trivial disagreement starts with a difference of views and continues because neither party is able to stand down from their position.

Individuals who are called upon to act as informal mediators need to be selected with care. In particular, the potential for aggravating an already sensitive relationship must be avoided, and anyone who may be seen as representing the organization's view of a dispute needs to be mindful of the potential to expose the organization to a liability that might not currently exist. Coercing someone to participate in a joint mediation session when it's known that an individual is susceptible to excessive stress, for example, might provoke a possible charge of injury to health that they might otherwise not be able to claim.

In the absence of specialized knowledge of employment law, or at a minimum, basic training, mistakes of this kind can be easily made. Where both parties wish to engage a mutually respected colleague who may be entering into mediation for the first time, it may be appropriate for expectations of what the mediator is able to do to be made clear, with the intermediary possibly being first briefed by HR (especially to recognize the potential risks for exposure, for example, where medical certification is needed to recall an individual for a meeting if the person is currently absent due to sickness).

'Informal mediator' third parties might also be sought from outside the organization when circumstances allow. Inter-company associations such as the International Conflict Management Forum encourage networking, knowledge and resource sharing between organizations to facilitate such interventions.

Engaging a conflict coach to work with each party

Coaches can play a powerful role in helping each party to articulate the basis for their perspectives on their disagreement, sometimes meaning that they are able to see a situation in a completely new light. Coaching might be defined as a process for helping individuals come to new insights and perspectives, and finding answers to the questions that they raise and problems they face. A coach asks the questions, helping a coachee to reflect, frame and think through what they discover, as opposed to 'giving' answers, guidance and the benefits of his or her own wisdom (as may be the case, for example, with mentoring). Since coaching facilitates the remarkable ability of the brain to revive itself – a concept described by neuro-scientists as *plasticity* – changed mindsets brought about through coaching after the prospect that negative perceptions of an opposite person in a dispute may be reduced or even removed altogether in the future relationship.

The practice of coaching usually plays an important role in all forms of ADR, and we borrow heavily from the lessons of coaching in the following chapters. As with mediation, coaching may involve just one coach or two working together. Tandem coaching can be especially useful if an individual suspects that a coach may have an inherent bias against them (eg due to gender difference).

A coach may be assigned to work with one or both parties (optionally, the same coach may work with both, or to ensure complete impartiality, a different coach may be offered to each party). The coach then helps each party to reflect on their perspective, gaining a deep appreciation of why they hold their point of view. The coach may not need to know much about either the business context in which the disagreement has occurred or its legal context. His or her primary role is to help support unprejudiced and clear thinking, allowing individuals to discover their own appreciation of their situation and their reasons for feeling the way they do.

Coaching is normally best introduced before a dispute reaches an advanced stage, but it can be used at any point. A coach may be very helpful in resolving a blockage, and he or she can help an individual who has become overwhelmed by the dispute to see and think more clearly.

Coaches may also play an important role in helping both parties in any joint dialogue. Again, the coach's main role is to help the parties explore their beliefs, consider options, and agree a way forward. The coach should be able to encourage productive thinking without directly leading any individual's line of thought. Nevertheless, well-trained and experienced coaches should have a good repertoire of knowledge and helpful approaches for addressing matters such as log jams. Their focus is usually predominantly forward-looking, and a coach may work with an individual or a group over a period of time. Coaching therefore offers more than mere *facilitation*.

Even a brief involvement by a coach can be invaluable, given his or her ability to help individuals grasp the reality of their situation and the consequences of pursuing different courses of action (such as a quest for 'justice' that may leave a trail of undesirable side-effects). In some cases, a decision not to continue the argument may be achieved after just one coaching conversation.

A coach should more easily be seen as a supportive independent than some other intermediaries, especially since coaching conversations are normally guided by strict rules of confidentiality. Coaches' 'rules of engagement' should be easy for most individuals to accept, such as their complete independence from any formal grievance investigation process. Coaching should shed light on the reasons the aggrieved parties disagree and on the outcomes that will satisfy them, in turn benefiting subsequent mediation or arbitration, if a dispute needs to escalate that far.

Where possible, it's preferable for an individual who's playing the role of mediator not also to act as a coach to one of the disputing parties. However, there are no hard and fast rules about this – time, cost and resourcing considerations must invariably be carefully balanced. Similarly, to insist that intermediaries operate within the strict limits of a role profile can hinder effective DR in some situations (it may also make sense to train in-house coaches as mediators to optimize their skills).

A mark of a DR professional is a commitment to developing their knowledge of other intermediary's roles, as well as being sufficiently gracious and self-aware to know when to refer to others for help.

Engaging one or more third parties to help broker a way forward

As in a one-to-one dialogue, a third party may be engaged at any point. He or she may be an individual known by and trusted by each of the disagreeing parties, perhaps a detached colleague or other person who might not normally expect to become involved in such a role (for example, a respected colleague called upon to broker a dispute between a manager and a member of his or her staff or other manager). Alternatively, bringing another person into the dialogue may involve a more formal approach. A mediator, either employed internally (for example, an HR professional) or engaged from outside the organization, may be called upon to step into the role.

A mediator's role includes helping the disputing individuals to shift their focus onto a realistic outcome, assisting them to form an awareness, and ultimately appreciation, of their different perspectives. Except in the case of evaluative mediation (which we'll discuss below), a mediator isn't engaged to act as a workplace therapist or adviser. We would strongly urge that caution is taken to ensure that this doesn't happen.

The intended role of a third party may be restricted to just one objective; for example, to help identify a way forward, or to help both parties pin down their objectives for wanting to pursue the dispute. A go-between may be a facilitator rather than a guide, may be invited to offer a view on the dispute or maintain strict independence from directly contributing an opinion in the argument itself.

One of the most common difficulties faced when engaging a single third party is that one party may be suspicious of the individual's true independence. For example, if an external mediator is hired by the HR department to help broker a dispute, the aggrieved employee may suspect that the mediator is really acting in the organization's interests. A similar suspicion may arise when a manager from another part of the organization is brought into the mix. One approach for overcoming this may be to involve more than one mediator. This is common practice in formal mediation. In this scenario, each party may work with one mediator. Private discussions don't influence the mediator's behaviour in a group (conference) session. Whilst not perfect, the separation of mediators improves the prospect of their impartiality being trusted.

Whilst mediation is often only considered following a formal grievance procedure or when the threat of litigation is looming, it can be a very powerful tool in the early stage of a dispute, before mindsets become locked and other parties become involved.

Engaging a collaborative legal process

A variation on the tandem mediation approach is to involve lawyers in mediation before a dispute finds its way into court. Two lawyers may be engaged, each working with one of the parties. Most experienced mediators will have at least foundation knowledge of employment law contexts in which most employment disputes occur.

A common reason for engaging lawyers as opposed to others as mediators is that knowledge of the possible considerations and outcomes were the matter to escalate into litigation may serve to help the parties better reflect on the value of protracting the dispute, given that their interests may be best served by reaching an early settlement. For example, an aggrieved employee may want to feel assured that he or she hasn't committed to a reduced settlement when he or she may have achieved more by pursuing litigation on what he or she sees as being a clear-cut case, and one in which the employer acknowledges some failing.

In practice however, in this type of ADR, the basis for deciding whether one party has been treated fairly or otherwise need not be reduced to just what is defined in law. In some countries, for example Australia, New Zealand and the UK, this form of ADR has become popular during recent years, being encouraged both by parliament and the judiciary.

The decision on whether to involve legal collaboration is therefore one that might normally be taken in light of the likelihood of the issue escalating into litigation and the legal complexity or ambiguity of the dispute. Lawyers should be engaged before any agreement is drawn up, even though all parties in a mediation process may have reached a point of consensus. This may be simply a matter of seeking a lawyer's advice and offering an employee access to legal advice for his or her own protection, similar to what might be offered before a compromise agreement is finalized as a settlement to other HR matters.

Moving swiftly to litigation

Attempts to resolve conflicts can be costly in terms of time and human resources. Many organizations may feel that they don't have the time to dedicate to informal DR and the pressure to move swiftly to litigation may therefore be strong. At least, organizations may opt to pick and choose which cases they feel justify going the extra mile to attempt to resolve the matter internally.

Recent research shows that many US organizations expect to undertake a number of court cases per year, and that this is an inevitable part of managing a workforce. Where they are certain that they can defend their position and there is little incentive to prolong the process in-house (especially if earlier attempts at ADR have not reached a satisfactory conclusion), this may be a tempting option. Some take the view that the risk of having to pay compensation if an employee is successful in their claim is more beneficial to investing the many hours of effort to attempt to resolve a dispute internally. As we've seen in Chapter 1, this can be a false economy; however, it's one that we've often seen entrenched.

Even though employees as well as employers may need to have demonstrated their commitment to attempting ADR before bringing a matter to court, some individuals may engage lawyers at breathtaking speed. Indeed, employees who are convinced of the invincibility of their case may be champing at the bit to have their day in court. Prolonged grievance processes and mediation delay this opportunity, and so may be seen as undesirable.

Engaging an arbitrator or informal tribunal panel to hear and reach a judgement

Arbitration involves a formal process for reaching a judgement on a dispute, normally adopting a principal used in civil law, that a decision may be made on the 'balance of probabilities' as opposed to being 'beyond all reasonable doubt'. An arbitrator is therefore empowered with a more decisive role than a mediator or coach. Arbitration may involve mediation, but if the parties who are in dispute cannot reach a conclusion through mediation, then it's for the arbitrator to reach a decision on closure, based on the evidence he or she has examined.

An arbitrator may pass on the content of a dialogue conducted with one party to the other, and may also alternate between the two, allowing for an option which both parties don't have to face each other at the same time. This might be appropriate, for example, where there is a strong risk of a conflict erupting into physical or verbal violence, or where one party is acutely sensitive to facing the other (for example, where an employee alleges harassment by a senior colleague).

A variation in arbitration is for a panel rather than an individual to reach a decision on how to conclude a dispute. In effect, this is an internal equivalent of an external tribunal. A panel-led arbitration may be most appropriate when there is ambiguity or complexity in the facts of a dispute. However, used inappropriately, it can serve to frustrate any prospect of finding a satisfactory solution for both parties.

Letting a line manager play the role of arbitrator

In an initial attempt at resolution, peers within a team are most likely to bring their disagreement to their line manager. This is usually appropriate, and in any event their manager should normally be made aware of the nature if not the detail of any dispute that has been formally escalated by a member of his or her team.

Front-line managers should also be best positioned to know how to manage their staff since they normally interact with them on a regular basis. They should be aware of individuals' motivations and likely responses to different types of intervention, assuming that they've built a relationship with the individual concerned and have the skills needed to manage difficult situations.

Unfortunately, this isn't always the case. Indeed, some managers find themselves in a new position in which they've responsibility for managing staff, but without having had any training in this area, whilst others may manage a virtual or field-based team in which they have limited interpersonal contact with members in their team other than to discuss purely task-related matters. It's these novice managers who are perhaps most vulnerable to making mistakes in attempts at DR, although more seasoned managers aren't exempt. Heavy-handed dealing of a situation, unconscious prejudice (for example, a bias toward a particular individual's side of the story), and an inability to properly listen and avoid rushing to assumptions are amongst the factors that might unseat the unwary. We'll look at these and other potential pitfalls in Chapter 6.

In contrast, a skilled manager can often bring a dispute to a speedy conclusion. Managers in the front line (as it were) having responsibility for interacting with staff on a daily basis, have perhaps the biggest role to play in ensuring that conflicts are quickly recognized and contained. We'll return later to consider what training and support can be given to managers to enable them to take on this role most effectively.

Anyone might be eligible for this informal mediator role, but not all will have the skill and knowledge to meet the challenge. Where an individual is proposed as a possible go-between, and assuming that he or she is available and willing to step into the role, it's important that he or she is briefed on the nature of a mediator's role, if they haven't already received training in this area. Indeed, the person might be persuaded to carefully consider declining the offer to mediate if they haven't received appropriate training.

Letting the dispute run its course

Just allowing a dispute to continue is rarely the best option. Unless conflict is properly channelled or brought to a conclusion, the negative consequences can be enduring. However, in some cases, a dispute may not follow a standard life-cycle, reaching a point at which the disagreement begins to defuse: in effect, a dispute may just fizzle out. This is most likely to be the case where the conflict was not intense and where the people involved have moved on.

Each of these approaches offers relative advantages and disadvantages, as shown in Table 3.1.

Table 3.1   Options for conflict resolution

OPTION	ADVANTAGES	DISADVANTAGES
Attempting to resolve a matter on a one-to-one basis	Avoids need to disclose the existence of the dispute to others (stays 'off the record')	Prospect for resolution may be slim unless both parties operate on same transactional basis
	May force a quick resolution as each party is shocked into recognizing the reality of their dispute	
	Puts both parties on a par (neither comes out feeling a 'victor' or 'vanquished')	Possibility of exposing individual and/or organization to litigation or harm ('unsafe')
Taking a direct approach	May force a quick resolution as each party is shocked into recognizing the reality of their quarrel	May trivialize and further entrench a significant grievance
	Puts both parties on a par (neither comes out feeling a 'victor' or 'vanquished')	May alienate a readiness for individuals to be forthcoming about a dispute in future
		May expose the organization to a charge of abdicating its duty of care
Engaging a conflict coach to work with each party	Offers an opportunity for an individual to talk about and come to terms with the issue they are facing and work through options without needing to open up about what they discussed outside of the coaching relationship	May miss important perspectives held by the other party or the wider context which may be crucial for both parties achieving a lasting resolution to their differences
	Likely to focus on achieving a realistic outcome which is acceptable for the individual	Coach may be regarded by other party as being biased toward their client
	May help an individual decide whether further ADR is appropriate, and if so, which type of intervention is most likely to help them move forward	
	May help individuals to reflect and so prepare the way for further ADR, saving time of a wider group of people than might otherwise be the case	

	Helps an individual to focus on what they really want to achieve, so potentially reducing the time needed for achieving resolution and increasing the likelihood that they will recognize the benefits of overcoming the suffocating influences of the dispute* (Berg, 1992; De Shazer *et al*, 2007)	
Engaging one or more third parties to help broker a way forward	Third party intervention should help stabilize a dialogue ('keep the peace'), help the parties retain a relevant focus and offer suggestions, observations and questions to help both parties reflect and arrive at a new appreciation or decision	
	Clearly bounds the amount of time the parties spend locked in discussion (may hasten a drive to reach a resolution)	Can be costly in time and money
		Parties may not be ready to convene, regard an intermediary as an agent of the organization, or simply are 'going through the motions' of participating in a dialogue to have been seen to attempt ADR
Engaging a collaborative legal process (evaluative mediation)	Gives parties who are set on having their 'day in court' their wish, without the frequent time delays, costs and restricted scope for agreeing forward actions that the latter involves	
	Cuts through any perceived imbalance of equality which may exist with many other forms of ADR (a benchmark for evaluating the case and any potential penalty is the Law: applicable for the organization as much as for the employee)	May be costly compared with some other forms of ADR
	Allows both parties to avoid the need to argue their case in a public forum	

	Likely to be less costly than allowing a dispute to escalate to a tribunal or court process	
Moving swiftly to litigation	Avoids time and energy spent attempting ADR	
	Forces an ultimate confrontation for the issue at dispute (cuts short what may be a false threat)	The opportunity to achieve a possibly more appropriate, lasting and quickly reached resolution isn't explored
		Likely to be costly
		May often involve a long period of time before a case may be heard
		Unlikely to result in an acceptable resolution for both parties
		Losing party may be penalized for not having attempted ADR
Engaging an arbitrator or tribunal panel to hear and reach a judgement	As for engaging a collaborative legal process	As for engaging a collaborative legal process
Letting a third-party manager or other colleague play the role of intermediary	May avoid the need to enact a formal DR process	Chosen intermediary may be inadequately trained or be unfamiliar with the role they've been invited to undertake (may unwittingly aggravate the dispute or expose the organization to a possible breach of employment law)
	A colleague who is approached without reference to HR is less likely to be treated with suspicion than might an intermediary who is appointed by the organization	
	May allow a quick resolution to be achieved	
	A mutually trusted mediator may be better able to help one or both sides show humility or compromise than might an unknown party	

	The individuals who act as intermediaries may themselves enhance their skills and better appreciate the practice of DR from their experience	
Letting the dispute run its course, potentially never reaching a definite conclusion	Avoids taking out time to attempt a resolution	Time saving in the short term may be a false economy as time is lost later as the dispute continues to vent itself, dampen motivation and cooperative working or reduce individuals' attention to their work
	May avoid opening up further possible causes for aggravating the relationship between the disputing parties as they air their views	A significant dispute may further escalate, possibly affecting people beyond the current parties and exposing a manager (or organization) to a charge of neglecting its duty of care
		Misses a possible opportunity to constructively channel the energy and passion which conflict produces
		Disputing parties don't gain fresh perspectives on their dispute and miss the opportunity for possible transformative learning

*In using brief therapy as a therapeutic intervention with their patients, Steve de Shazer and Insoo Kim Berg found that a solution-focused approach enabled a patient to focus on a real underlying issue more quickly than with other methods (ie, to uncover what they actually wanted to achieve), and consequently, fewer clinic sessions were required. For example, individuals who set as their objective 'to lose weight' may actually want to be perceived as being more attractive when meeting potential partners and so overcome their loneliness, get fitter to improve their chance of living to see their grandchildren grow up, or get back to a time when they were able to wear a favourite outfit.

HORSES FOR COURSES?

As we've seen, the choice of which DR approach should be taken may depend on the stage the dispute has reached. More informal methods may often be most appropriate during the early stages of a dispute's emergence, whilst formal approaches such as mediation are typically more relevant at a later stage. This recognizes that the involvement of a third party and formal process may be expensive, but also that a conflict can be resolved quickly and locally.

We might then question when it may be appropriate to invoke a formal DR process or engage informal mediation, and what benefits the early involvement of a third party could bring. As we've already seen, mediation can take various forms – informal or formal, with a specific purpose or central role in the DR process, involve one or more intermediaries, brought from inside the organization or hired for their independence and specialism in a particular field. The question of whether and when to begin mediation or some other intervention therefore relies on a number of considerations:

- Whether it's clear what role the mediator(s) is expected to play.
- If their role is to facilitate a way out of a logjam, whether a colleague who is detached from the dispute that both parties respect might play this role.
- How intense and time/resource-consuming the dispute has become or may become (as well as what impact it has had or may have on the people involved and others).
- Whether there is any basis for mediation that both parties can agree with.

The decision on whether to embark on any formal mediation process – or indeed to attempt an informal mediation – might normally rest with HR professionals. Of course, line managers or others may also wish to take this decision, especially if they are required to pay for the service (as well as to face the consequences of not resolving an ongoing issue satisfactorily). For example, guidance given to managers and individuals, in a staff handbook or grievance procedure, should make clear what options are available for resolving disputes.

Formal mediation doesn't tend to be used until standard grievance procedures are exhausted. Many organizations have established mechanisms for investigating alleged unfairness, as well as an appeal procedure that may be invoked if necessary. We have encountered examples in some organizations where a virtually continuous chain of 'fairness at work' investigations may ensue, allowing disgruntled employees to continually raise fresh grievances if they feel that their concern has not been addressed to their liking. Clearly, this isn't a satisfactory means for resolving conflict, serving no one's interests well.

Ultimately, a judgement has to be made on the relative advantages of involving a third party versus allowing the dispute to continue. The financial benefit may be hard to pin down, although previous experience may help in forming a view on the likely course a dispute might take. Where a specific (perhaps 'one-off') role has been identified for the mediator, it should be relatively easy to predict what his or her time involvement should be and therefore to assess the costs this will involve. At any rate, it may often be desirable to specify a time limit for mediation, giving a clear focus for the parties to reach a satisfactory outcome. Of course, time invested in the process must also take account of the time involvement of the disagreeing parties.

More difficult is predicting the cost of allowing a dispute to continue. It may already be apparent that much time and energy has been spent in attempts to knock the disagreement on its head, but the hidden costs of conflict may be much more difficult to uncover. These may include the impacts of preoccupation, anger and stress on the individuals involved, potentially affecting their productivity, decision making and work quality. At worst, the psychological burden of conflict can induce high levels of stress or illness, sometimes being long-lasting and with expensive consequences for both the individuals concerned and the organization.

The impacts on others also need to be taken into account. Bad feeling within a team, for example, can impact on the performance of an entire group. We shouldn't forget either that the consequences of allowing a dispute to continue may be to sustain unease over a long period. Indeed, left unresolved, the emotional impacts may become more deeply entrenched.

However, it's not just the financial consequences of whether or not to engage third-party intervention that need to be considered. Involving mediation at the right time can have a significant benefit for both the organization and for the individuals involved. The benefits may be more motivational in nature for the individuals concerned – by which we mean not just the person or persons who have raised a complaint, but line managers, HR professionals, internal mediators and those representing the organization's interests, as well as others affected by the dispute (such as those working in an environment in which there is a continuously tense undercurrent). Reduced frustration, improved self-esteem and a sense of relief may all be by-products of a successful resolution.

Offering a coach, for example, and allowing time for safe, private conversations, may demonstrate an organization's commitment to fairness and staff well-being. Engaging a process of mediation, by contrast, might similarly show that no one's side is automatically assumed to be more valid than another's. Some individuals may also benefit from the process by gaining greater self-understanding, including those who may come to recognize the real issue driving their feelings. A manager may come to see how his or her own behaviour, words, or leadership style impacts on others, and so in turn gain a better self-understanding, to the benefit of others with whom he or she regularly interacts. Individuals prone to bursts of anger may be encouraged to explore training or other options for controlling the way they channel their emotions, whilst long-standing barriers preventing an open rapport between two individuals may be removed. Such transformational effects aren't inevitable consequences of DR, but they are not uncommon.

For the organization, benefits of controlled DR may include avoiding potential embarrassment or a damaged reputation if a genuine grievance finds its way into the public domain (for example, if a dispute is only ultimately resolved in court). It can actively demonstrate, rather than just describe, a commitment to support the interests of all staff (a process that involves listening to individuals and engaging with them), and making it easier for individuals to feel that they can raise concerns at an early stage, allowing potential problems to be addressed sooner rather than later.

Case study: Behind closed doors

Veronica was the branch manager of a bank, Molly a financial adviser. Both were of the same grade and pay band. Molly was contracted to work from 9 am to 5 pm. Being conscientious, she would always begin working earlier.

Each evening, Veronica let staff out of the building before locking the doors to check the day's accounts. However, she always seemed to have an excuse for Molly to stay until she was ready to leave, and consequently Molly could never leave on time. For Molly, this appeared to be a deliberate game. Molly's requests for Veronica to unlock the doors were always met with the response: 'in a minute'. Typically, Molly would need to stay for more than 20 minutes beyond the time she was ready to leave.

This pattern continued for more than a year, whilst Molly became increasingly frustrated and affected by the way she felt treated. Her sense of being undervalued was made worse by the fact that she had received excellent feedback from customers and had achieved the highest targets for attracting investment to the branches.

Finally, Molly approached her area manager with the concern, but was told that the pair were 'two grown women' and so should be able to sort the matter out themselves. Molly then approached Veronica, explaining how she felt, that she shouldn't have to hang around for no good reason. Veronica replied that she was branch manager and so Molly would leave when she decided. Molly pointed out their equal grading, but was ignored.

Soon after, seeing no end to the situation, Molly resigned, moving to another bank. The bank had lost an excellent and otherwise very committed member of staff, whilst Veronica's behaviour remained unchallenged.

In this case, a clear flag was raised by Molly to a manager whose lack of interest in becoming involved in informal mediating on the matter ultimately lost the bank a talented employee. Time pressures, a lack of appreciation for the seriousness of Molly's concern or a belief that 'grown women' really should be able to resolve their own disagreements may have influenced the manager's reaction; however neither of these can be used as an excuse for not keeping a check on the issue once it had been raised: the signs of a potentially divisive dispute should have been plain to see.

WHY CONFLICT MANAGEMENT SHOULD BE A CONCERN FOR ALL MANAGERS

The costs – both financial and non-financial – of allowing a dispute to run its course can be very high. Conflict management must therefore be a matter of concern for all managers. It's they who 'walk the floor', and so are normally the first to see the signs of potential unrest. They are in the front line to be approached by disgruntled employees, and ultimately they are charged with the responsibility of managing staff and all that entails. Managers of staff may also find themselves acting as intermediaries or protectors between their staff and other individuals, for example when another department confronts them. Managers too are often those charged with breaking any bad news to staff, and with it, the potential for resulting friction.

Even those who don't have staff management responsibility should be concerned about the potential of any policy they propose or influence to unsettle relationships. Many conflicts begin in larger organizations where an ivory tower mentality prevails; in other words, where there's a wide gulf between what might seem to be a sensible policy, and appreciating the impacts this might have on individuals. Any policy making or decision making that has the potential to impact individuals' motivation should take account of possible triggers and sensitivities. This of course means considering how a proposal or statement is worded and what method is used to communicate it.

Unfortunately, many managers and policy/decision makers aren't naturally sensitive to potential conflict triggers. Indeed, many who succeed in achieving promotion are those who are most competitive, self-assertive, and (in some cases) the most aggressive. Managers may misunderstand those who are less assertive, quiet and apparently content individuals. However, those who may be less likely to rush to complain can also be those for whom tension becomes most entrenched, and for whom a disagreement is already well formed when the camel's back is finally broken.

It's not just those with authority who should be concerned about preventing and containing the potential for conflict arising, however. Every person can help to avoid the often unnecessary unpleasantness associated with conflict by being better at recognizing their own capacity to identify and positively manage the early signs of confrontation. By being more self-aware, and having the techniques to deal with mounting unease, individuals should be better able to prevent unnecessary escalation of the issues that present themselves. At the same time, having the skill to present their feelings or perspectives constructively and assertively may prevent unnecessary quarrels kicking off.

APPROACHES TO MEDIATION

Mediation may be offered in a variety of ways, each representing alternative forms of ADR that may be appropriate to use according to circumstance and the preferences of the disputing parties.

Narrative mediation

This approach encourages the parties to focus on constructing the 'story' they would like to see play out; putting emphasis on envisaging their future relationship and situation, rather than dwelling on what has gone before. For example, participants might be asked:

- If you were standing and observing this, what would you see?
- Imagine you have watched this in a video – what did you actually see and hear?
- If you were telling this story to someone else, what would you say?

Similarly, for considering the outcomes individuals desire, the following might be suggested:

- What would make the difference between the way things are in the picture you describe and the way they are now?
- What would this look like? What would you see, hear, smell, feel?

Nagao and Page (2005) distinguish three elements in the process of conducting narrative mediation: engagement (during which each party presents their own story), deconstruction (where the conflicting issues in each story are highlighted and dismantled, helped by mediator intervention) and construction (in which the new story is put together). Some time after mediation, a follow-up review is conducted to determine how much of the new narrative has been put into practice. The mediator plays a very central role in helping the parties to deconstruct and rebuild a new story, employing skills of reflective questioning to help individuals identify the sources of conflict and rationalize why they want to swap the stories they've described with a new narrative.

Our experience with narrative mediation isn't using it as an overarching approach for mediation, but rather as a technique that can serve a useful purpose at different stages during any part of a DR process. Indeed, we believe that story-telling can be used with powerful effect during the initial 'Golden Hour' of an emerging conflict, and it's therefore equally relevant in managing conflict 'at the front end'.

Similarly, narrative is something that we've found can be regularly brought into coaching conversations, especially when working with individuals who prefer to describe their hopes and experiences in visual terms. Encouraging an individual to tell a story is a very gentle way of leading into qualifying and prob-ing questioning, including the way in which the person may be inclined to reflect on different points of interest. This is similar to the way that eight different witnesses to a road traffic collision might offer eight different perspectives – some commenting on the speed, the make or model of the vehicles, who the occupants were, what happened afterwards and some proposing explanations of how the collision occurred.

We also like the future-oriented perspective taken by the use of narrative. This brings us to another attractive approach or rather technique that can be used at any stage in conflict management: the outcome-based approach to mediation.

Outcome-based approach (solution-focused approach)

Outcome-based mediation owes its existence to the 'solution-focused' method commonly used in coaching and psychotherapy contexts, which in turn drew upon the earlier thinking of the eminent US psychiatrist Milton Eriksson, the French-Canadian communications specialist Fletcher Peacock, and solution-focused therapists Steve de Shazer and Insoo Kim Berg, amongst others.

As with a narrative, the outcome-based approach puts emphasis on envisaging a desired, target future – the so-called 'future perfect'. It encourages individuals to test their motivation for achieving this new state and challenges them to take small steps towards achieving it. The use of the word 'outcome' is deliberate since this suggests an ongoing situation rather than a snapshot event, such as when a particular goal is achieved.

Whilst encouraging individuals to look forward, the approach nonetheless takes account of past experiences that have brought them to their current point, including a mix of what was right and what was wrong in the past. The practice it then encourages is for individuals to do more of what works and less of what doesn't.

To become accomplished in outcome-based mediation, a mediator needs to become proficient in using a mix of communication styles and techniques advocated by Ericsson, Peacock and others. For example, mediators should know when to use what Peacock (2000) describes as 'the miracle question' – the single question that starts individuals thinking in a completely different way and begins the process of unlocking the narrow and superficial perspectives they may currently hold. We'll introduce a few of these in later chapters.

In coaching too, solution-focused concepts have been shown to be especially powerful and have gained increasing popularity in recent years. The teachings of Jackson and McKergow, Greene and Grant and others have created a strong following amongst coaches.

Facilitative mediation

As the name suggests, facilitative mediation involves mediators primarily playing the simple role of facilitator. They may propose a structure for conducting the mediation, but their main contribution is questioning, playing back and helping the disputing parties to move forward and acknowledge when decisions have been taken. This isn't to minimize the value of facilitation, nor its potential effectiveness or advantage over some other approaches.

A facilitator needs to exercise skill in helping individuals to reflect and achieve understanding, to manage time efficiently but not restrictively, and to avoid influencing the parties to follow in a particular direction. As with other forms of mediation, a facilitative approach may involve dealing with strong emotions, resistance, biting accusations and impasse. What's more, the mediator usually has less control over the course of the conversation, since facilitation encourages the parties to choose the approach they prefer for finding a resolution and to determine the way forward they believe is most appropriate. It requires that they 'own' the outcome of their discussion, with the mediator serving to help their interchange and decision-making happen effectively. Of course this doesn't preclude a mediator making suggestions, for example when individuals appear to be stuck or have no strong feelings about how their discussion should be structured. Necessarily, facilitation requires both parties to be involved in a joint discussion, although private conversations may also need to take place outside of a facilitated dialogue.

Depending on the nature of the causes of a dispute, this type of mediation usually avoids the uncomfortable provoking of raw emotion that the transformative approach often brings about. One other possible advantage is that facilitative mediators need not have a strong background in DR, opening up the possibility for involving a wide range of people in this role.

Evaluative mediation

In this approach, mediators act as both listener and adviser. They hear the arguments put by both parties, much in the same way that they might be presented to
a tribunal, but subsequently mediators offer their opinion on the arguments
presented to them, especially with a view to anticipating how a court or tribunal
might respond to them. Mediators performing this role are normally experienced
in law or qualified to consider the legal merits of the arguments presented to
them, extending to making suggestions about how one or both parties may wish
to proceed with their case.

Evaluative mediation offers a relatively quick means for moving the process
forward, being less likely to involve prolonged discussion between the two
parties than, say, 'shuttle mediation'. Individuals may reach a quick decision on
whether to proceed to litigation following an evaluation hearing, or may come to
a quick and stark recognition of the merits of their particular complaint and so
choose to back off.

The evaluative approach may therefore be most appropriate when it's clear
that neither party believe that a compromise is possible or one of them seems
intent on pursuing his or her cause to the bitter end. However, since it focuses on
the strength of legal arguments rather than endeavouring to diagnose the underlying causes of the dispute or unpack the psycho-emotional turmoil that this may
have produced, evaluative mediation may offer only a limited chance of achieving a lasting peace.

Judicial mediation

Judicial mediation has recently been piloted in some countries. Similarly to evaluative mediation but occurring once a case has reached court, mediation occurs
in situ at court, where the judge acts in the role of a mediator rather than presid-
ing over the hearing and reaching a judgement. The option to continue to a full
hearing remains available if the case doesn't reach an agreement, although the
same judge will not preside over the case in such event (Gilhooley, 2009).

Transformative approach

The transformative approach was introduced relatively recently by Bush and
Folger (2004) and further enhanced by Cloke (2001) to consider a mediator's
role as extending beyond facilitation to one of being a reflective guide who interacts directly in the discussion. The transformative approach has been described
by Epstein (2009) as offering 'a passionate, in your face plea for exploring
the difficult process of mediation, truly digging into the roots, the skin, the
pores of people's, group's and organization's conflicts'. The basic intention of

the approach is to help individuals reach a deeper awareness of their response to a conflict, with an aim of transforming their thinking and, in particular, achieving a better understanding of the other party's perspective. Bush and Folger argue that by achieving this, individuals may not only find that they can re-evaluate the current situation they find themselves in, but will also have grown as individuals, developing their emotional intelligence and ability to relate to others.

The essential change agents required for transformation are empowerment and recognition of each other; for the mediator, most attention is normally focused on the first of these – making sure that individuals can feel safe to explore their own thoughts and feelings, probing deeply to improve their awareness of personal value systems and core beliefs. Empowerment seeks to give individuals an enhanced sense of self-value and so be more confident about confronting unpleasant or challenging situations. With a stronger belief in their self-worth, they should be more ready to listen to their opponent and to recognize and ultimately have knowledge of their perspective. This puts the human concerns of each party into a context that both parties can begin to understand and therefore attend to, moving from an adversarial position to one of cooperation and empathy.

If either party concludes that they cannot comprehend the other's perspective, this is nevertheless a useful step forward in mediation. The fact that we cannot understand everything about the way others see the world, with all their differences of experience, mind and personality, is something to be acknowledged as being positive.

A mediator may need to help individuals break through a series of barriers to achieve this end, including confronting their fears, exhibiting humility and coming to an apology. They are likely to need to help individuals to overcome their resistance to making change, tame their appetite for seeking revenge and contemplate the notion of asking for forgiveness. We'll look at some practical ways for achieving these needs in Chapter 8.

So too for the mediator, the experience can be quite raw. As Cloke (2001) explains, 'mediators need to bring a deep, dangerous level of honesty and empathy to the dispute resolution process'. For the parties involved, the experience is 'dangerous' because it requires them to give up an entrenched position for something that is completely unknown – not only letting down their guard, but potentially also baring their souls and facing up to some hard self-truths.

However, this uncomfortable and sometimes lengthy process should pay dividends. The prospect for keeping a lasting peace should be high, individuals should be better equipped to manage their emotions in future situations in which conflict is threatened, and both parties should normally feel able to work effectively together and put the dispute behind them.

In pursuing a transformational approach, mediators might find themselves brushing against the role of a counsellor or psychotherapist, contrary to the normal boundaries of their role that we have suggested should be sacrosanct. Weinberg and Coyle (2003) suggest that the mediator's role as envisaged by Cloke 'isn't simply a facilitator. He or she is a coach, an interactive party to the process who gives recommendations, and at times even evaluates and provides instruction'. However, in the right hands, this may be too limited. In facilitating a mindset change, it's certainly true that roles may become blurred – conflict coaches may just as readily find themselves playing this role, and often one-to-one coaching may be a preferable intervention over mediation for this purpose.

The transformative approach has not avoided criticism. Quite apart from the potentially lengthy process involved – something which may be more acceptable in a quest for a lasting peace between warring nations or in settling a domestic dispute than in most workplace disputes – the approach offers no guarantee of a satisfactory outcome.

In losing their neutrality, mediators can become party to unwitting criticism, unless both parties are ready to approach the exercise with full openness and honesty. They risk becoming embroiled in the dispute rather than acting to facilitate a resolution, may be criticized for favouring one party over the other (often the 'weaker' side) and may not end up protecting the fairness and integrity of the DR process.

For some people, an initiative that aims to change people may seem to be too idealistic an idea to be true. Therefore before proposing this approach, a mediator should recall our first principle – that both parties should not only be ready to play their part in mediation, but believe that the process has a reasonable chance of succeeding.

Insight mediation

Not unlike the transformative approach, insight mediation works towards both parties coming to realize that they are on course to achieving a resolution, based on having sufficient insight into the other party's interests and perspective, and so having a shared understanding of what is needed to reach a conclusion.

Ideally, the outcomes that each party wants to achieve from DR should be defined at the outset; however, their reasoning may very often not be clear to the other party. Insight mediation isn't just about both parties coming to a belief that a resolution is possible. Rather, it's about getting to the point in the forest where a shaft of light can be seen penetrating from the outside – and with it, the path ahead becomes clear, even if it involves crossing a few more 'fallen branches' and other hazards before emerging into open ground.

The approach was pioneered in Canada by Melchin and Picard (2009). The mediator plays a crucial role in the process of helping each party to achieve an understanding of the underlying nature of their dispute. This usually involves five main stages:

1. contracting (agreeing ground rules, determining the process, and so on – as we've already discussed);
2. stating hopes and their perceived problems;
3. seeking insight (exploring individuals' anxieties and reasons why a gulf has opened up between them);
4. collaborating (confronting these anxieties and moving each party to a point where they feel able to cooperate); and
5. making decisions.

As with transformative mediation, the insight approach aims to pinpoint and eradicate the fears that one or both parties have in making what they may see as uncomfortable concessions, confronting self-truths and unblocking entrenched mindsets. But as with the transformative approach, getting to the point of insight – the 'eureka!' moment that marks the turning point in mediation – may take considerable time and calls upon well-honed skills. In some cases, reaching this point may prove impossible within the bounds of mediation and what individuals are prepared to open up to in their workplace.

Problem-solving mediation

Problem solving[1] focuses on joint analysis of a dispute, with each party being guided by specialist third parties in a workshop. The workshop may be structured to examine each stage in the development of a conflict, taking account of the circumstances in which different conversations, actions or mounting beliefs occurred, and the interpretations and feelings that resulted. This can be especially effective for helping each party to understand the other's perspective, to check their own interpretation and, when relevant, offering a face-saving context in which to revise their views. Having worked through a comprehensive analysis of the situation both parties find themselves in, there should normally be scope for suggesting ways of moving towards a resolution. The problem-solving approach benefits by its inherent need to involve both parties in a shared exercise of establishing understanding, even if neither may recognize themselves as acting as a team!

The approaches compared

Each of the approaches described above has advantages and disadvantages, whilst the circumstances or objectives of a dispute may favour one approach over another. For example, available time may limit the opportunity for adopting a transformative approach or both parties may be under pressure to achieve a final resolution after a lengthy series of appeal and grievance hearings. Skilled mediators are able to mix the 'good' from any or all of the approaches in the DR process they adopt, as well as knowing when it's appropriate to abandon one approach in favour of another.

A further factor to take into account when deciding which approach may be most appropriate is to recognize the extent to which organizational rather than human interests are being represented by one party. Where the subject of a complaint is a department, group of people or 'the organization', the individual(s) representing the side's interests may have considerable detachment from the emotional nature of the dispute. Indeed, their professional role may require them to quite regularly represent the organization in similar situations, and so participating in a mediation discussion may be seen by them as being 'all part of the job'. Role expectations or political expediency may therefore be greater motivators for some parties than wanting to achieve a lasting peace or overcome a major grudge.

Summary

Deciding how to respond to a workplace dispute inevitably involves a 'resource and risk' type assessment, normally being guided by such matters as the stage the dispute has reached, the readiness of the disagreeing parties to participate in a dialogue, and the desire or need to reach a speedy conclusion. Informal mediation by a trusted third party might be considered before further escalation, as may engaging a conflict coach to work with individuals on a one-to-one basis.

When the need for formal mediation arises, there are further choices concerning the form of intervention that is most likely to be helpful or relevant. In some cases, such as evaluative mediation (in which the strength of individuals' cases is weighed up by a specialist with legal case knowledge), this may be driven by the determination of one or both parties to pursue litigation, though normally greater flexibility exists to choose a form of mediation that might focus on problem solving, facilitation or having a solutions focus.

Note

1.   Mitchell and Banks describe the application of problem solving in international conflict resolution in Mitchell, C and Banks, M (1996) *Handbook of Conflict Resolution: The analytical rather than solving approach*, Pinter, New York.

4

RESOLVE – The Janus perspective

INTRODUCTION

Having introduced 'RESOLVE' in Chapter 2 as a model that can be used when mediating any dispute, we now turn to consider each part of the model in more depth.

RESOLVE is more than a useful framework to guide a mediator and, as we'll see, it's more than a catchy pneumonic too. Indeed, RESOLVE can be used in virtually any stage of conflict management, including what we call the 'Golden Hour'. Similarly, when a dispute has been formalized and reached a point at which third-party involvement is inevitable, the model can be applied in arbitration, conflict coaching and of course mediation.

THE JANUS PERSPECTIVE

Figure 4.1 may help you to memorize RESOLVE, depicting what we like to describe as the 'Janus perspective'. Janus was the Roman god of gates, openings, beginnings and endings. He was often worshipped at the time of a birth, marriage or new harvest, and famously gives his name to the month of January – of course, the first month of the Gregorian calendar year and a time of resolutions to begin anew.

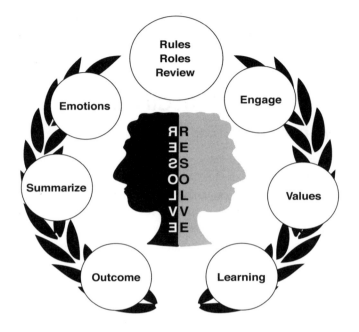

Figure 4.1   'RESOLVE': a model for managing conflict

Janus was also associated with transition, such as the period of changing from young to old. Perhaps it's because of this that the god is normally represented by two heads, each looking in opposing directions. The idea of looking back to the past and looking forward to a brighter future is an aspect of the Janus image that we believe applies in CR. Some of the elements of RESOLVE focus on looking backwards – reviewing, summarizing and acknowledging emotion, whilst others take a mainly forward-looking perspective – outcome, learning and engaging, for example. Considering the past is important since it offers a foundation for learning, helping to inform a better way forward.

Just as might be expected of a good mediator, Janus was celebrated as a hero for bringing peace to Latium and for instituting a new rule of law. In no small sense, as King of Latium he presided over a new 'golden age' in the history of Rome. Perhaps so too (if a little idealistically), mediation might seek to move individuals toward a golden future of their own.

As protector of Rome, Janus saved the city from an attempted siege by the Sabines and as a result, the gates of his temple were always kept open during times of war so that he would be able to intervene when required. Conversely, the gates were closed during times of peace. So too, the doors of a mediator or other intervener might be thought to be always open when there's a prospect of resolving a dispute, while his or her services may not usually be called upon during a time of peace. So it's against a wonderfully dramatic backdrop that we set about describing the model. Below we look at each element in detail.

RESOLVE DECIPHERED

R – review, rules and roles

The 'R' represents not one but three elements of mediation, which we like to refer to as 'the 3 Rs'. More than most other components, each of the 3 Rs is most likely to be covered during the opening stages of a joint dialogue. Each may need to be revisited later, and in particular reviewing is likely to recur as the discussion proceeds. All three are intended to provide a common understanding amongst the parties and the discussion can be used as a baseline.

Review

This ensures that both parties are given reasonable space to put their point of view across. It may help either party better understand what is at the root of their dispute, by having an opportunity to think about and with some degree of expectation to clearly articulate what is causing their concern, or by hearing the main substance of the other party's viewpoint.

It allows the scope of the dispute to be jointly defined and therefore the key points that need to be addressed by mediation to be identified. It can also help individuals say things they want the other party to hear, and in the process vent pent-up emotion. Ultimately, *review* concerns finding answers to the questions, 'Why are we here (today)?', 'How did we get to this point?' and, 'What outcome do you want to achieve from this process?'

When used as a later stage in the dialogue, *review* allows individuals space to reflect on their thinking and to articulate why they've formed that particular point of view. It's an important lever for encouraging individuals to reflect and to listen. Unsurprisingly perhaps, a mediator can often borrow questioning techniques from the coach's repertoire, for example:

- What's your understanding of this situation?
- How have you reached this view?
- How do you know that?
- I've heard you say... please correct me if I've misunderstood.
- What do you think will be the consequence of not resolving your disagreement?

In an initial contact between a mediator and an individual involved in the dispute, *review* is an essential starting point for a mediator to understand what the context for the dispute is and, in turn, to be able to suggest whether mediation is likely to be an appropriate means for finding a resolution. This qualifying of understanding isn't only relevant when liaising with those who will sit across a table in the mediation room, but also when seeking to understand the perspectives of all other stakeholders.

When used during the opening of a joint session, *review* might be considered to be the equivalent of an exchange of opening statements in a court trial – though we don't want to push this analogy too far. By allowing each party an opportunity to introduce their perspective in a structured and controlled way, discussion can then quickly move on to identifying common objectives for mediation and, in turn, the ground rules that should guide discussion. Quite often, this alone is sufficient to open the door to an effective solution.

A mediator may propose quite specific guidelines to ensure that each party is given a fair chance to present their position. For example, it might be agreed that they can take a certain amount of time to make their 'opening statement', and it should also be stated that the mediator will be strict in ensuring that this open space is respected by the other party. The mediator might want to spell out this common understanding that both parties are expected to respect, perhaps along the lines of, 'You each will have a fair chance to put across your view without any one of us interrupting to pass comment, but remember also to tell yourself that when it's your turn to listen, "I will not interrupt".'

Rules

As we've seen earlier, ground rules need to be agreed between the parties who are locked in a dispute to ensure that mediation flows effectively. Ideally, the rules should normally be proposed by the individuals themselves; however, one party may object to proposals put by the other. A mediator may therefore need to be ready to propose possible principles that both parties might wish to consider, for example:

- respecting each party's right to speak;
- having an irrefutable presumption that both parties want to reach a satisfactory outcome;
- recognizing when discussion is diverting from matters that may be most relevant or are not helping each party to move forward;
- respecting the role of the mediator as an impartial intermediary whose aim is to support the best outcome for both parties.

At this time, attention might also be given to ensuring agreement by each of the parties to keep all points discussed confidential to those present. Reference might also be made to the values that guide the mediator and are offered for others to share (this should also serve as a reminder for the mediator of the ethical code that underpins their work).

Establishing ground rules shouldn't normally require much time, but it's important that this task isn't rushed. Clear and unambiguous ground rules that can be referred to later in the discussion may save considerable argument and frustration. For this reason, it's important for a mediator to check that both parties understand and accept each point, and acknowledge that if they dismiss the agreed baseline later, they may jeopardize the possibility for mediation to continue.

It's perfectly acceptable for a mediator to question or challenge the intention of any proposed rule, although irrespective of a mediator's opinion of its value, the proposal should be accepted by both parties. Alternatively, where both parties are at loggerheads over agreeing a proposed rule, a mediator may seek to establish why the proposal is important to the individual who has raised it, and suggest an alternative that might achieve the same end, if appropriate. With the mediator taking 'ownership' of the new proposal, the other party may more readily accept the suggested alternative.

This is also an appropriate time for a mediator to make it clear that the points discussed will not be documented or reported to any other person outside of the mediation room. The shared responsibility to maintain the confidence and the acknowledgement that whatever is discussed will not be used to prejudice any subsequent dialogue should also be pointed out at this time.

One exception to the 'no documenting' rule is that a single-line record that mediation occurred can be put on file. Notes may be drafted during discussion to help the mediator keep track of the dialogue, and information can be written up on flipcharts and whiteboards. However, even the restricted way in which these will be used may need to be highlighted, to make the point. A ground rule could be established that any notes taken by the mediator are torn up in front of the group before closing the session.

This 'R' doesn't just apply to rule setting. For a mediator, a ground rule may need to help navigate discussion and resolve points of order when the dialogue becomes stuck. For example, a ground rule could be that if the discussion becomes distracted on to a single point of detail for more than 20 minutes, the mediator will ask both parties to agree whether they wish to continue with this discussion or to 'park' it for possible reconsideration later. This gives a mediator a reasonable justification for intervening if such a situation arises. Similarly, reminding the parties that they had agreed a rule to allow the other an opportunity to present their view may be usefully called upon in situations where one party is repeatedly interrupting the other.

In rare circumstances, it may be appropriate to refer to a ground rule as a check on discussion, asking the parties whether they still wish to abide by the rule. This risks undermining an important means of controlling the course of discussion, but can be telling should both parties believe that ground rule should be abandoned. For example, a decision to abandon the right of each person to be heard may indicate a deterioration in the dialogue to a point where a positive outcome may no longer be possible, justified by comments such as 'This has become pointless when they [the other party] aren't able to listen.' When encountering such circumstances, a mediator may wish to ask the parties whether they feel that the dialogue has broken down to a point where there's limited prospect of them reaching agreement, in other words, to question whether there's value in mediation continuing unless a new order can be restored in the discussion. However, if it becomes helpful for both parties, rigid adherence to the ground-rules can be relaxed.

The following types of intervention may be useful to help 'navigate' or control discussion:

'Are you finding this process useful?'
If yes – 'what exactly are you finding useful?'
If no – 'what would you find useful?'

Roles

Making clear what the roles of mediation and mediator are at the outset is intended to avoid possible misunderstanding by one or both parties. In turn, this should enable them to set reasonable expectations of what they hope to achieve from the process. The purpose of mediation and its boundaries should normally have already been discussed before each party enters into a joint dialogue; however, it's important that there's a shared understanding, and therefore for the nature of the roles to be repeated at the start of a joint dialogue. A possible way for a mediator to set the scene might run on the lines of:

> This has been discussed with you privately; the reason we are here today is to work towards achieving a resolution. My role in this process is to help guide this discussion, and I would like to offer you my assurance that my role is to help facilitate your discussion.

The functions that a mediator plays will depend on the type of mediation being conducted (facilitative, narrative, etc). These can be described, as should the boundaries for mediation. Where two mediators are involved in the discussion, their respective roles and means of interacting also need to be explained. The following might feature as boundaries for mediation:

- not offering direct advice (except in certain circumstances or where the form of mediation requires this, eg in evaluative mediation);
- not acting as a judge (except when acting as arbitrator);
- not offering personal opinions.

Crucially, an important role for mediators is to be able to listen without interruption, unless intervention is required to help the discussion move forward. Similarly, they should be at pains to resist any indications of bias, for example being careful to control their body language to avoid unhelpful transference (unconsciously directing feelings about a person onto another). As a reminder of this principle, we particularly like the words of the UN Peace Medalist Jiddu Krishnamurti that 'observation without evluation is the highest form of intelligence' (Krishnamurti, 1929).

Boundaries that may apply to what any party may discuss include:

- not offering to counsel another person;
- not entering into legalities;
- not bringing in personalities;
- not bringing in personal views, remaining neutral.

This pen-picture of the mediator's function might extend to explaining points of order on which they may intervene, their role in reminding a group of the time available for discussing particular points, and offering summaries of the progress made as the discussion proceeds.

Any of the '3 Rs' may be called upon in informal conflict management. For example, a line manager who is attempting to defuse an apparent disagreement between two members of a team might label the boundaries of their role, such as, 'I'm not here to say who is right or wrong, but to help you move forward to a realistic outcome' or, 'I want to help you appreciate why [the other party] sees things the way they do.' Similarly, a manager might informally call upon an unwritten rule when an unproductive argument is in full flow: 'You're giving me the impression that this discussion isn't getting anywhere. Am I right?' or perhaps, 'Can we stop a moment and take stock?'

E – emotions

RESOLVE stresses that it's important to acknowledge emotions – the physiological and mental states we all consciously experience as feelings, moods or impulses and associate with attitudes or states of mind.

Strong emotion is a major ingredient in the mix that drives individuals into a dispute. One or more of the 'primary emotions' may be at work – happiness, sadness, fear, anger, surprise and disgust; but so too may less obvious ones, such as jealousy, guilt and pride. What's more, it may not be clear even to the individuals themselves what emotions they are feeling. One powerful question that may help tease this out whilst also forcing each party to acknowledge the emotion is: 'What is the strongest feeling you are experiencing in the situation you have with each other?'

Emotions are undoubtedly an important part of what makes us human, but so too is the instinctive need to release pressure when we feel under stress. Whether it's Michelle Larcher de Brito delivering a grunt in tune with her volley at Wimbledon, a racing driver punching the air as he takes the chequered flag, or a football crowd's collective sigh when an opposing team's shot at goal is deflected, letting off steam is a necessary part of releasing emotion.

Emotions can quite often be suppressed over a long period of time. Only when the pressure of deep anger, resentment or whatever other emotions are at play reaches breaking point, does the full strength of what an individual is feeling become apparent to others – often as an unexpected explosion of rage, bursting into tears or other intense outpouring. The growing power of a suppressed emotion might be compared to a small air bubble in water starting its journey towards the surface. Whilst at depth, the bubble may be quite small, compressed under the intense pressure of the liquid around it, but as it rises into shallower water, it will start to grow, increasing in size until, when it reaches the top, a sudden miniature whirlpool appears on what was previously a calm surface.

A basic principle of cognitive behavioural psychology, discussed in Chapter 1, is that feelings are a consequence of a pattern of thinking. Being able to identify and articulate exactly what such feelings are is not always straightforward. Amongst other complications, the influence of a personality trait or psychological disorder may have an important influence.

Obsessive compulsive disorder (OCD), paranoia and narcissism especially are more common in the workplace than might often be assumed. As many as 2.5 per cent of adults in the United States suffer from OCD (NIMH-ECA, 1982–84), which can manifest itself in a relentless need to pursue a particular line of action such as a quest for justice. Paranoia has been described by Daniel and Jason Freeman as 'the 21st century disease', with hallucinating being five times more likely to occur amongst people who are suffering from stress (Freeman and Freeman, 2008). Narcissistic personality disorder, meantime, is diagnosed in up to 16 per cent of the US population in clinical settings (APA, 2000), whilst in a recent survey of workers in Australia, 73 per cent identified their bosses as being the main source of bullying (*Human Resources Leader*, 2006).

The common incidence of such conditions presents a potential problem for a mediator, especially if a condition is declared. Where individuals have stated that they suffer from a particular condition, employers and those they engage to act on their behalf must be acutely sensitive to avoid aggravating the condition. Quite apart from the legal protection afforded to employees against an injury to health in many countries, mediators must also be mindful of the ethical code that underpins their work. Clearly, putting pressure on an individual that may exploit or worsen his or her condition would raise a serious ethical question for a professional mediator. Where any doubt about an individual's state of health exists, occupational health, chief medical officers or other specialists need to be called upon.

A mediator would be ill-advised to form assumptions about an individual's emotional state. Individuals vary in the way they express emotion and in some cases may harbour very deep feelings that may not be obvious to others. Some individuals with autistic spectrum conditions are among those whose physical, facial and eye language may give limited clues to what they are really feeling. Similarly, cultural norms may encourage deflection of eye gaze, especially when deferring to a person of a perceived higher status.

An objective for conflict management is to help individuals to acknowledge and channel their emotions in a positive way. The influence of emotion becomes unhealthy when it begins to consume an individual and restricts their ability to think objectively and clearly.

In allowing emotional expression, a mediator may also occasionally need to label an individual's behaviour. For example, if an individual continually returns to a particular, unsupported allegation that is based on suspicion when this is not appropriate to a question being discussed, a mediator might sensibly ask the individual to reflect on whether the points he or she is raising are appropriate for the moment.

Emotional outbursts can sometimes be quite prolonged, but necessary. Before intervening, and subject to the ground rules agreed by each party when starting mediation, a mediator's most useful interaction is usually to remain silent, observe and allow the exchange to blow itself out, so long as both parties are reacting in a way that indicates they are ready to engage in such a dialogue at the time. Careful observation of the interaction and noting how the words are received are important.

Possible questions to help an individual express emotions include: 'Tell me your grounds for feeling like this. How have you reached that conclusion? Why do you feel that way...?' It may also be relevant to label an emotion to help a party recognize the effects of what they say, for example: 'Did you notice Connor's reaction? I noted that when you said... he flinched.'

The Thought Pattern Critique approach described in Appendix 2, which draws on cognitive-behavioural constructs, might also be offered to help individuals articulate the emotions that are most affecting them and to consider possible reasons why such feelings have arisen. Appendix 1 offers several possible question structures to help individuals consider others' viewpoints. Any of these techniques may be appropriate in informal as well as in formal CR.

S – summarize and reflect

Summarizing is often used as a means of punctuating a conversation. It can also be useful at any stage to:

- Help clarify understanding – both for the mediator and for individual parties. Testing to ensure that they've built up an accurate understanding of what has been said is especially important when a mediator believes it's time to suggest moving the conversation onto another point. Left unchecked, misinterpreted comments can have a bad habit of unsettling attempts to reach agreement later.
- Help signpost a dialogue, using the opportunity to state not only what has been achieved but the point the discussion has reached on any route map that may have been proposed earlier, and linking into the next topic for discussion.
- Help isolate common ground between the parties, points that have been agreed or other areas where progress has been made in discussion (this may be especially helpful where the perception of what progress has been achieved by those in the room is limited or where a complex topic needs to be broken down into its constituent parts).

Summarizing might routinely be used both before and after a break in discussion, as well as following an intense discussion on a single theme (such as one of the key points the mediation aims to address or following discussion of a former sticking point). It's of course logical to summarize in closing out mediation, but the decision on whether to disclose any of the conclusions drawn or actions committed to must remain with the participating parties. Example summary structures are included in Appendix 1.

A summary need not be lengthy or have to follow a significant 'triumph' or milestone in discussion, but should be more than a general recap. A mediator might suggest a summary; for example, 'This would seem to be a useful point for me to summarize what you've agreed.' The summary should then be brief, sticking to what has actually been discussed, and using the language expressed by participants themselves. To be useful, a summary must be specific, precise and comprehensively describe what needs to be summarized. However, precision may sometimes need to be sacrificed in the interest of moving discussion forward; at times it may be enough just to question: 'Is this about right?' In particular, quarrels over precise wording should be avoided unless they alter the meaning of what has been proposed.

'Reverse summaries' may also be used, inviting one or both parties to state what stage they believe the dialogue has reached. For example, a mediator might ask, 'Please would you like to summarize where we are?'

One risk inherent in summarizing is to unwittingly invite individuals to reopen points of discussion that have already been closed out. In some cases this may be necessary – for example, to correct a misunderstanding or if significant information has been revealed since previously agreed points were discussed and which have an obvious impact on what was agreed. In such cases, any fresh conversation must be carefully managed, ensuring that the focus is kept solely on what needs to be clarified or revisited. A new ground rule may need to be agreed with the parties to time-bound and restrict the scope of such diversions.

O – outcome

It may be an obvious point, but both parties must want to achieve an outcome for any attempt at a resolution to succeed. Without having a clear view of the outcome each party wants from mediation, it's very difficult for anyone to know when a successful conclusion to the process has been reached. The value in considering outcomes is therefore to both define and remind individuals of what it is they are seeking to achieve as the discussion progresses.

The task of identifying desired outcomes should have started before mediation is convened, once individuals understand what the role of the process is and so are able to identify what they wish to achieve. A mediator may be able to help individuals define the outcome they envisage in fairly general terms quite quickly, although time and additional support may be needed to help them form a very specific view. A coach may be able to help facilitate this thinking.

Perhaps the most useful tool for encouraging individuals to describe what they want to achieve is simply to ask them to imagine what their situation will look like following mediation. In building up this 'picture', specific details about what is different to their current situation can be explored – the picture will have more resonance for them if it can be described in tangible terms (what can be seen, touched, heard, spoken, and the like). The *Imagine Role-play* approach described in Appendix 1 offers a variation on this technique.

The scene that is depicted might refer to the individual's relationship with the other party with whom he or she is currently in dispute. For a mediator or coach listening to this description, useful insight can be obtained about the way the individual wishes to reframe their current relationship. To some this may still seems like a difficult relationship, but perhaps one in which both parties can feel that their past differences should not be a cause for prejudice or a lack of cooperation in moving forward. Of course if an individual feels that a satisfactory situation is one in which the other party doesn't feature, then this too puts a clear stake in the ground about what kind of 'future' is expected.

A mediator may encounter a situation where an individual is unable to articulate the outcome he or she would like, or face individuals whose expectations are unrealistic. In the latter case, we have come across several examples of individuals feeling that only the dismissal or removal from their current post of their perceived opponent would be sufficient for them to feel satisfied: a strong quest for 'justice' often goes hand-in-hand with a belief that the guilty should be punished. But whilst disciplinary action may be a possible outcome of a grievance process, it has no place in mediation. Unrealistic expectations of this kind therefore need to be quickly addressed.

In the case where individuals are unable to identify the outcome they desire even for themselves, the value of launching mediation needs to be questioned. In such circumstances, coaching might be considered as a means of helping the individual to uncover what will satisfy him or her.

We prefer to talk about the notion of an 'outcome' as opposed to objectives. In our view, an outcome is something that not only results from taking part in an activity such as mediation, but which is enduring. That implies that some transformation might very often need to take place, such as an individual rethinking their perspective or taking on a new mindset.

Objectives, by comparison, tend to conjure up the idea of quite specific, 'SMART' goals that are achieved at a particular point in time. These are often not appropriate when in the midst of mediation, putting emphasis on precision and process. An easier guideline for considering an outcome is to ensure that it fits with the '3Ms' – that it's motivating, manageable and measurable (the concept of the '3Ms' is credited to Julie Hay (Hay, 2007)).

Objectives are more relevant as criteria for deciding when mediation has achieved its purpose; for example, answering questions such as, 'Can we see a way forward in which we can work together?' and, 'Is there further scope for mediation to realistically resolve the differences between us?' Note that this is a different type of outcome to the kind described in a picture – in other words, one that is a living situation, played out over time after mediation has been completed.

Following individual reflection, once mediation begins and both parties come together, time should be given for each to describe what their desired outcomes are. Normally, this will logically follow their review of the disagreement, and may often form a part of their 'opening statement'. Allowing each person to have their say and to acknowledge that it's their right to have a different point of view helps encourage mutual respect and preserves each others' dignity. Scaling (which we'll discuss later in this chapter) can be a powerful tool to use here.

Once both parties have spoken, it should be clear if any common ground exists between them and where there are significant differences. Realistic objectives may then be set for mediation itself – in other words, the criteria that can be checked to know whether mediation has achieved its desired end. From the shared outcomes, the key question that needs to be answered at this point is, 'Is there a joint outcome which we can realistically achieve?' (Examples might include allowing others to benefit from learning gained, individuals may have built a stronger relationship than when their dispute started, or have a clearer view about how they might better handle themselves in a disagreement in future.)

Again, the ability to identify common ground and qualify the depth and importance of areas of disagreement should help produce an answer. If it's felt that there's a very low prospect of achieving an outcome that both parties can be satisfied with and within the time made available for mediation, then the justification for continuing the process may need to be assessed.

In seeking to identify areas of the desired outcomes on which both parties agree, a shortcut is for a mediator to list what he or she perceives as being the common ground. This should normally avoid the risk of increasing disagreement if the task is left with the disputing parties. Being objective and emotionally detached from the content of the discussion, a mediator may also be better positioned than either of the other parties to see 'the wood for the trees'.

Outcomes that both parties can accept need not achieve a perfect world. Small changes and compromises may often be sufficient for both parties to feel that they can move on from the dispute. For example, they may be able to commit to respecting each other or treating each other politely, or agree that when it's practical, they will endeavour to talk to each other rather than engage in lengthy e-mail exchanges.

Recalling the Janus perspective, the advantage of including *outcome* after *review* in making opening remarks is that it helps balance a look to the past with a strong focus on the future. Both for the individuals involved and for others in the organization, it's what happens in future that must be seen as being most important, a point that can usefully be suggested to the participants in mediation.

L – learning

Learning is often missing from CM, but is the most important element for ensuring that organizations can achieve the greatest benefit from the experience of resolving a particular dispute. Learning is the only means for breaking the phenomenon of conflict.

For individuals too, learning may be recognized even from before a cause of a dispute took hold, and it can make sound business sense to help those coming out of a dispute to reflect on what they've learnt for themselves. As independent from both the mediation meeting and the participating individuals' management structure, a coach is normally best positioned to help each party draw out their own learning through honest reflection.

Learning is likely to happen as mediation proceeds: insights arise from fresh understanding, a sharing of more information than may previously have been known and as a result of the frantic mental and subconscious processing of all the new 'data' that mediation usually involves. It's not just in formal mediation either that individual and organizational learning should result – even in the briefest of conversations, there may be cause for reflection and sharing of new knowledge.

Through learning, individuals should develop better self-awareness of their ways of thinking and responses to different circumstances, and come to recognize the possible influence they may have on others and their potential to trigger new disputes with others. By being more mindful of such sensitivities 'in the moment', individuals may be better placed to exercise strong control when they detect that they may be veering onto a course that could lead them into dispute.

Helping individuals to enhance their 'emotional intelligence' – at least their self-awareness and self-control – may be supported both by coaching and through appropriate training. Common learning that may often result from reflections on a dispute include: gaining a better understanding of how others perceive us, recognizing the power of language in impacting others' responses to requests and poorly channelled emotions, and appreciating that there are often alternative explanations to the conclusions and assumptions that we may be prone to jump to. To 'live and learn' may even be seen as a secondary benefit of mediation, and for individuals who are able to acknowledge this, it is a possible softener when the outcome of mediation is otherwise disappointing for them.

For an organization, the biggest challenge is often knowing how to act on what has been learnt. In the first instance, agreement must be reached amongst the disputing parties that generalized learning can be reported back to the organization, perhaps in combination with learning arising from other conflict discussions, fairness at work feedback, recommendations to be fed back through training and the like.

Assuming that this potential barrier can be overcome, to obtain value from the exercise the organization must be ready to put the learning into practice. This may involve changing procedures, training managers or staff in new ways or even seeking to adjust elements of the organization's cultural 'recipe'. We'll look at this important topic in some detail when we come to consider conflict management strategy in Chapter 9.

Finally, mediators are not beyond being able to gain new insights from every dispute they are called upon to broker. It's through personal learning that mediators can build their own competency and awareness of the potential pitfalls and ways of approaching different situations that may arise during mediation. We therefore strongly recommend that every mediator takes time to reflect on their own learning following every dialogue that they mediate.

V – value

To value or express appreciation for each individual's contribution takes no more than a moment, but it can be very powerful in affirming the achievements that have been made. Whilst being particularly important when a compromise is offered, admissions of misunderstanding or failing are acknowledged or when concluding mediation, valuing may be relevant at virtually any time when new ground has been broken in discussion.

That said, for a mediator's words of encouragement to be believed, they must be authentic. Simply repeating a statement of praise routinely will not fool anyone. Similarly, praise that is overdone or offered too freely will have limited credibility.

In expressing value, mediators should avoid crediting themselves in remarking on how progress was achieved, rather putting the emphasis on the results achieved by the other parties, and using authentic, affirmative language. Example phrases that might be used include, 'Look how far you've come since starting this conversation today,' 'Look what you've achieved,' 'Not many people can be as open and honest about how they feel,' 'You've not only named the elephant in the room but chunked it down'.[1]

It may be hard for some individuals to accept praise, especially at a time when what may have been a prolonged period of emotional turmoil seems to be reaching a conclusion, so it's not unusual in what may be quite an affecting moment for tears to flow. Whether these are tears of joy, emotional release or pure confusion we don't know, but they can be quite moving moments nonetheless! One of Jackie's favourite observations in mediation that often seems to fit such moments is to remind both parties that 'If you didn't care, you wouldn't be here!'

As with all other elements in the RESOLVE model, valuing plays a crucial role in informal conflict management situations as well.

E – engage

In our model, *engaging* refers to the task of inviting participants to take part actively in mediation and also to committing to carrying forward any decisions or actions that they agree. Engaging goes beyond just motivating individuals to utter the words they think you want to hear to inspire action.

The process of encouraging individuals to play their part should start before a convened session, and is perhaps best combined with exploring the results each individual hopes will arise from mediation (the *outcome*). A mediator may need to suggest potential benefits from giving mediation a fair chance to succeed, for example that so doing will demonstrate a commitment to reaching a positive outcome and will offer the best chance for completing mediation quickly.

In this initial encounter, individuals might also be told what to expect when they come together with the other party, appreciating that they too may find the process to be uncomfortable and may naturally be inclined to approach discussion with some reservations. Individuals' suspicion and hesitation about opening up on their position may be reduced by giving assurances about the confidential nature of mediation – in particular, that it's a discussion that takes place exclusively within a closed room and that points discussed are not discussed with others or put on record.

Once the parties come together, further highlighting the 'prize' of mediation and the necessary part that each must play to achieve this will be relevant at the outset. Allowing time for individuals to present their *review* and then for both to offer suggested ground rules and to identify the key topics that mediation should address should allow time for both parties to settle.

The extent to which individuals put into practice what they say they will do should become apparent quite quickly as the mediation dialogue progresses. A tendency to give one-word answers in response to open questions, a lack of proactivity in responding to overhead questions that are put to both parties, and a general air of negativity or lack of interest are all possible indicators of a reluctance to be forthcoming in the discussion. Mediators should anticipate a possibly brusque and stilted start to mediation, as each party weighs up the extent to which the other is prepared to be open, and finds their own comfort zone.

The very presence of an intermediary who, hopefully, can be trusted by both parties should help create an easier dynamic than were both parties to face each other alone. The mediator's skill in facilitation needs to come to the fore to help instil an atmosphere in which both parties feel comfortable to speak openly and feel encouraged to do so. A possible way in which a mediator might help facilitate this includes offering the view: 'This is your opportunity in a controlled and confidential environment to get your concerns out into the open.'

As discussion proceeds, one or both parties may need to be re-engaged in the discussion from time to time. A retreat into periods of silence, deviation from the principles of respecting each other or recognizing the benefit of being open in sharing views are amongst the situations where re-engagement may be needed. Possible interventions that could be used to help re-engage include: 'Let's please remind ourselves of the rules we agreed to respect,' or, 'Can I suggest that we might be moving away from the agreements we made earlier to be open with each other?'

Apart from needing to initially engage those involved in mediation and occasionally to re-engage them, an aim of mediation should be to encourage deeper engagement as a discussion proceeds. By encouraging each party to not only buy into mediation, but also to set aside any unnecessary barriers that prevent them conversing and working effectively together later, a stronger foundation may be laid for their ongoing relationship. Deepening engagement should happen naturally by encouraging open conversation, reminding each party of the values and principles they identified as ground rules, and acknowledging when individuals have made an uncomfortable disclosure.

When it has become clear what the parties have resolved to do in moving forward from mediation, they might be encouraged to further engage with each other to put into practice what they've agreed (unless of course mediation has reached an ultimate stalemate from which the participants' preferred way forward is to instigate litigation). At this point, both parties can be brought back to considering what the benefits will be of taking the intended way forward, for example in terms of their emotional costs. In looking forward, any prospect of a positive and lasting engagement requires a genuine commitment on the part of both parties, not for each just to play lip-service to the conclusions they've reached.

Scaling and action

To help move individuals towards such a commitment, the mediator can both invite and challenge each party to qualify what they agree to. This may be simply a matter of them agreeing to respect certain principles, or perhaps agreeing to a mutual review of their progress some weeks or months ahead.

A mediator may encourage individuals to consider simple steps they will take in the days immediately following mediation as well as those intended for the longer term, for example by asking, 'What will you do? By when?' Individuals might also be asked to scale their level of commitment to the actions they've agreed: 'On a scale of 0 to 10, how motivated are you to carry this action through?' (0 usually means 'not at all', whilst a score of 10 would indicate 'total commitment'.)

Responses that give a middling score might be challenged with a further question – 'What would enable you to move from a 5 to a 6?' for example. As always, a mediator needs to use his or her discretion to know whether posing such a question might be counter-productive to closing out the discussion if it seems clear that the individuals have gone as far as they feel comfortable to. The scorings for agreed actions that have resulted from a compromise or that otherwise fall short of what an individual had previously hoped for are far less easy to 'push up the scale' than may be the case when coaching individuals who have a clear motivation to achieve a particular objective.

Note when using scaling questions you shouldn't be tempted to trivialize.

Similarly, when asking individuals to consider the importance of their current situation over the longer term, be careful not to create an impression that the situation shouldn't be seen as important to them now (or worse, that you or others might view their quarrel as being of little significance within the grand scheme of things). So too, the way in which individuals set their ratings is very much a personal matter and not one for a mediator to pass judgement on: someone's interpretation of a 2 score might be equivalent to 9.5 for someone else! Ultimately, whatever is agreed must be 'owned' by those who will need to live with the decision. For this to happen, commitments must be proposed and rationalized by the participants themselves.

Further scaling questions that might be used in concluding mediation include:

'On a scale of 1 to 10, where are you now from when we started the session?' (If the response is higher than before, ask: 'What is it that's changed that has got you to this? What's happening to get to this?')

'How committed are you to making this happen?' (If the response is lower, try: 'What's made it change?' This may help reveal a core issue.)

In addition to asking individuals to rate their intentions, further questions may be used to help them make their readiness to act public to both the mediator and the other party. For example:

'Would you send me an e-mail/give me a phone call when you've achieved …?'

'What will you do in the coming week?'

'What will you do if you find yourself going off track?'

Further examples of questions that use scaling are included amongst the microtools listed in Appendix 1.

Engagement might also encourage individuals to plan later time for reflecting on what they've learnt (in other words, putting *learning* into practice).

RESOLVE REVISITED

RESOLVE isn't intended to be followed as a series of sequential steps – reviewing, processing emotions, and so on; rather it serves as a means of conceptualizing the various aspects of mediation that may come into play at somepoint during DR. Not all elements may always be relevant and, of course,some may be called upon more frequently than others at different points in mediation.

Whilst being completely flexible in how it's applied, some natural sequencing might normally be expected. As we've seen, a description of an individual's hoped for *outcome* might logically follow their *review* of the current situation; *summarizing* and *value* may punctuate a point of progress in the discussion; and *engaging* should occur before joint mediation is convened, as well as at the start, the end and throughout the process.

Nevertheless, being able to envisage the combined elements of RESOLVE as a single, holistic approach should help anyone called upon as an intermediary in a dispute to stay on top of what can often be a very busy and distracted dialogue. It helps a mediator keep the focus of a dialogue on achieving a lasting resolution, whilst being sufficiently flexible for him or her to call any element into play at any time.

The model helps to steer mediation along a course that will ensure that all relevant bases are covered within the available time. For a manager or mediator, a quick safety check on which element is in play at any point in the dialogue and which have come before should help highlight where a dialogue might need to move to next: momentum can therefore be maintained without the mediator struggling to know what he or she might need to do next. This momentum to help discussion to continue moving in a positive direction can in turn help minimize or cut across unproductive arguments and wasteful idle time.

For each element, the emphasis is on sustaining each party's engagement and moving toward a positive end. Whilst not infallible or always appropriate in every mediation, RESOLVE provides a comprehensive reminder of a mediator's tasks and the guiding principles that are known to usually produce a satisfactory resolution.

Summary

RESOLVE provides a simple model to use in dispute resolution, considering the past perspectives that have brought individuals into a dispute and focusing on the outcomes that they wish to achieve. It may be used at virtually any stage during the development of a dispute, including the 'Golden Hour' opportunity for early, informal mediation.

RESOLVE offers a reminder that DR usually provides an opportunity for defining a new beginning for the disputing parties, and hence the model recalls the 'Janus perspective', or the perspective offered by the Roman god of new beginnings.

Note

1. In this phrase, an 'elephant' represents a significant issue that one or both parties are likely to be aware of but aren't comfortable to acknowledge publicly.

5

Preventing conflict

THE MEDIATOR WITHIN EVERY MANAGER

There's a line to be drawn between what is normally sensible for a front-line manager to address and what may more appropriately be passed to another person or specialist. Quite where this line is drawn will vary from person to person, organization to organization and situation to situation. For example, some organizations' HR policies make clear which types of complaint need to be promptly escalated and detail the process for subsequent investigation. We'll have more to say about this in later chapters.

For now, we'll focus on the concerns that are most relevant for those who are in the front line and usually the first to encounter an emerging disagreement – line managers, team leaders, supervisors, site leaders and the like. Managed correctly, an embryonic dispute may be quickly defused, avoiding significant time and effort that might have been expended had it escalated further. CM is therefore a fundamental concern for managers, as is the goal of developing 'the mediator within every manager'.

As we've seen, the original trigger for a dispute may often appear to be quite mundane. However, it's when individuals' positions become entrenched and a game of bat-and-ball begins between two increasingly diametrically opposed parties that the task of reaching a quick and easy resolution becomes challenging. Time is usually of the essence: a front-line manager needs to be able to recognize when an unhelpful dispute is brewing and to intervene quickly in a helpful way. This is what we call the 'Golden Hour' (we've devoted a section later on to consider how to identify and optimize the opportunity offered during this critical period). Managers need to be equipped to deal with emerging conflicts, requiring both finely honed interpersonal skills and a range of techniques to confront the unexpected (what we call 'micro-tools').

COMMUNICATION STYLES AND MANAGER CHOICES

Managers, as much as anyone else, can choose from a variety of ways for communicating with another individual. When imparting information, a choice may be made between being directive, stating a clear view or instruction; or participative, inviting suggestions and comment from the other person. A directive or 'tell' instruction doesn't need to be made curtly, as though issuing an order. For example, the command, 'You'll finish your report by Monday' might better be framed as: 'I need your report by Monday so that I'll be able to finish the briefing note for Tuesday's board meeting.'

Making a demand without an explanation can be interpreted as an unreasonable order, lacking two-way respect. Compare the impacts of the statements: 'I feel disappointed because you said you would finish it and you didn't', with 'When you said you'd finish it and didn't, I felt disappointed because I want to be able to count on you', or 'Have I given you everything you need to know?', and 'Is there anything else you might need from me?'

Similarly, managers can choose whether or not to be participative in listening to what others have to say. They may keep an open mind, genuinely consider the points raised by others, and be ready to challenge and change their own thinking. Alternatively, they may remain resolute in their views and, consciously or otherwise, filter out anything that contradicts this or which they don't want to hear: listening to instruct rather than listening to engage.

Introducing these two basic functions in communication – saying, writing or otherwise imparting something you want another person to hear or read, and being on the receiving end of someone else's message – highlights a potential for failed communication. A simple illustration, which you may have come across before and is illustrated in Figure 5.1, shows the potential breakpoints between 'sender' and 'receiver'.

The choice of words as well as when, how (voice intonation, situation, etc) and by what means (verbally, by e-mail, in a team meeting, etc) a message is communicated is therefore something to get right. So too is the way in which we listen.

Unfortunately expediency, or defaulting to a preferred communication style, is normally the master when communicating in the moment, although applied practice can break this natural instinct. What's more, many managers are hesi-

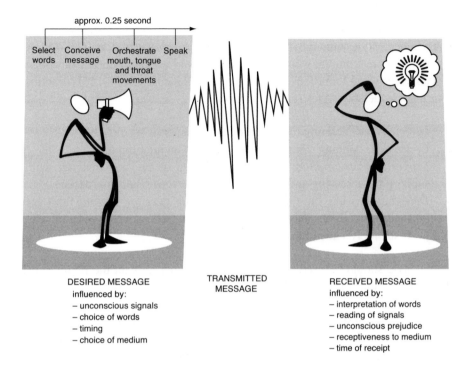

Figure 5.1   A familiar picture: the send-transmit-receive syndrome

tant about using communication styles they aren't familiar with, especially if they perceive that these may undermine their position of power within a team. It can take courage to move from a situation in which barking out orders is the normal, preferred way of interacting with junior staff, or to admit to not knowing all the answers in a team, yet such change can often reap rewards.

Where managing conflict is concerned, effective communication is all the more important. Taking a passive assertive position (for example instructing someone who is obviously consumed with anger to 'calm down' or 'not make such an issue of something that isn't really that important') may at best silence a disgruntled employee for a while, but will most likely cause the issue concerning them to become more firmly internalized.

Similarly, offering a listening ear but not following up with any feedback or action is unlikely to reassure an unhappy team member. Failing to take follow-up action may often lead to the issue being turned back on a manager, leaving him or her and the organization vulnerable to a criticism of not acting when the issue was first raised.

How a manager communicates in the moment is therefore closely related to the way he or she chooses to manage the situation. Much has been written on management styles, though perhaps one of the most useful models for our purposes comes from the well-known 'situational leadership' theory developed by Paul Hersey and Ken Blanchard (Hersey and Blanchard, 2008). This describes four main leadership styles (or behaviours):

1. *Directive/Tell:* defining roles, setting tasks, supervising closely.
2. *Coach/Sell:* defining roles and tasks, but also inviting input.
3. *Supportive/Participative:* delegating a degree of decision making, whilst supporting, observing and being ready to intervene when appropriate.
4. *Delegate:* passing on greater discretion for decision making and task management, largely leaving the individual to seek advice/guidance when he or she feels a need for it.

Which style should be used, the model suggests, depends on the performance development level of the person being managed, one of being:

- Unable and insecure or unwilling: the individual lacks both the ability to decide how to approach a task and the motivation or confidence to do so.
- Unable but confident or willing: as above, but where the team member has confidence or motivation.
- Able but insecure or unwilling: confidence may be lacking, motivation may be poor, although the individual has the competency to see through the task.
- Able, confident and willing: the best of all worlds – the individual shows positive levels of motivation, confidence and ability.

For example, a 'tell' style is recommended when an individual is unable and insecure or unwilling to take on a task, whereas a 'participative' style is more relevant for someone who has ability but lacks security or motivation, encouraging him or her to take decisions and build their confidence. The key to being an effective situational leader isn't just knowing which style to adopt to suit the circumstance, but being sufficiently adaptable to skip from one style into another.

A further way to categorize relevant management styles for managing conflict is according to the degree to which an individual has a workable idea for resolving his or her disagreement, his or her current emotional state (and so ability to think objectively), and the extent to which it's appropriate to ask questions or give answers. The main options are shown in Table 5.1.

Table 5.1 Management styles

Counsellor 'You do it; I'll be a reflecting board'	**Coach** 'What do you want to achieve?' 'How will you achieve this?' 'What will you do?' 'How committed are you to seeing this through?'
Facilitator 'You make the decisions; I'll help smooth the process'	**Teacher or Trainer** 'Here are some hints and techniques you can use for this task'
Reflective observer 'You try; I'll observe and reflect back what I see'	**Adviser** 'I'll answer any questions when you hit a problem'
Mentor 'First, tell me what you think. If you wish, I'll then offer suggestions based on my experience'	**Collaborator or Partner** 'We'll try this together and learn from each other'
Hands-on expert 'I'll do the task; I'll tell you how to do this'	**Modeller** 'You watch me demonstrate. Learn from me'

It is nearly always necessary to mix interventions; however, the following are most commonly used in managing conflict:

- coaching;
- facilitating;
- mentoring;
- counselling.

Note that our use of these terms here refers to management styles rather than to other meanings attached to the same words (for example, 'coaching' may be used to refer to an ongoing relationship between two individuals working toward a common end, guided by clear principles and boundaries).

Coaching

Coaching is most powerful in helping individuals to develop their thinking, change mindsets and take on challenges such as breaking out of their comfort zones. It aims to help coachees think clearly about how they can help themselves and then feel inspired to take action.

Coaching relies on asking appropriate questions, carefully listening to responses, and helping individuals pull together the different insights they gain. When coaching, a manager seeks to encourage reflection, and challenge and probe an individual's thinking.

Typical questions that indicate a coaching style include:

- Gathering information: 'What are the options you've considered?', 'What have you achieved since we last spoke?'
- Exploring a thought chain or idea: 'What would you like to gain from this?', 'What might [your opponent] feel like if this were to happen?'
- Directing and focusing attention on relevant topics: 'What is it best for us to focus on now?'
- Clarifying points for the manager or challenging the individual to clarify something for him or herself: 'I'm not sure I understand why you believe this explains your disagreement. Can you explain this for me?'
- Challenging behaviour: 'What stops you doing this?', 'How would you feel if you were able to say sorry?', 'What evidence is there to suggest the opposite?'
- Pinning things down: 'What are you committing to do?', 'When will you do this?'
- Challenging ways of thinking: 'What other ways could you look at this?', 'What might others make of this?'

Facilitating

Facilitating involves providing the resources, encouragement and support necessary for an individual or group to achieve their objectives, whilst not taking control, decision making or responsibility away from them. Bob Keisch of the Xerox Corporation offers the following helpful definition:

> Guiding without directing; bringing about change without disruption; helping people self-discover new approaches and solutions to problems; knocking down walls which have been built between people whilst preserving structures of value, and above all, appreciating people as people. All of this must be done without leaving any fingerprints. (Keisch, 1984)

When facilitating, a manager should balance praise with constructive criticism, show real interest in individuals, and inject energy and drive into the conversation. This requires deep listening skills, demonstrated understanding, and an ability to ask timely, appropriate and powerful questions.

Typical questions that indicate a facilitative style include:

'Is there anything I can do that would make it easier for you to explain this?'

'Is the approach we're taking helping?'

'What do you think is the best way for getting to the bottom of this?'

Mentoring

Mentoring aims to help individuals become clear about what they need to do to move forward from their current situation. It seeks to answer a 'How do I break out of this...?' or 'How do I achieve...?' question.

When mentoring, a manager offers wisdom, knowledge and an understanding of the political and organizational structures and processes that might affect the courses of action open to the individual. He or she may offer suggestions and act as a source of information or reference point for contacts, but his or her greatest contribution is to help individuals develop their own understanding of their potential and to identify the pitfalls and the opportunities they may face. This may involve filling in gaps of knowledge and acting as a sounding board, suggesting how others may perceive a situation and what might be a useful way forward.

Typical phrases that indicate a mentoring style include:

'Let me outline how I see this...'.

'Something you might want to think about is...'.

'Who would you like me to speak to about this?'

Counselling

The term 'counselling' can be used to describe various interventions, ranging from ad-hoc advice given in conversation to remedial discussions and therapy. Here, we use the term to simply mean a 'sounding board' and we don't advocate that managers should attempt to play the role of counsellor in the sense of offering advice on personal, social or psychological problems.

The focus in counselling is often backward-looking and tends to be more directive than most other intervention types, though not exclusively so. As with coaching, counselling relies on listening and questioning rather than 'telling', but the individual being counselled is likely to ask for the counsellor's opinions and observations, and usually wants to hear what you have to say. As a counsellor, you're entitled to offer advice and thoughts based on your own reflection and experience.

Counselling can also involve playing a devil's advocate role, taking alternative perspectives to individuals and challenging their thoughts to help them validate their views. Questioning can then be used to explore what the individual wants to talk about, help him or her reflect (devil's advocate) and offer suggestions.

Typical examples of questions that indicate a counselling style include:

'What's on your mind today?'

'But what if...?'

'How would this impact...?'

'What would [a person holding a different view] make of this?'
'How have you come to this view?'

Ultimately, whether asking such questions with a coaching, facilitating, mentoring or counselling style doesn't really matter – it's the thinking, insight and action taken by the individual being spoken to that counts.

THE POWER OF LANGUAGE AND ITS IMPACTS

The impacts of what and how we communicate can be very profound for others. Even by simply uttering a single word (and sometimes by not saying anything at all) or just presenting a certain look can send a strong message, whether or not the sender's intention has been interpreted correctly.

We might look to the world of advertising to see how much emphasis is put on getting the words right for triggering desired reactions. Words such as 'shine', 'dazzle' and 'sparkle' may give rise to quite different emotions to, say, 'light' and 'bright'. Words that convey a negative meaning may give rise to more subdued reactions than more positive ones; compare 'frustrated', 'depressed' and 'miserable' for size against 'happy', 'brilliant' and 'wow!' Or consider what some 'favourite' business buzzwords do for you, such as 'viral', 'value-add' and 'paradigm'.[1]

Longer or multi-syllable words may often have a less spontaneous positive effect than shorter ones: a point that might be of special interest to readers whose mother tongue is English, given that it's often said that those who prefer words with a Saxon origin tend to cut to the chase, whilst those who more readily use Norman-inherited terms tend to be more wordy.

Of course the way a message is delivered can also have a strong impact on a receiver. Similarly, the way sentences are framed can make a difference to how words are received. This isn't just a matter of style or avoiding possible ambiguity in the way a message may be interpreted, but also concerns the ordering and weighting that may be put on particular words. 'Only you seem to be saying...' might be used to suggest that a recipient is alone in the view, whereas 'You seem to be saying only...' might indicate that the recipient has only one point to make on the matter, or perhaps that his or her point is a trivial one.

Even the number of times an individual uses the singular pronoun 'I' and exclusive words such as 'but' can reveal whether they are likely to be relaying their full, true story, since it's thought that individuals who are trying to conceal something are generally not very good at coping with 'cognitive overload' (Dönges, 2009; Krakovsky, 2009).

Of course it's not just what is said that impresses upon a receiver, but the often unconscious non-verbal cues we display as well. Some even suggest that we give off an invisible energy that can be detected by others, whilst some speak of people having a 'presence' about them.

The way we position ourselves to others, both in our posture, angle of facing and proximity to another person also communicate messages about our feelings and/or intentions towards them. Eye contact too can convey strong meaning, as can the assumptions we form about what others are thinking. We'll return to consider these topics in the next chapter.

Non-verbal communication can be very subtle in its effects. Clive, a passionate horseman, has experienced the thrill of 'joining up' with a horse, having an animal voluntarily follow him around a field without having any physical or verbal contact with them. This skill is quickly learnt by individuals who have no interest in the equine world, simply by appreciating the rules of non-verbal communication known to horses in the wild, such as the meaning of the smallest movement of the eye, positioning of the ears, body positioning and proximity.[2]

Single words can serve to either defuse or escalate feelings and intentions, so it's important for managers to be aware of likely hot triggers. This calls for strong emotional awareness, or a commitment to continual self-awareness, personal influence and self-control.

The eminent peace-maker Marshall B Rosenberg (2003) reminds us that in every interpersonal exchange we act as observers, in turn giving rise to feelings about what we observe, which are themselves being impacted by our core values, needs and wishes. Acknowledging these observations, feelings and needs allows a request to be made of another person that will be satisfying to the sender. But a key for building successful relationships is to do likewise when listening, to tune-in to the needs and feelings of others, appreciating the substance of their request.

The implication for managers working with parties in conflict is that they must tread carefully in how they communicate, as well as watching carefully to note how others are interacting.

Triggers

Words can trigger memories, thoughts and emotions (and often these three may follow in close succession). Whether conjuring up an image, voice or feeling, triggers may often be unknown to a sender, having planted their roots in an individual's long-term memory. Seeking to avoid using strongly emotive language, a manager should also aim to build awareness of the sensitivities of an individual by observing his or her reactions over time.

Other common management phrases that may unwittingly antagonize include:

I'm thinking of you [or the organization] when I say this…'.

'With the greatest respect, I think you're [wrong]…'.

'Let me give you a word of advice…'.

All too often, the exact opposite of what is said is meant, and the receiver will invariably detect this.

A MANAGER'S CONTRIBUTION TO CONFLICT

To be effective in managing conflict, managers need to be aware of the capacity they have to unknowingly contribute to the onset and growth of disputes. As we mentioned earlier, management and communication styles can play a significant part in fostering unease amongst team members. Apart from the words they use, an inappropriate management style is a regular culprit in this regard.

Manfred Kets De Vries (2006) suggests that there are five main clusters of behavioural and personality types often seen in the management ranks; those who:

1. seek attention and believe that they are worthy ('dramatic');
2. are hypersensitive and protective of information ('suspicious');
3. deliberately isolate themselves from others ('detached');
4. undervalue themselves and lack confidence ('depressive'); and
5. are domineering, dogmatic, lovers of rules and insistent on perfectionism ('compulsive').

Each of these offers potential for fostering unease amongst team members, as well as for conditioning individuals' behaviours. For example, if an 'obsessive' manager constantly puts down a creative individual's suggestions, he or she is likely to become quickly frustrated. Unless this frustration can be vented through constructive channels, he or she may become predisposed to expressing his or her tension in conversation with another individual, including colleagues who may be close at hand.

As we've also seen, a poorly chosen comment from a manager can intensify rather than help calm a disagreement: observations such as, 'Sometimes I think I should bash your two heads together', 'Is this really worth quarrelling about?', 'I'm in charge, my decision is…', and 'I don't want to hear about this any more' may serve only to strengthen each individual's resolve to fight out their differences.

It's therefore important for managers to recognize the aspects of their own personality, preferred language and management styles that might give rise to conflict. Honest self-appraisal and strong emotional intelligence are needed to heighten this awareness.

Hard conversations

Sometimes tough talk just can't be avoided. It may be that an individual is causing disruption to team stability beyond a point that is acceptable, doesn't recognize when he or she is crossing a line or, perhaps, is deluded in his or her assessment of their own virtuosity.

Many managers find straight talking with others difficult. By definition, this involves describing things as they are. By being open, honest and direct, a manager may often best help an individual gain awareness of the reality of a situation. But uncomfortable home truths may not be received graciously, especially if an individual is already in a state of heightened anticipation and uncertainty. Tough talking may easily trigger feelings of insecurity, denial and defensiveness.

Knowing whether it's appropriate to broach a difficult matter and choosing the time to do so must be primary concerns for managers who believe that it's time to take the bull by the horns. Cutting to the chase is normally a preferred strategy. We've suggested a micro-tool that might assist with this task in Appendix 1 ('SAW') and a possible approach for structuring a hard conversation ('ILRAG'). In our experience, individuals are often not surprised when presented with an uncomfortable truth, perhaps perceiving that a hidden issue had been hanging over them or anticipating an uneasy air that needed to be cleared.

Managers need to be able to make their point clearly and assertively, explaining why they're confident in their beliefs, and referring to examples to illustrate their point where possible. Managers who invest time in building relationships and who work hard to listen and engage with their staff are more likely to be given respect when a tough conversation is needed (rather like maintaining an emotional 'bank account'). In turn, their intervention is then more likely to be seen as being strong management rather than 'bullying'.

Inevitably, most individuals will need time to process what they've heard, and may be unable to give their attention to anything else until they've digested the implications of what's been presented to them. It's therefore essential that reasonable time is allowed for this to happen. Managers should avoid engaging in a defensive argument if the individual responds in an attack. Such responses might reasonably be expected, just as may a reaction of withdrawal or not wishing to pursue the conversation further at the time. Not too much store should be put upon anything that is said in such circumstances, but rather to calmly suggest that the individual takes time to reflect on what he or she has just heard, and to offer an opportunity for a follow-on conversation sometime later.

Recognition

Being able to recognize the early warning signs of a possible dispute is obviously key to knowing when and how to intervene. Sometimes, individuals will quickly make known their differences; however, most won't want to present themselves as potential malcontents and so won't be as forthcoming. Potential indicators include:

- *Communication:* unusually limited, absent or reluctant responses to suggestions and requests; lack of proactivity in initiating or engaging in communication or new activities (when this is out of character); observations of unusual behaviour fed back by other colleagues; reluctance to engage in team social activities; talking over others in meetings.
- *Physiological:* unusual and frequent agitation; isolating or combative body language (eg frequently crossing arms, indicating a possible barrier); avoidance of certain people/meetings; frequent complaints of headaches; avoidance of eye gaze; apparent hesitancy when a particular person's name is mentioned.
- *Performance:* greater than normal incidence of mistakes; fall in productivity; evidence of poor concentration; higher than normal frequency and duration of sickness absenteeism; taking longer lunch breaks; showing reluctance to work more than minimum required hours.
- *Emotional:* subdued mood, introspective, hints of tearfulness, suggestions of poor sleeping, withdrawn, defensive, frequent negativity/propensity to criticize or dismiss another's views in conversations and meetings; sulking; irrational and aggressive outbursts; apparent sensitivity to mention of some topics or named individuals.

We must stress that these are just potential indicators of unease at work. By themselves, they don't provide a reliable guide to an individual's emotional or psychological state, and of course don't invariably reveal what may be causing any unusual behaviour. A wide range of factors and various nuances may be at play, notably anxiety, depression, psychological or neurological activity, and these may very often be prompted by events occurring outside of the workplace.

A combination of a number of these may strengthen the likelihood that a dispute has arisen. When suspecting this possibility, a manager's first action might be simply to check whether each individual perceives a problem, leaving open the opportunity for either party to feel that they may approach the manager should they feel they've any concern (something team members should feel able to do anyway). In itself, this simple exchange may be revealing. Even when an individual claims that all is well, his or her non-verbal language may suggest otherwise. Of course if, when questioned, both individuals respond differently, it's possible that both have a different impression of the nature of their disagreement.

If what at first seemed to be a possible indicator of unease appears to intensify, a manager needs to more closely observe and be ready to intervene again, to question once more whether there is still a normal peace between them. The need for a third intervention normally means that a manager should make clear why he or she has formed his or her impression of what may have become an uneasy relationship, then invite the individuals concerned to comment on this observation.

The 'Golden Hour'

Even when it takes an individual to make known a disagreement, the 'Golden Hour' opportunity need not necessarily have passed. Disputes can still be stopped dead in their tracks before they escalate into a vicious circle of intensifying positions, closed mindsets, and firm resolve.

In the 'Golden Hour', a manager's main task is to help both parties understand what underpins their dispute and to encourage them to see the benefits of resolving it as swiftly as possible, even if this may involve making a compromise. Both parties need to be quickly brought together following an initial private discussion with each, common ground between them needs to be identified, the origins and reasons why a dispute has started to develop needs to be uncovered, and both parties need to be engaged in a mindset of wanting to bring the matter to a speedy close.

A manager then needs to cram what might otherwise require several days of mediation into a brief conversation. To compound this challenge, time may not be available to plan a breakout, make private meeting room bookings, and allow each individual to prepare before coming together, especially if work demands are pressing. Delay isn't normally something that we encourage, since this can give an opportunity for a further deepening of the disagreement and strengthening of the opposing positions. However, it's sensible for a manager to be prepared for an unexpected diversion into a 'mini mediation' session. To help, a range of micro-tools is provided in Appendix 1.

Managers should verify that individuals are satisfied with the way they've handled their complaint, making sure that they look after their own backs. The more manipulative dissenters can have a nasty habit of turning words around to point the finger of blame at a later time, for example, accusing a manager who attempted to resolve their quarrel of bullying.

Brief meetings shouldn't be expected to achieve a satisfactory conclusion in every circumstance, but should at least help to broach what might otherwise remain a closed dispute and take the immediate heat out of what may have become an uncomfortable standoff.

Group dissent

Indicators of potential unrest within a team include:

- reservation or push-back in responding to suggestions or requests;
- predominance of 'cliques' and group isolation of some team members (or others, including managers themselves);
- a higher than normal frequency and duration of sickness absenteeism;
- reduced productivity;
- lack of creativity and proactivity;
- poor engagement with team or organizational initiatives;
- higher than normal incidence of errors;
- general reluctance to engage in some activities involving others;
- prevalence of 'group think' – individuals rallying behind a single point of view, normally voiced by a single or limited number of spokespeople;
- subdued team mood (eg reluctance to engage in social activity outside of work).

Case study: The Starbucks star

What may appear to be a simple thing can cause distress. Jackie recalls a story told by a former colleague of hers who, as a member of a senior management team, was continually left out of invitations to go for a coffee. Being repeatedly ignored dampened her self-esteem, sufficiently to cause distress. Her breakthrough came by her taking the initiative to ask her colleagues whether they wanted to share a coffee. This invitation was taken up by only her boss initially, which then marked her out as a colleague who could engage in social conversation, and so encouraging others to do the same.

In this case, a turnaround relied not only upon the sensitivity of a boss to the unhappy colleague's motivation, but also his readiness to take up the invitation to respond in a way that showed a willingness to be 'on side'. Managers may often be those best placed to act outside of current group behaviour, though good role modelling by anyone who appreciates the cause of discontent felt by a colleague that they could simply alleviate should be encouraged.

For a manager, directly confronting a suspected grievance in a team is generally easier than approaching the topic of a suspected conflict with an individual. Managers ignore the task of managing conflict at their peril. Strategies that may be used include questioning one or more individuals privately, on the basis of showing respect for their readiness to comment on any issues they perceive affecting the team, and stating ('labelling') the perception of unease in a team meeting, and inviting comment.

In both cases, it needs to be made clear that the reason for raising the matter is because it's a matter of concern and one for which there is a desire to help find a resolution – in other words, to be empathetic and supportive. Managers who have developed open and non-directive relationships with their teams should find this an easier task than those who have not. For these, the 'SAW' technique described in Appendix 1 might often be used when cutting to the chase on a difficult matter is required.

RECOGNIZING AND CHANNELLING CONSTRUCTIVE CONFLICT

Not all conflicts are unhealthy. Constructive disagreement within organizations can help prevent dogmatic and misguided leadership, as well as allowing alternative approaches for tackling a problem or achieving a project or task goal to be discussed and compared. And by sharing organizational learning, similar situations might be prevented from occurring.

Open, managed debate of different points of view is a healthy, normal activity, and one which many executives claim they want to hear! As Don Hewitt, the late veteran news anchor and pioneer of the CBS TV programme *60 Minutes* put it: 'It's good to like people who disagree with you, even though you may always take the decisions' (CBS, 2009)! A readiness to consider conflicting ideas may trigger fresh thoughts and allow individuals to further develop and articulate their propositions, whilst sometimes, 'agreeing to disagree' is a satisfactory outcome, especially if elements of the alternative proposals can be combined to produce a better whole.

It's therefore imperative for managers to be able to distinguish constructive conflict from the unconstructive kind, and to know how to channel each most appropriately. This distinction is actually quite simple to make: by questioning whether the motivation of each opposing side is well intentioned or not. Disagreements in which individuals seek to win over another person for reasons of personal gain are usually unconstructive in nature; those that aim to defend a good idea, propose the best way for achieving a team or task objective, or otherwise bring about improvements within the organization are invariably constructive.

There are a variety of ways for channelling constructive conflict, though whichever path is chosen, a manager should take care to ensure that the motivation of individuals whose ideas are not carried forward isn't dampened. Proposals may be debated in a team discussion, separately critiqued or used as a platform for launching wider analysis. They may be referred to others within the organization or recorded and acknowledged as being helpful but reserved for consideration at another time.

Ultimately, it's for a manager to decide how best to escalate constructive conflict as much as it's for him or her to decide how to progress unconstructive conflict. Which route is taken may often depend on the nature of the disagreement, whether it's appropriate to discuss the different viewpoints in any team forum or whether to refer them to others who have an obvious stakeholder interest in the topic of disagreement.

PREVENTION

An overriding aim of CM is to limit or prevent disputes from arising rather than focusing exclusive attention on fire-fighting. For obvious reasons, prevention is almost always better than cure – avoiding the time and resources, negative consumption of energy and (usually) higher costs associated with addressing a dispute (not to mention offering a manager a chance for a 'quieter life' – well, maybe!). Not only is prevention better than cure, but it also fits with an ideal that we'll explore a little later – the concept of building a 'happy company', or one in which there is a high level of cooperation and harmony.

It may be unrealistic to expect that all potential conflict can be identified and prevented. However, efforts dedicated to prevention can significantly minimize the risk of conflict emerging and developing.

Prevention incorporates three elements:

1. Having a heightened early warning system of potential disputes.
2. Equipping managers or others in the 'front line' with the knowledge and skill to broker a swift resolution as soon as a dispute emerges.
3. Limiting the conditions in which conflict is allowed to thrive.

To be successful, these rely to a large extent on the organization's culture, management style and training, and appropriate communication. Initiatives to encourage self-awareness amongst all employees and making it easy for individuals to feel able to express any concern without fear of criticism should ideally complement the mix.

Changing cultures and transforming managers' styles are by no means straightforward, as many well-intentioned HR and Learning and Development professionals will testify! However, this shouldn't preclude an attempt to influence a changing perspective, especially if the value of building a 'happy company' can be recognized by the organization's top team. The business case for taking strong steps for managing conflicts should be relatively easy to sell, and as we'll see later, is also one that lends itself to a relatively simple evaluation process.

Notwithstanding the 'big steps' that might be taken, much can also be achieved at a local level for limiting the onset of conflict. Any individual can be a champion for the anti-conflict campaign within their team and others with whom they interact, whilst both staff members and managers can sharpen their awareness of potential conflict signals and adopt a readiness to address these at an early opportunity.

Later, we'll consider possible training options for managers and staff. For now, let us return to consider each of the three main prevention steps in more detail.

1. Having a heightened early warning system of potential disputes

Early warning depends on three factors:

a. The ability of managers in the front line to detect the possible signs of unease, and to have the intuition and tact to know when to question whether anything is wrong.
b. The readiness of individuals to be open about their concerns, especially if these are only just beginning to form.
c. A general awareness that accessible, non-threatening mechanisms exist for sounding out concerns, including confidential channels that are independent of the line management structure.

These imply the need for appropriate manager training, which should help managers to identify not only potential indicators of a growing problem, but to equip them with the ability to gently and non-invasively test their suspicions (as well us to be mindful of possible alternative explanations).

It may be the case that a manager observes unease even before individuals have admitted this to themselves. To begin a conversation about a matter that hasn't yet assumed significance for an individual might easily provoke on unhelpful reaction, not to mention the potential to cause an individual to question others' perceptions of his or her behaviour and personal presentation. At an extreme, this could even induce a mild paranoia.

Our observation is that it's therefore wise to avoid rushing to assumptions, and to avoid making an attempt to broach the subject until there are very clear indicators, ideally not before more than one indicator is apparent. Possible strategies for testing the water and questioning whether everything is alright include:

- Introducing action learning sets at a team event, inviting suggestions about how the team can be more effective.
- Asking: 'How can I help and support you more in your role?'
- Reframing an observation as a question, eg: 'How can I help you to have your say more at meetings?' softens the possibly provocative observation, 'I've noticed you don't speak up in team meetings'.

2. Equipping managers or others in the front line with the knowledge and skill to broker a swift resolution as soon as a dispute emerges

Once an individual has acknowledged his or her unease with another person, team or organization, a manager needs to consider how to help alleviate their concern. This may be a simple matter of offering reassurance; clarifying points that may have been misunderstood and given rise to anxiety, or helping an individual to reframe his or her perspective.

A decision may need to be taken on whether to approach the individual or individuals who are the subject of the concern, if relevant. Due consideration needs to be given to the timing and way of approaching the issue, making initial contacts via any other line managers involved. The perspective(s) of the subject(s) should then be sought, without judgement. Discretion may be needed to determine how much of the detail of the allegation to present to them for response, including whether or not it's relevant to name the individual who raised the concern. At least sufficient information should be given about the reason for approaching them with the matter, to avoid the risk of causing them undue worry or to set the seeds for a host of suspicion-led rumours.

Again, it may be that misunderstandings can be clarified and perspectives of the effects of words and behaviour on others might be reframed. Such initial discussion may also lead a manager to question whether other factors are at play in initiating the unease, for example, a history of disagreements between the individuals involved. If the matter remains unresolved at this point, some form of third-party intervention might need to be considered.

As we saw earlier, managers need to be honest about their own potential to fuel disputes, and to work to adapt their management and communication styles if necessary. Managers might also benefit from reflecting on their previous experiences of managing conflict: there's rarely likely to be a time when there won't be something new to be learnt!

Appropriate management is essential at this stage, without which unwary managers can easily help to aggravate a relatively minor issue or alternatively walk away from addressing an issue which later boils over into a full blown dispute. The next chapter is dedicated to considering how managers can develop the appropriate skills needed to avoid this.

3. Limiting the conditions in which conflict is allowed to thrive

Implementing and communicating the mechanisms that make it easy for individuals to raise concerns should help limit the conditions in which conflict is allowed to grow. The basic principle here is: provide every reasonable opportunity for concerns to be raised without fear of any negative consequence.

A mutually supportive and cooperative team culture will obviously further reduce the potential for conflict developing, albeit the task of creating this is usually beyond the potential of any one individual.

Summary

Managers can be unwitting contributors to the life of a dispute, both in triggering unease in the first place and in helping an emerging dispute to grow. Choice of management and communication style is especially important, whilst the actual words that are spoken can have very profound effects on others, even single words (and sometimes by not saying anything at all).

Normally, stemming the flow of a disagreement at the earliest opportunity is appropriate; however, managers should recognize conflicts that are of the healthy kind and know how to channel these effectively. In turn, they may further themselves by recognizing the conditions that often trigger unhealthy conflict, and work towards removing or at least reducing these to the minimum.

Notes

1. A light-hearted look at uses and abuses of business clichés is offered by John Hollon (30 August 2009) 'Most overused business buzzwords? Here are some you may know and love', *Workforce Week*, 10 (32).

2. The US horse trainer Monty Roberts pioneered the concept of 'join-up' as a means for training horses. See Roberts, M (1997) *The Man Who Listens to Horses*, Arrow Books.

6

Managing conflict from the front line

A MANAGER'S ROLE IN DISPUTE RESOLUTIONS

Responsibility for DR typically sits with front-line managers during the early stages of a dispute, with DR specialists being more likely to be called upon in later stages. In considering a manager's normal main role in resolving conflict, it's therefore useful to understand the perspectives taken by the disputing parties during these early stages.

An emerging dispute

As the first signs of a possible dispute appear, stakeholder perceptions are likely to be ones of heightened awareness and caution, rather than believing that a disagreement is inevitable.

The main aim of a manager who detects early hints of unease should be to defuse the situation. This may mean intervening to speak to the individuals concerned, which may take the form of understanding what their concerns are, being explicit in acknowledging why they perceive potential unease, and seeking to correct any false perceptions. Where the emerging dispute concerns individuals within the same team, a manager may determine that private conversations aren't enough, and move to take more direct action to bring the disagreement to an end.

At this stage, the individuals who perceive a cause for grievance may similarly be watching with caution. Already suspicious, some may actively seek out evidence to support their beliefs (what psychologists call having a 'confirmation bias'), though they may not have mentioned their concerns to anyone else. During this emerging dispute stage, stakeholder interests are likely to be limited to just the individuals who are on the centre stage of the dispute, as well as their managers and potentially others working within the same teams. This is often a point when individuals who are peripheral to the dispute start to take sides and some may feel sufficiently engaged to take direct action themselves; for example, colleagues in a team who see one person pursuing a complaint feel that it's the right time to raise a grievance of their own.

The perspective of the assumed 'subject' may be difficult to determine, and it may well be the case that they are themselves yet unaware of the friction they are helping to create. A lack of appreciation for the sensitivities of others, combined with a difference of views on what is acceptable behaviour (for example, indulging in what they see as being light humour), may further limit their ability to recognize their contribution to a growing disagreement. Humour can nevertheless be a powerful diffuser. For example, in concluding an intense mediation session and after judging the mood, Jackie commented when both parties mentioned they were then planning to take annual leave that she hoped that they were not going to the same place! This greatly helped to lighten the mood, though of course required sensitivity to guage whether such a comment was appropriate at the time.

The perspectives of these various parties are likely to change as the dispute becomes more apparent. The 'originator' will become more certain of the basis for their grievance, the 'subject' will eventually become aware of the part they've played in their process, and manager(s) will become more convinced that informal and non-direct action will be unlikely to resolve the dispute or prevent it escalating.

Case study: No job for a woman

When Jackie was a uniformed police sergeant, she was responsible for booking-in prisoners brought into custody. On one occasion, overtime was offered for a sergeant to arrest several subjects. Jackie volunteered, but was told that the operation was 'not an appropriate deployment for a woman'.

Jackie told her inspector that she worked at the sharp end of policing every day – why, when it came to overtime, should this operation be any different? The inspector replied that it was not a good situation for a woman to deal with. Jackie told him she did not agree, then spoke to her senior manager who offered to talk to the inspector.

Jackie and the inspector later met again over a coffee. He explained that he felt protective and hadn't deliberately denied overtime out of a sexist or any other motive: he was just 'old fashioned' and wanted to 'look out' for Jackie. Jackie accepted this explanation, but told him she was quite happy to do any tour of duty, and could look after herself. She appreciated his concern, but still felt patronized. Reluctantly, Jackie was allowed to complete the operation, and complete it successfully. The pair remain good working colleagues today.

In this, as in many situations that give rise to conflict, a misinterpretation of intention was to blame. The readiness of Jackie to say clearly why she felt the way she did and her boss's honest and candid response not only dealt with this matter quickly, but also helped build trust and openness between them. For this to be achieved, the readiness of an individual to be open about his or her feelings needs to be respected by the person who is being challenged, and met with readiness to be open in turn.

A declared dispute

The point when the various parties stop keeping their thoughts to themselves and acknowledge these in conversation with others represents a significant milestone in the journey toward resolving a dispute. Candid discussion allows views to be aired, and so opens the possibility for finding a resolution.

At this stage, the originator may make a veiled complaint or present the reasons he or she feels aggrieved to his or her manager or other trusted third party. In the mind of the originator, the grounds for feeling unhappy are real, as is the perception that the emotional impact the dissatisfaction has had will be apparent. His or her hope may be that the manager (or other person approached) will be sympathetic to his or her views and act quickly to resolve the dispute. He or she may have had some hesitation about raising the issue, through fear of aggravating the relationship with the alleged subject.

For managers, a determination to resolve the matter effectively should of course continue. However, the way in which this is approached may become a bigger concern for them. Consideration might need to be given to the need for formal escalation, for example, if the alleged grievance might need to be treated as a disciplinary matter, whilst they may be uncertain of the boundaries of their role for resolving particular types of dispute. Managers might also be anxious about passing on a hot potato to the HR department or a coach, especially if their own performance measurement takes account of how effectively they handle conflict. At least managers must now acknowledge that it's an issue that must be addressed, even if this is something they feel uncomfortable doing. Knowing how to approach the alleged subject is likely to be uppermost amongst their concerns.

The 'subject' will of necessity now be fully aware of the existence of the dispute, and have heard the basis of a complaint made against him or her. He or she may greet this in a variety of ways: with total surprise, with a desire to play down the importance of the allegation, or with a flat denial. He or she may be anxious about the possible consequences of being found to be at fault, blotting his or her copybook or even facing disciplinary action, and so may quite naturally feel a need to defend him or herself.

MANAGING DEVELOPING DISPUTES

Disputes that cannot be prevented or nipped in the bud early on may begin to escalate to a point where more concerted management attention is needed. This is potentially a point at which involving an intermediary might first be considered, depending on the nature of the dispute and the manager's skill and ability to remain a neutral broker between the two parties. This might be the case, for example, where a dispute involves two individuals from different teams, perhaps led by managers who feel a need to support their team member. Coaching and informal mediation may be especially appropriate at this stage.

As a dispute begins to form, sides will begin to be taken, the positions or 'battle-lines' of each party will become more entrenched, emotions will become highly charged, the motivation to pursue the dispute will be more likely to increase, and so too will the intervention needed to bring about a lasting resolution be more likely to demand increasing skill. Those involved in earlier attempts to constrain the dispute therefore need to be sufficiently self-aware to know when the limits of their own capability to resolve a dispute have been reached.

In practice, this may not be quite so easy to take on board. Managers may be wary of involving others at what they may see as still an early stage, whilst some will be very eager to pass the issue on rather than attempt to resolve it themselves. For some, a sense of duty and the right to address conflict in their teams may be jealously protected. And where two or more strong-minded managers are locked in their determination, jointly they offer the potential to add to the intensity of a dispute rather than to defuse it!

So too, the individuals who are embroiled in a dispute may be nervous about the prospect of third parties becoming involved in their dialogue too early, recognizing that escalation usually equates to a formal process, with all the connotations of trial, judgement and character-marking that may involve. This is of course a false perception, but one that many are likely to hold. Furthermore, involving a conflict 'expert' in what may still be seen as a private disagreement may be seen by some as an admission of failure.

HR advisers or others responsible for supporting conflict resolution have a role to play in correcting any such false perceptions. In countering managers' concerns, this means being proactive in highlighting the value of available guidance or third-party intervention at an early stage; for staff, this means selling a notion that involving others doesn't invariably mean escalation to a grievance procedure (indeed, many organizations' grievance procedures state that formal investigations wouldn't normally be launched without one party requesting them).

The aim at this developing stage is still to bring the dispute to a satisfactory close without the need for further escalation. It's incumbent on managers and the disputing individuals to recognize this imperative, and to be ready to accept when involving a third party offers the best prospect for achieving this.

Case study: Reluctant rivals

A member of staff who had been running a team for several months was very frustrated and bitter when a new manager took over. The new broom completely changed and overhauled the system, never consulting with the member of staff. It appeared to the team leader that everything he had engineered was cast away, overridden and dismissed.

The two were at complete loggerheads, nearly coming to blows one evening and very bitter toward each other. Meanwhile, different loyalties began to form within the team, and one concerned team member eventually made the HR department aware. Informal mediation was offered and accepted.

This resulted in an open exchange of views. The manager disclosed that she felt overshadowed and threatened by what she perceived as the other's competitiveness. She had felt she had to show everyone who was the boss and had to prove she was in charge. She believed that this was showing strong management. For his part, the team leader explained how hurt and inadequate this had made him feel, how his loyalty to the organization was being repaid unkindly. He said he wanted to support the manager and in fact was relieved to have the pressure of running the team taken off him and appreciated how the manager must have felt coming into the team, whilst conceding that there may have been a clash of egos between them.

This was the breakthrough in the impasse that was needed, resulting in them both accepting each other's apology and expressing appreciation for their different perspectives. They subsequently worked collaboratively, managing a very healthy functioning team.

This mediation took place in little more than one hour.

This example illustrates the compounding issues that often result when two strong characters can't see eye-to-eye, not least the division of team loyalties that they can attract. As with many other cases that we've seen, mediation need not be lengthy to achieve a breakthrough – quite often it just needs to happen (with of course both parties recognizing this need). Honesty and openness by each of the conflicting parties, combined with the good grace to accept another's humility and apology, made the difference in restarting what was to become a supportive relationship.

Grievance investigation

Grievance or fairness at work investigations usually mark a formal stage in the progress of a dispute, but still one that may precede the possible need for formal mediation and may make a considerable call on a manager's time.

All organizations should have an established grievance procedure or approach for investigating alleged fairness at work disputes. Typically, this is invoked when attempts to resolve an individual's complaint locally (ie, normally by a front-line manager) have failed. A key objective of the procedure is to ascertain whether the complaint has substance, and if necessary to warn 'offenders' of their contractual responsibilities to other colleagues.

The task of investigating a grievance is normally the responsibility of HR, although it may be delegated to a trusted third-party colleague. Whoever takes on the task plays an important role in the DR process, and therefore should be familiar with both DR principles and practice.

Investigation may involve interviewing not only the person bringing the grievance and his or her alleged 'subject(s)', but also other colleagues and potentially others outside the organization. E-mails, documents and other types of 'evidence' may need to be inspected. Investigations may be time-consuming and risk making an allegation public when this might not be desired, something that may often be unavoidable. The success of a fairness at work investigation depends not only on the quality of the investigation and reasoning for the decision reached by the investigator, but also on the extent to which the rival parties trust the integrity of the investigator and the investigation process itself.

The process of formalizing a grievance can itself trigger further conflict, as form-filling and preparing a case take over from taking time to talk through and work through the problem. Complainants often don't allow a cooling-off period before raising a grievance, even if an internal process encourages this. However, a cooling-off period can allow time for tempers to settle and for other information to come to light. Conversely, managers may be concerned about advising an individual to take stock when dealing with an obviously serious matter, for fear of being seen not to have given due attention to the matter.

Worryingly, many grievances result in appeals. If an initial investigation has been conducted comprehensively and correctly, an appeal is unlikely to be upheld; however they absorb additional resource and effort nonetheless. We've encountered situations in some organizations where virtually perpetual appeals or new fairness at work investigations can be raised, perhaps because the originator feels that they haven't been treated properly or his or her complaint hasn't been properly understood in an earlier investigation. The original investigator can then find him or herself being asked to explain how they reached their conclusion by another colleague, and in some cases this can lead to friction amongst investigators.

One common reason why grievances don't achieve satisfactory conclusions is that insufficient evidence may be available to substantiate the complaint. The 'one word against another' scenario is all too common. Similarly, it's always possible that an investigator can reach the wrong conclusion, perhaps based on a majority view of those interviewed.

The way in which grievance procedures are implemented cannot be taken outside of the context of a CM strategy. There should be criteria for selecting investigators similar to those used for mediation or other intermediary roles (see Chapter 10). In particular, investigators must be impartial and non-evaluative, have an open mind to the likelihood of an allegation being true when they set about investigating it, and a desire to achieve what's right and fair for the individuals concerned. Investigators need to work to establish the trust of individuals they are questioning, and to be free of influence from powerful 'lobbyists' such as senior managers with vested interests.

Grievances invariably inflame emotions and heighten anxieties amongst others. They create a worry for either party that their relationship will never be the same again, whatever the outcome of the investigation, and concern for the alleged subject(s) that they may forever blot their copy book if found guilty.

ESSENTIAL SKILLS FOR RESOLVING DISPUTES

The key stages described above set the context for a manager's normal role in dispute management. Their success or otherwise in preventing further escalation depends in part on the skill-set they can call upon.

Amongst prerequisite competencies, the skills of questioning, listening, engaging and building rapport are paramount. These are frequently covered in management training courses, as well as being central themes in a wide range of management texts. This shouldn't be too surprising – they are after all essential skills!

We won't spend significant time repeating information that is widely available elsewhere, but our brief coverage shouldn't mean that working on 'the basics' isn't important. Whilst the theory may be readily understood, for many, practice is often more difficult, so recalling some basic principles should be valuable even for those who consider themselves to be excellent communicators. It's these key points that we provide here.

Listening

- Listening isn't the same as hearing. To hear is to be aware that someone has spoken and usually to register the general theme of what has been said if not the actual words; to listen is to really engage with what is being communicated.
- Human beings have two ears and one mouth – generally, we should use them in equal proportion!
- To listen involves observation of non-verbal as well as verbal messages, to 'listen between the words' (see later in this chapter).
- There are several levels of listening – Whitworth *et al* (1998) propose a model involving three levels:
  - level one gives attention to what is being said, but with an emphasis on what the message means for us; this self-interested focus is removed in level two;
  - in level two there is a high level of concentration, demonstrated interest and appreciation of the context in which the individual is making their point, recognizing the actual words and turns of phrase that they prefer to use;
  - level three listening goes one stage further by involving an all-round sensing of how an individual is communicating, taking account not only of his or her body language, emotional expression and demeanour, but also to the environment and circumstances in which he or she is speaking.
- You will only truly know the question an individual has heard when you hear the answer they give in reply![1]

Listening involves showing that you have received and understand what individuals have communicated correctly, by acknowledging, summarizing and playing back what has been absorbed. As Alan Greenspan once put it: 'I know you think you understand what you think I said, but I'm not sure you realize that what you heard is not what I meant!' (cited by Saxe, 2009).

When posing any question, it's important to listen not only to what's being said, how it is being said and what might not be being articulated. It may not be necessary to know the detail of an account, but rather to appreciate what an individual is thinking and how his or her attention is focused.

The best interviewers are often those who say the least. When used appropriately, pregnant pauses can be especially powerful in encouraging individuals to reflect and speak, giving time for them to think through an answer. Irrespective of the theory, putting this into practice is quite difficult for many.

One possible technique to keep in mind when you might feel tempted to speak is to wait at least 15 seconds before speaking again. The image of a drum being beaten slowly three times (indicating speaking, thinking, response) might be useful to call to mind when feeling a strong urge to break the silence. Another person will almost always feel the need to fill the gap, and the information revealed can be very helpful for moving the discussion forward. In her previous career as a police officer, Jackie often faced arrested suspects whose only response in interviews was to utter 'no comment'. By an interviewer leaving silence, individuals would often begin to fill the silences.

Sometimes, of course, body language cues may lead us to form an inaccurate view of what an individual may be thinking or saying, even when combining several types of evidence. For example, an individual may be unusually restless not because they are struggling to control what they say, but because they often experience ticks when they feel under stress.

Questioning

- A question should serve a useful end, being relevant to the purpose of the conversation.
- Closed questions invite one-word answers (eg, 'Do you feel any sense of responsibility for this?') They are sometimes useful to confirm a point but rarely encourage individuals to reveal why they think the way they do.
- Leading or weighted questions are likely to result in 'led' or biased answers.
- Socratic questions encourage individuals to reflect on what they've said, helping them to work through their thinking and check their assumptions.
- Probing is a form of Socratic questioning that aims to uncover what an individual really believes or what has led him or her to form a particular view.
- An individual who poses a question should allow reasonable time for the receiver to process and give an answer, whilst not dwelling on which question to ask next.
- To ask a question but to fail to listen to the response given serves little purpose – by listening, not only may an individual's perspective be better understood, but also subsequent questions may be better informed.
- One useful memory-jogger questioning approach often quoted in management training is *TED-PIE*: 'Tell me, Explain to me, Describe to me – Previously, In detail and Exactly'. For example:
  - 'Tell me what has brought you here [or] to this?'

- 'Explain to me what will be useful [or] what it is you want to achieve', 'Explain to me how this has come about';
- 'Describe what you are thinking/feeling/experiencing.' 'What if... then describe how you'd feel... ?'
- 'Previously, before this kicked off, what was going well?,' 'Previously, how was your working relationship?' (Note the emphasis here is on what was right, not what's wrong);
- 'Detail on a scale of 1 to 10 how you feel about this idea...'.

Another familiar questioning mnemonic prompt is 5WH (What?, Why?, Where?, When?, Who?), borrowed from Rudyard Kipling's (1902) famous *Just So* story, 'The Elephant's Child'. *TED-PIE* and '5 WH' are amongst the micro-tools included in Appendix 1.

Whilst seeking explanation is fundamental to appreciating the root of a dispute, 'why?' questions may need to be framed carefully, to avoid being seen as challenging or provocative. To illustrate: 'What difficulties are you facing managing your current work load?' invites reflection without judgement, whereas asking 'Why are you not managing your current work load?' can imply criticism. Inappropriate use of 'why?' questions can quickly stop an important line of dialogue.

When challenging an individual, it's better to frame an invitation (eg, 'What are you thinking when...?') rather than a point of view (eg, 'I feel there's something you're not saying'). A careful choice of language here can prevent a manager from unwittingly putting pressure on an individual to say something that they may not be ready to, rather than challenging them to reflect on the same issue and choose for themselves whether it's appropriate to raise.

When using questions, a manager may often seek to help individuals access their own base of knowledge to find answers to the challenges they are struggling with. Questions that aim to help individuals achieve this most effectively might be termed *direct route* questions, whereas those that lead away from finding a resolution can be thought of as *possible deviations*. Clearly, it's in both parties' best interests to focus on a direct route rather than unproductive deviations. Examples are given in Appendix 1.

Engaging

■ The aim of engagement is to encourage an individual to actively and willingly participate in conversation.

■ To engage conversation, it's first desirable to know that a dialogue is welcome. All too often managers pressure individuals to talk without taking account of their readiness to do so.

■ Where intervention is appropriate but individuals are reluctant to speak, a stimulus for engaging in conversation may be required – a manager may need to 'sell' the benefits of being open to conversation ('Would it help to talk to someone who's not involved in this...?'), provide reassurance that to engage is safe ('Would it help if we went and found a quiet place for a coffee?', 'I'm not here to judge'), or offer a challenge ('It doesn't seem to me that you're making much headway sorting this out alone. Can we talk?').

■ Occasionally it's right not to intervene, or at least to choose the right moment to do so. Individuals may well be able to resolve their differences alone, although a manager needs to keep a close watch to ensure that the 'Golden Hour' opportunity isn't missed.

■ When all else fails and intervention is required, a 'push' rather than a 'sell' approach may be required: there's a time and a place for a manager to be directive.

There is of course quite a difference between engaging in a dialogue and merely communicating, not least when relying on e-mails and text messages rather than actually speaking. It's all too easy for an author of an e-mail to feel that he or she has made his or her point, and so rush to hit the 'send' button. It's quite a different matter to observe how recipients may interpret a message before themselves possibly responding in kind. Disputes cannot be properly settled without interpersonal communication, invariably meaning that a verbal dialogue is necessary.

Building rapport

■ To have rapport is to be 'in tune' with another person.

■ Building rapport is a normal prerequisite for establishing trust, and so allowing individuals to feel able to express how they really feel.

■ To create and sustain rapport involves active listening, demonstrated interest and association with the other person's preferred communication style, body posture and conversation pace.

■ Verbal association may be demonstrated by recognizing whether an individual prefers visual, hearing or feeling language (VHF) – for example, someone with a visual preference might like to describe a thought as something that they picture, using language such as 'I can now see clearly what's going on here'; a preference for hearing might express itself through language such as 'What I'm hearing from you is'; whilst someone who prefers a feeling or kinaesthetic style might make regular reference to how they feel about something.

■ By recognizing which type of language an individual prefers, greater rapport can usually be built by adopting a similar style, for example, by using a metaphor to paint a picture, such as, 'It appears to me that you're trying to climb this mountain on roller skates!'

- Non-verbal rapport can be built by demonstrating interested and 'tuned in' body language – maintaining eye contact and adjusting body position to match or mirror that of the other person, though not to obviously replicate their every move.
- Empathy is an often misunderstood concept. A model developed by the eminent scientist Simon Baron-Cohen (2003) distinguished three components of empathy, with some degree of overlap: affective empathy (feeling appropriate emotion triggered by observing another person's feelings), cognitive empathy (appreciating what someone else may be feeling), and sympathy (relevant when someone is hurting, a desire to want to alleviate their suffering).

LISTENING BETWEEN THE WORDS

The ability to read or 'listen between the words' is a rare but universally valuable skill to have. We've already mentioned some of the more obvious ways of detecting what might be being said: observing body language, noting whether an individual may be displaying defensive body language, and quickly gaining an impression of their mood. However, an accomplished listener needs deeper skills, which we'll now explore.

Speech patterns

The pace, intonation, pitch, tone and volume of someone's voice can send strong messages. It takes little to notice likely agitation when a normally calmly paced and quiet-speaking person suddenly becomes more frenetic in his or her dialogue and starts shouting to make a point, but loudness and speed of delivery may convey less obvious messages from someone who is normally an energetic speaker.

Eye-accessing cues

John Grinder and Richard Bandler, the creators of neuro-linguistic programming (NLP), studied the way in which individuals appear to shift their eyes according to the type of language they use (visual, hearing, feeling) and the mental processing they are undertaking at the time (eg, recalling a distant memory, trying to picture how something might be in future). Whilst not to be treated as an absolute rule, they concluded that there does appear to be a strong correlation between the way individuals shift their eyes and their mental activity, as if they were 'looking' for an answer (Bandler and Grinder, 1979).

Building on this thinking, one model suggests that the position of the eyes can offer a strong clue to what a person is mentally processing:

- Eyes pointing upwards and to the left suggests that an individual may be picturing an image they've seen before, whilst pointing to the right may indicate that they are constructing a picture (such as envisioning the way things may be in future).
- Eyes that point to the left or right on a level horizontal plane are usually associated with auditory activity (such as being especially attuned to a noise from outside).
- Eyes pointing down and to the left may suggest that a person is locked in an internal dialogue, whilst those pointing right often suggest that a concept has been understood or connected with (as if being in touch with a feeling).

Of course not everyone responds in the same way. For example, there appear to be different eye-accessing cues displayed by right- and left-handed people, and people from different cultural backgrounds may also react differently.

The language of the eyes

Individuals vary in their ability to interpret the emotions and intentions revealed by the eyes (Baron-Cohen, 2003). This is a subject that has been researched very carefully across a wide range of cultures. Astonishingly, the different emotions that some people can reliably detect breaks down into 412 discrete emotions, a finding that is remarkably consistent across different cultures. However, most of us are normally only able to distinguish a small fraction of these.

Quite apart from the meaning conveyed by a particular glint of the eye, the positioning of the eyebrows, tensing of the facial muscles, pace of blinking and tendency to hold or avert gaze may all reveal telltale messages about what a person is thinking. Arched brows, for example, are often connected with appreciation and intrigue, whilst down-swept ones are thought to indicate a plea for help. However, as with all sensory processing, care must be taken before assuming that a particular type of eye gaze carries a definite meaning: eyebrows can be cosmetically shaped, people from some cultures are trained at a young age to cast their eyes down when presented to an elder, and autistic people are thought to avert their gaze because their cerebral cortex is easily aroused by gazing into the eyes of another person.[2]

Theory of mind

An ability to form a theory of mind might be thought of as putting yourself into another person's mental shoes. As we engage in conversation, our brain kicks-off a series of simulations about what others with whom we're conversing may be thinking and feeling, and so creates a theory of what's motivating their thinking.

This happens every time we interact with others, and indeed neuro-developmental scientists believe we are hard-wired with this ability. The problem is that we don't always form the right theory. As such, managers who rush to assumptions based on the theories they form may completely misread what an individual is really experiencing. Those who trust their own gut instinct 'never to be wrong' may similarly be wrong-footed. This suggests a need for managers to regularly check themselves, even as their theories are forming, and to search out other lines of evidence to see if these support their initial beliefs.

Of course, when 'listening between the words', a manager needs to judge how individuals are reacting to another's participation in the dialogue. Some may react to an admission of personal failing with humility, whilst others may want to retain the moral high-ground; a concession made by one party may persuade another to offer one in return, but conversely, it may embolden his or her resolve to fight tough.

WHEN AND WHAT TO ESCALATE – AND TO WHOM

If disagreement can't be resolved in the 'Golden Hour', then third-party intervention and probable escalation normally follow. Some matters will always be escalated: claims of bullying, harassment and potential criminal activity amongst them (although managers should be guided by their organization's HR policy or staff handbook guidance on such matters, if available). The difficulty is knowing what this 'point' is. Unfortunately, the advice given by the former British Prime Minister Edward Heath (BBC, 1998) doesn't apply in our case: that when asked whether you agree with a viewpoint on which you have no opinion, reply 'up to a point' – no one ever asks what that point is!

There are several unambiguous circumstances where escalation is appropriate:

- when the dispute is getting out of hand – descending into ever more bitter disagreement, or possibly marked by regular emotional outbursts by one or both parties;
- when it's clear that an individual may potentially have a claim against the organization that could expose it to litigation;
- where either party decides that they wish to formalize a complaint;
- when the organization's HR procedures say that it's necessary to do so (eg, in the case of a serious disciplinary matter).

Less clear bases for escalation include a desire by an informal mediator to stand down from the role, an apparent lack of progress toward resolution using informal methods, and when a dispute has reached an impasse. For these, a judgement must be made on what next step is appropriate, consulting with the individuals who are involved in the disagreement to review their preferences amongst the alternative ways forward available to them. These may include:

■ taking no further action, recognizing that the dispute has reached a point of impasse;
■ making another attempt to resolve the matter informally;
■ concluding that formal escalation is inevitable or necessary.

In helping individuals to review their options, they should be encouraged to consider the consequences of following each suggested path. For example, if no further action is taken, individuals will need to consider how they will live with a continuing impasse, accepting that the organization had taken reasonable steps to attempt to resolve the matter and provided an opportunity to hear their complaint. This might not preclude them from raising a similar concern in future, but normally only if significant new evidence to support their complaint has emerged.

Managers too need to weigh up the relative advantages and disadvantages of the different courses of action available to them. In this task, a decision may not always be clear-cut: continuing to attempt a local resolution may prove to be less time-consuming than escalating, or it may not; informal peace brokering may better allow two individuals to overcome their disagreement, but it may just delay an inevitable impasse.

Managers need to be honest in recognizing when it's appropriate to call upon the involvement of others rather than dealing with an issue themselves. One of the most common cries that we hear from HR managers is that often quite mundane disputes are escalated to them too quickly, sometimes without an obvious attempt having been made by a manager to resolve a matter locally. This can place a significant burden of work on HR, whilst front-line managers don't develop the ability to handle future 'Golden Hour' opportunities.

If both managers and the disputing parties all agree on the next step, it makes sense to move swiftly. Where there is disagreement, a manager must ultimately decide what action should be taken next. A disagreement on this next step amongst managers should normally prompt a third party's involvement.

But deciding whether to engage a third party is more complex where a conflict involves a team member and his or her manager, even at the informal (emerging conflict) stage. A third party should normally be quite quickly involved if it's clear that the manager and team member are at risk of falling out or are simply unable to resolve the disagreement between themselves. Unfortunately, managers may be reluctant to open themselves to a level playing field with a subordinate, especially if they may possibly be held accountable for their actions.

Team members may also be reluctant to invite a third party's intervention from fear of undermining their manager's credibility and so risking an uneasy relationship with him or her in future. A strategy of 'stand-off' may be seen as being preferable. However, storing up unresolved differences may prove to be ultimately destructive, like a silent time bomb that ultimately explodes with devastating effect. Similarly, organizations that assume that a fear amongst workers during a period of recession may deter many from initiating disputes may be ignoring the time bomb that threatens to explode when easier job mobility returns.

Case study: Storm in a teacup

A small group of personal assistants were responsible for making tea and washing the cups used by visiting guests and bosses throughout the day.

It was an unwritten rule that the assistants would take alternate turns to wash up. One new member took umbrage at this, announcing it 'was not in [their] job description', refusing to wash up. The others responded badly and the newcomer soon found herself the subject of regular corridor gossip.

A manager who observed the disagreement decided to install a coffee machine, which dispensed paper cups. However, the restored peace was short-lived, as one of the senior managers took exception to using paper cups and insisted that the contents be poured into a china cup, re-igniting the quarrel over washing up duties.

Conflict usually begins with small matters, but ones that can quickly generate a furore. In this case, an insensitive or deliberately uncooperative senior manager upset a calm that had been easily won, illustrating the importance for all who contribute to such uncomfortable situations to be made aware of their impact and of the collective responsibility for restoring peace.

THE SEVEN RULES OF COMMUNICATION

Throughout the chapter we've emphasized the often complex nature of interpersonal communication and how it can affect the course of DR. To complete our discussion on this theme, we'd like to share a wonderfully powerful set of principles for communicating in challenging circumstances.

Dick Wolfenden, a former colleague of Jackie and previously a senior hostage negotiator for the UK government, advocates using 'the seven rules of communication'. We like to think of these as forming a charter for good DR practice. The seven rules are:

1. listen;
2. empathize;
3. adopt appropriate attitude;
4. be sincere;
5. respect others' dignity;
6. build trust;
7. show compassion.

These are also included in Appendix 1.

Summary

Managers in the front line have the greatest opportunity for preventing disputes from deepening. Suitable intervention during this 'Golden Hour' opportunity requires managers to be capable of recognizing the early signs of an emerging dispute, know what and when to escalate, and have the sensitivity and knowledge to choose how to mediate informally.

Many of the skills required for 'Golden Hour' interventions are no different to those that might be expected of a good people manager, including strong emotional intelligence and an ability to read beyond the words that people speak. To help, a range of simple techniques and principles (such as TED-PIE and 'the seven rules of communication') can be usefully brought into play.

Notes

1. This observation is borrowed from De Shazer, S and Berg, I K (1995) 'The brief therapy tradition' in J Weakland and R Wendel (eds), *Propagations: Thirty years of influence from the Mental Research Institute,* Haworth Press.
2. A comprehensive study of the 'language of the eyes' is provided in Marshall, E (2003) *The Eyes Have It – Revealing their power, messages and secret,* Citadel Press. A version of an eye-reading test is included in Baron-Cohen, S (2003) *The Essential Difference – The truth about the male and female brain,* Basic Books.

7

Escalated dispute resolution

A FULL-BLOWN DISPUTE

Whenever an attempt to reach a conclusion to a dispute that could not be solved locally involves informal or formal intervention by a third party, all parties involved should be able to recognize that they've entered into a new phase of their disagreement. A complete impasse may have been reached between the differing parties, and the consequences of not achieving a satisfactory outcome may have broadened to include the organization's reputation and potential financial penalty.

Managers, grievance investigators and other intermediaries involved in the earlier life of a dispute may no longer be on the centre stage, but the same interests that they have for finding a resolution to the dispute will continue, if not inten-sified. At the same time, battle lines will have been drawn between the parties who are in disagreement.

Perceptions of their innocence or right to feel aggrieved may have become entrenched, although by this stage other factors are likely to be at play in influencing each party's thinking. Overt game playing will be all the more likely now that the stakes for each party are higher; indeed, the will to 'win' may exceed a rounded sense of the current reality.

Disputes that arise with a lack of clarity on what is right or wrong may well perpetuate after a grievance process and subsequent appeal. Where such disputes progress to mediation, it's possible that the party bringing the complaint will no longer be the originally aggrieved but the 'accused', such as an individual who has been disciplined but who believes that he or she has been wronged by the process and is now anxious to clear his or her name. In such cases, the organization rather than a particular individual may now have become the subject of complaint. Even if it's believed that there is no prospect that the organization might be exposed to potential litigation over the matter, a duty of care remains for the individual who remains aggrieved. Indeed, in extreme cases, someone who feels falsely disciplined may succumb to mental ill-health. In any case, an individual's motivation, physical health and psychological contract[1] are likely to be adversely affected, and this cannot be satisfactory from a manager's perspective.

From an organization's point of view, the stakes are now much higher for finding a resolution quickly, especially given the clear commitment of time and resource diverted to it in an attempt to achieve this end. Employees may be more relaxed about the time and cost of the process, but their quest for 'justice', recompense or clearing their name is likely to remain as steadfast as ever.

Given the potential for the dispute to escalate into the public domain, a wider range of stakeholders may now have an interest in the outcome of the DR process. These may include more senior managers than those who've been previously aware of the disagreement, potentially involving board-level interest. Depending on the profile of the dispute, further interests may include those with responsibility for the organization's public relations, press management and publicity, and commercial advisers. Trade union representatives, colleagues of the originator, and other supporters and advocates may also contribute their views, each offering the potential to influence the thinking of the main actors involved.

It now becomes critical to ensure that individuals' objectives and expectations are clear, and that each person is committed to helping the process work. Engagement is now crucially important to get right: without a common will to move forward and a readiness not to obstruct a fair exchange of views, mediation is doomed to fail. At the same time, with the range of stakeholder interests now likely to be energized and the potentially complex and hidden motivations of the main players, any intermediary charged with the task of resolving the conflict must undertake a robust stakeholder analysis.

Achieving clarity of expectations may take time. Either party may be reluctant to participate in the process in spite of recognizing this as being a logical next step, whilst in some cases it may become apparent that it's wise for them not to do so. We should turn our attention to understanding what stakeholder perspectives are and to the crucial task of engagement.

Case study: Sent in error

Abbie was an administration officer for a large team, referred to by her manager Joseph as 'the AO', but very rarely by name. Abbie was put out by this and wrote an e-mail to a colleague to express how she felt. Mistakenly, the e-mail was sent to Joseph rather than the intended colleague.

Realizing what she had done, Abbie went hot and cold with shame. On reading the e-mail, Joseph called her in immediately, demanding an apology. Abbie became upset and said that what she had written was real, that she didn't feel treated like a person.

Joseph stormed out of his office, bellowing that she 'was out of order'. A full-blown argument ensued, whilst all around buried their heads in their work, pretending not to hear. Abbie was in tears, but Joseph continued his attack in full flow. Shocked, Abbie ran out of the building and then remained sick with stress for four months before lodging a grievance accusing Joseph of overbearing conduct. All of the team were interviewed, as was Joseph, who himself subsequently became sick with work-related stress.

Abbie later said that her only wish was for Joseph to apologize for referring to her as 'the AO' and losing his temper; Joseph wanted an apology for Abbie's critical e-mail. Neither spoke to each other again, with Abbie transferring into another team and Joseph carrying a cloud over him, being seen as overbearing and brutish.

Permanent stand-offs can have very extreme consequences, as in this case, when a timely 10-minute conversation might otherwise allow things to end very differently. Once Abbie's complaint had become formalized, an unsatisfactory ending may have been likely unless she could be assured that her interests would continue to be protected, for example, if she felt unfairly treated by Joseph again in the future.

Similarly, Abbie might have felt more ready to raise her grievance earlier had she felt assured that by doing so she wouldn't be marked out as a malcontent or trouble-maker by the organization (in other words, if the HR department had been able to impress on her that out-of-turn bosses are just as accountable for their behaviour as anyone else). Counselling, training or reminding Joseph of the organization's shared values (even under discipline) may similarly have been appropriate in this case.

STAKEHOLDER ANALYSIS

A wide variety of techniques exist for considering how to identify and engage with different stakeholders. Most of these emphasize the relative influence and importance of each stakeholder group, both as they may currently perceive the dispute and how this perspective may be likely to change should the dispute escalate further.[2] A template that may be used in this analysis is included in Appendix 2.

Setting aside the relationships that might exist between disputing parties (as we outlined in Chapter 2), we should also consider the quite specific perspectives that both they and other stakeholders may adopt. We'll start by considering the possible viewpoints taken by the primary players in a dispute.

Perspectives in the 'inner circle'

'The originator'

Role: The individual(s) who brought the concern to the table.

Possible objectives: To seek justice, fair recognition, rebuke for the 'subject', achieve a change in their current situation, and be vindicated.

Possible perspectives: Blinkered, wanting to win over intermediaries, self-confident/believe they have the moral high-ground, base their views on limited facts, fear the consequences of escalating their dispute (whether their complaint is upheld or not), believe that they may (or may not) have support from their organization depending on how they perceive they are regarded or owing to their status.

'The subject'

Role: The individual(s) who is the subject of the dispute, who may in turn represent a particular group, prevailing point of view or the organization itself. Note that an originator may be a 'subject' of complaint by the other party, and both may potentially initiate a concern.

Possible objectives: To achieve success at any cost (even if this requires avoiding telling the truth), vindication, maintaining dignity/reputation, avoid rebuke or disciplinary action.

Possible perspectives: Wanting to win over intermediaries, embarrassment, fear of the consequences of being found against, game-playing (eg, wanting to distract from or play down the real issues, suggesting that the originator's perception is 'their problem' or exploiting small weaknesses in the other side's argument), believing that they may (or may not) have support from their organization.

Intermediaries

Role: Those brought in to broker a resolution to a dispute, either a single mediator or arbitrator, two mediators or an arbitration panel.

Possible objectives: To achieve what the sponsor and/or parties view as an acceptable resolution or to demonstrate that the dispute is irresolvable beyond the stage they've reached, within the terms of their engagement.

Possible perspectives: Giving honest advice (evaluative mediation), helping individuals gain a clear perspective of their situation and options for moving forward, keeping an open mind, unconscious bias, strong focus on achieving progress, strong time management, awareness of the interests of stakeholders outside the room, reputation, commercial opportunity for selling-on further services.

Beyond the 'inner circle'

Slightly more peripheral to the key roles we've just described, may be others who have a direct part to play in the DR process. Each of these two is likely to have a mix of personal objectives and differ in their psychological contract with the organization.

Conflict coach

Role: Engaged to help one or both parties to objectively evaluate the conflict they believe themselves to be facing.

Possible objectives: To achieve their client's objective, help the client form a clear perspective and choose a way forward that best serves their interests.

Possible perspectives: Having a strong client focus, desire to move the client forward, may (or may not) be focused on sponsor interests, probably detached from the interests of the other party, commercial opportunity.

Advisers and lobbyists (directly engaged to support, represent or advise the inner circle)

Role: lawyers, medical specialists, trade union representatives, supporting colleagues and others who advise or support one of the disputing parties (usually, though not invariably, in isolation from convened mediation[3]).

Possible objectives: To achieve their client's best interests, to achieve their own or the objectives of members they represent.

Possible perspectives: 'The client is always right', playing devil's advocate to the client, wanting to give frank advice, protecting their own reputation, personal concern for the individual's wellbeing (or) being detached from concern for the individual.

Advisers and lobbyists (not directly engaged)

Role: Supporting colleagues, family or friends who offer informal advice and support.

Possible objectives: To achieve their ally's best interests, to actively demonstrate their support.

Possible perspectives: Saying what they believe their friend wants to hear or what they believe will encourage or show support for them (may be driven by a personal ulterior motive, eg, a partner who feels the need to express allegiance to protect the strength of their relationship), satisfaction from seeing someone other than themselves take the organization to task.

Front-line managers and heads of department of the parties involved

Role: Have a duty of care and management responsibility for one or both of the disputing parties.

Possible objectives: To obtain a resolution to a distracting activity as soon and as simply as possible, get what they perceive as a troublesome person 'sorted out', limit or prevent potential fallout within the team.

Possible perspectives: bias, concern (or a lack of concern) for the individual, concern for the team and other stakeholders, protecting their own staff (being competitive with other managers), being driven by a desire to be seen as a 'strong' or 'supportive' manager.

HR or other custodian of Dispute Resolution policy and process

Role: Oversee corporate DR policy, engage intermediaries, manage costs and risks, and advise on DR options.

Possible objectives: To ensure fair treatment for the parties involved, ensure that proper process is followed.

Possible perspectives: Wanting to avoid escalation to litigation, desire to achieve a lasting settlement, see themselves as power-holder as the representative of 'the organization'.

Note that we've suggested a range of alternative perspectives in some cases (it is to be hoped that most fellow intermediaries won't have a sell-opportunity at the forefront of their minds, but unfortunately this may not always be the case). Whilst not automatically assuming the worst, it's sensible to keep in mind that not all stakeholder perspectives may be explicitly displayed or conform to an expected pattern.

In addition to those who may play an intervening role in a dispute, several other stakeholder interests may need to be considered, including:

- other members of the team or group in which the conflict has arisen;
- individuals working in other groups who regularly interact with one or both of the disputing parties;
- public relations staff, concerned with protecting the organization's external reputation;
- individuals who may be considering raising grievances of their own (eg, those who keep a close watch on the outcome of a high profile dispute in progress).

Quite apart from having an interest in the dispute, it may be necessary to obtain the cooperation of any or all of these, for example to ensure that they can support the agreed outcome of the DR process.

Diversity perspectives

One further but no less important perspective to consider is the potential influence of diversity. The way in which individuals perceive that their gender, sexual orientation, physical or mental disability, ethnicity, age or other difference influences the way in which others treat them can have a significant bearing on the onset of conflict, even if it's not a central issue. Clearly, it's important for anyone attempting to broker a resolution to a dispute to take note of such influences and assess their potential to be either real, perceived or deliberately promoted to ensure sensitive treatment by the organization.

The incidence of disputes in which diversity plays an explicit part seems to be on the increase.[4, 5] The strengthening or introduction of new legislation in many countries, as well as the high profile that a number of cases have attracted, may in part have encouraged this.

An originator's perceptions of the significance of potential discrimination are likely to be deeply held. The way in which we develop our self-concept is typically established very early in life. For example, gender identity, and beliefs about the relative opportunities available for men and women in work, can be established as early as the age of three (Skelton and Hall, 2001). Similarly, the prevalence of deep-rooted unconscious prejudice is perhaps more common than we might like to believe.[6]

ENGAGING THE INNER CIRCLE

Rules of conduct

To engage warring sides in dialogue needs a basis for coming together to be agreed with each; in other words, the 'rules' of play are mutually accepted. In workplace mediation, such rules should:

■ define the ground rules for both private conversations and those in which both parties are involved (what we refer to as 'convened sessions');

■ make clear the limitations of what may or may not be brought into mediation;

■ make clear what the roles of mediation and a mediator are, and the reasons why it should be in the interest of each party to play an active part in helping mediation to succeed;

■ give assurance of confidentiality, that what is discussed in mediation remains private (ie, observing the principle of holding a discussion 'without prejudice', which should encourage openness without fear of this candour being taken advantage of if the dispute were to escalate further);

■ make clear how it will be decided that mediation should be brought to an end.

For a convened group, the following topics might be considered as possible ground rules:

■ respecting the need for structure in the dialogue, and allowing the mediator(s) to facilitate this;

■ recognizing that some topics may need to be 'parked' to allow the course of discussion to flow without distraction, but not precluding the opportunity to return to such topics later;

■ allowing the other party time to speak, especially when individual airtime is built into the structure of the discussion;

■ not allowing unsubstantiated criticisms (eg, ones that don't refer to examples that others should be aware of);

■ avoiding direct personal attacks;

■ avoiding emotional outbursts;

■ respecting the confidentiality of what is discussed (other than revealing the outcome of mediation publicly – the 'Chatham House Rule');

■ not distracting from the scope of the dispute unless appropriate;

■ saying when any ground rule or the basis for concluding mediation is misunderstood or ambiguous;

■ recognizing that uncooperativeness will be letting both mediator and themselves down;

■ respecting each others' time, honouring pre-agreed meetings and other agreed commitments;

■ agreeing clear criteria for knowing when to end mediation.

Ground rules might be established more quickly if individuals are encouraged to consider what's important to them before coming to the dialogue and to be ready to propose guiding principles of their own. It's of course totally reasonable for mediators to propose ground rules themselves.

To be helpful, ground rules need to be generally accepted rather than reluctantly agreed to. It may not be possible for all individuals to accept all proposed points. Ultimately, a mediator can only try to encourage cooperation; by explaining the reasoning for suggesting each point, listening carefully to and responding to any objections.

Engagement should ideally happen quickly, but not at the expense of failing to uncover the real issues at stake in an argument, or leaving the door open for a protracted dialogue or 'scope creep'. Time spent during engagement may often save many frustrating hours of exhausting effort later.

Unlike most agreements, the terms of engagement for mediation shouldn't normally be written down. The only formal log that may be put on record is that mediation occurred.

Contracting

An early step in the engagement process of formal mediation is to 'contract' with each of the disputing parties. This may need to distinguish what is discussed in private and what may be brought to a convened dialogue. *Contracting* usually takes the form of a verbal agreement between mediators and disputing parties, giving assurances about confidentiality and the ground rules and boundaries for mediation. This may involve helping individuals to prepare themselves for re-visiting issues that may be sensitive to them or to confront others who are the subject of their complaint (although in some cases, face-to-face contact in a single convened meeting may not be desirable or possible – for example, where an employee alleges harassment by a colleague).

Through engagement, a mediator seeks to establish not only what an individual's ideal outcome is, but also what he or she might be prepared to compromise, and understand the circumstances in which he or she may accept a resolution. Of course it's important that a mediator makes clear the reason for exploring this possibility, to avoid individuals fearing that they may default to these rather than seeking to achieve their most desirable result.

In private conversation, mediators seek to understand what an individual expects to achieve from mediation, to assess his or her readiness to take part in the process, and provide the necessary reassurances. They should also aim to obtain acceptance on a variety of possibly uncomfortable matters, which in turn may form a part of their verbal contract:

■ recognizing that openness and honesty will serve their best interests, as well as helping a process to run smoothly;

- recognizing that anything may be brought for discussion in a convened session, except matters that a mediator may need to make public to avoid harm to another individual or to conform with the law;
- understanding that challenging and probing questioning may be necessary to help a mediator's understanding of perspectives, although any such probing is intended to be helpful;
- recognizing that discussion may become uncomfortable, requiring individuals to move outside their comfort zone;
- having an open mind to possible ways of resolving the dispute, including ones that may involve compromising a 'must have' mindset;
- having the humility to admit to mistaken views and misdirected emotions, such as making false accusations or shouting uncontrollably.

Despite this informative role, a mediator's primary task in private conversation remains to observe without evaluating, to listen without judging. His or her questioning approach should therefore be exploratory, aiming to gather information and confirm his or her understanding (see Appendix 1 for a range of question types that might be employed for this purpose).

Contracting is also relevant where two mediators who may not normally work together are engaged to broker a dispute. Clearly both will need to quickly establish a modus operandi for conducting the mediation, including considering how the process should be structured, which role each will play, what ground rules should be proposed, and whether there actually appears to be a need to convene both parties in a joint dialogue.

Selling the basis for engagement

As mentioned above, a mediator may often need to play the role of a salesperson to help individuals see the value of allowing mediation a chance to work. Selling points for mediation include:

- highlighting that mediation provides the best opportunity for achieving a satisfactory outcome, outside the boundaries of legal constraints and burdens of proof;
- pointing out that mediation can help prepare the way for a satisfactory working relationship between the parties after their differences have been aired, irrespective of whether one is at fault (something that is unlikely to be on offer should the dispute escalate to litigation);
- suggesting the value of being able to share what is learnt from mediation, allowing recommendations to be made based on specific dialogues whilst maintaining confidentiality;

- reflecting that the offer of mediation indicates the organization's desire to consider the dispute fairly, to help support those involved and without bias;
- making clear that the organization also has important objectives for encouraging mediation – to quash the dispute fairly and as quickly as possible, as well as possibly being legally obliged to ensure that a genuine attempt to resolve a conflict has been attempted;
- making clear that mediation aims to protect the dignity of all parties it involves.

Engagement is often hard: requiring a mediator to play the roles of both a salesperson and a coach; persuading an individual to recognize the value of falling into line with a particular structure, but doing so in a way that allows them to appreciate the reasoning for themselves.

Convening mediation

Convening is a formal stage in mediation when the disputing parties come to a joint dialogue. It's essential that this process is managed effectively. Much of what might be discussed during this session may already have been previewed with each side, for example ground rules they may wish to suggest, and objectives and outcomes they are ready to make known.

In convening, a mediator's role is partly one of facilitator and partly one of chairperson. He or she may both propose an agenda and invite participants to add to or substitute it; and he or she may set the scene by summarizing the nature of the dispute as he or she understands it and invite each party to summarize the main points of their arguments and state their objectives for the process. Depending on the type of mediation being practised, the process the group wishes to adopt may then either be discussed (with the mediator acting as a facilitator) or be prescribed.

Mediators may play the role of facilitator for much of the time. In this role, they serve to help the group form its own conclusions and move forward progressively. Facilitators pose questions, offer reflections and invite comment on suggestions. They provide the resources and as far as possible endeavour to engender a conducive atmosphere within which the dialogue can take place. Facilitators can play the role of time-keeper and otherwise maintain discipline, and they should help the group draw their own conclusions and commit to any actions, typically requiring them to summarize the main points of the discussion at regular intervals.

However, mediators offer more than facilitation. They are integral to finding a resolution and aren't detached from the discussion, and therefore should be at liberty to make observations, offer proposed solutions, and exercise authority as a keeper of discipline. For example, a mediator should be able to point out when the criteria for concluding mediation have been achieved and to initiate close-out.

CRITERIA FOR CLOSING OUT MEDIATION

Criteria for ending mediation are important to establish early, to help clarify what individuals are prepared to accept as a valuable outcome of the process. The most common situations in which mediation should normally end are when:

- an agreement has been reached that all are satisfied with;
- it's clear that there is an entrenched impasse, irreconcilable differences or complete breakdown of relationships;
- there is non-participation, including 'going through the motions';
- it's recognized that another intervention is more appropriate;
- one or both parties recognize that they have reached a stage where a compromise is their best outcome;
- serious disciplinary or criminal acts are admitted to or threatened, including matters to which a mediator could subsequently be called as a witness in court;
- the individuals involved recognize the benefits of concluding the discussion and abiding by the pledges that they agree as an outcome;
- time or budget caps are reached.

Views may differ between the parties on when such criteria have been satisfied. However, by setting them out at the outset, as well as referring to any others that may be suggested by a sponsor of the DR process, a mediator should be able to refer back to them when a difference of opinion occurs.

An often challenging task is to define what is meant by an agreement that all parties can be satisfied with. This of course doesn't mean that either party will necessarily be perfectly happy with an outcome, but can recognize that what is agreed is fair and represents the best outcome that they might realistically hope to achieve given what has been brought to the table, or that the risks, time and energy involved in pursuing the matter further are not in their best interests.

MEDIATION STRATEGY AND PLANNING

The decision on whether to focus on one-to-one, group or shuttle mediation (see below) may be informed by some of the following factors:

- considering who the stakeholders are, what perspectives they hold and what outcomes they want to achieve;

- how individuals feel about taking part in group mediation;
- the history of the dispute – how issues raised by the party have been investigated, the nature of arguments they have presented and the responses offered in reply;
- which intermediaries may be available;
- the wider context in which the dispute has developed (for example, being one of a number of similar complaints raised by others, such as individuals coming forward with claims of racism for any perceived discrimination following compensation settlements offered to others);
- how much time, how many sessions and what involvement of people may be required;
- when mediation can be arranged and what facilities may be needed (eg, break-out rooms).

Where physical hostility breaking out is a realistic possibility, some organizations such as Amnesty International have even constructed special rooms where both parties aren't able to reach each other without considerable difficulty. The prospect of a dispute erupting into physical combat should not be taken lightly; neither should other illegal actions such as taking managers as hostages (a tactic used during some recent industrial disputes in France).

It may make sense to follow a standard checklist when planning mediation, such as the one shown below.

Mediation planning checklist

- How much time, how many sessions and what involvement of people may be required.
- Which venue to use for discussions (eg, using a neutral, quiet and not overlooked room – a challenge in many open plan environments in which conference rooms may be separated from an open office by just a thin pane of glass).
- Whether it's appropriate to commence mediation with opening statements or to assume a clean slate.
- What ground rules may be appropriate to propose as a basis for guiding the dialogue.
- What resources may be useful to have to hand (eg, flipcharts and markers, paper and pens to help individuals with their reflection, and supplies of drinking water).
- Whether an open circle seating arrangement is preferable to separating each side across a table.

Tandem mediation

In formal mediation, the involvement of two mediators is common, indeed in some organizations, 'tandem mediation' is *always* used in formal mediation.

Both to maintain a high level of impartiality and to share some of the burden of what can be a very intense process, co-mediation can offer significant benefits. Tandem or co-mediation can help maintain an equitable relationship dynamic, and limit the risk that one party may feel that a mediator favours one side's testimony over the other. In turn, this may encourage greater trust and provide greater assurance of safety in the discussion. For both mediators too, having the support of another reduces the burden of keeping track of a potentially busy dialogue.

Given the potential benefits, tandem mediation may be considered in virtually any dispute, provided the disputing parties see both mediators as being impartial. Recourse to solo mediation is normally only driven by a budget constraint.

Each mediator will usually converse with each party before discussing their joint roles, allowing each mediator to share the perspectives they have formed in their one-to-one conversations. In this way, they may often be able to develop a clearer understanding of the disputing parties' perspectives than might otherwise be the case.

Co-mediators may be familiar with working with each other, especially if they share an employer or operate in a joint practice, or they may be recruited from different organizations. In either case, it's important that their respective roles are properly defined in their terms of engagement, and how they intend to conduct the convened session and the modus operandi they will establish between themselves and their client. For example, this might mean agreeing to alternate the roles of key mediator and secondary facilitator/observer and agreeing who will lead on different stages of the process (in the same way that two facilitators of a training course pre-agree who will manage each session).

When playing the role of 'key mediator', the focus may be on moving discussion forward, proposing and keeping parties on track within the structure agreed for the session, and closing down agreement on specific points. A secondary facilitator/observer may play a more supportive role, offering suggestions that might be missed by his or her fellow mediator, such as relating points discussed both within and across a number of sessions, and helping to remind the group of points that had been reserved for later discussion. They may also be better able to observe possible messages given in individuals' body language, which may suggest possible areas to probe. In effect, their role is to provide a second pair of 'eyes and ears' as well as a 'second brain' to the key mediator.

The agreed roles shouldn't align one mediator with a particular party – both mediators should act as 'go-betweens' for both subject and originator. Neither mediator should act or appear to have a more prominent role than the other across the session as a whole.

Shuttle mediation

There's often a good reason for conducting private discussions with each party, sometimes avoiding the need for group dialogue altogether if new perspectives and ways forward can be reached through private discussion. It may also be necessary to hold separate discussions if one party is reluctant to participate in a group dialogue with someone he or she perceives as an aggressor (for example, where an accusation of harassment has been made).

In shuttle arbitration or mediation, the intermediary takes proposals to and from the discussions of each party (located in different rooms). This can be an exhausting process, but one that can produce surprising results. In an amusing example we encountered in a marital dispute, the mother of a daughter who was filing for divorce grabbed the cloak of the barrister representing her daughter to prevent her rushing to make an offer as compensation for the estranged spouse's prized stamp collection, suggesting that a better approach might be to allow him to propose the collection's value. A swift response was given, with the barrister returning to the daughter with a significantly better offer!

Circumstances in which one-to-one coaching or arbitration may be more appropriate to convened mediation include:

- when group discussion continues to stall on specific points;
- where particular sensitivities for one or both parties are exposed;
- where a highly emotive dialogue becomes the norm in a joint session, with a focus on verbal attack rather than constructive dialogue;
- where either party requests it (with good reason).

Group mediation, by contrast, allows both parties to hear the other's perspective in their own words and (when appropriate) to offer a direct response. It can make efficient use of time and allow decisions to be made more quickly than when a mediator needs to shuffle between meeting rooms. Bringing both parties together can also help to break the ice in a strained relationship and ultimately, once agreement is reached, mean that there is a common, public understanding of what has been agreed.

Mediating team disputes

Increasingly, organizations are using mediation where a dispute has arisen in or between entire teams. Clearly, the negative impacts of entrenched disagreement within a team are no less severe than those that may arise from disputes between individuals. Tandem mediation is almost always preferable in this case, although the principles for mediating effectively are the same as those that apply in one-to-one disputes.

PREPARING FOR MEDIATION

As we've seen, there must also be some common ground in agreeing what the actual basis of the dispute is. A mediator may be able to help establish this understanding; however, this is best identified before mediation starts, if possible. By encouraging individuals to conduct their exchange about an explicit issue of dispute means that it should normally be possible for each party to be clear about the outcomes they desire and to agree criteria for assessing when mediation has achieved its purpose.

One crucial principle that must be fully clear at the outset is that the parties coming to mediation are doing so voluntarily, having a genuine readiness to play their part in helping the process to work. Mediation can never succeed if one party doesn't wish to participate, whether he or she has been coerced into giving the process a try, isn't prepared to meet his or her opposing party across a table, or is sceptical about mediation achieving a satisfactory end.

Earlier investigation may have identified what can be evidenced as being fact and what remains unproven or a matter of perception. Perceptions may be true, but they may as easily be confused by faulty memory or emotion. Feelings are arguably the most difficult influence to unravel in a dispute, not least because the reason an emotion has been triggered may not be clear even to the person it affects.

PERCEPTIONS, REALITY AND LIES

Let's remind ourselves of the various scenarios that might apply in a dispute:

- the views of both sides are equally valid and not for anyone to judge;
- one party is at fault but can't recognize this;
- both parties should take their fair share of the blame for the dispute reaching the point that it has;
- the issue in dispute has been largely invented and exaggerated as the disagreement has evolved; and
- one party knows that he or she has a case to answer, but remains resolute in pursuing his or her line of argument out of pride or a desire to avoid being rebuffed.

In each of these, the explicit premise is that each of the disputing parties believes that they are in the right, even when they know that they may have pushed a point too far to acknowledge a weakness in their argument. Apart from this latter case, a belief in being right can arise for several reasons:

- an individual believes that he or she has been genuinely wronged;
- an individual is hooked on a single narrow point of view, unable to see the wider context; and
- an individual's perception of reality isn't real (eg, he or she has constructed a false memory or become convinced of his or her own hype).

Sceptics might want to question the last of these, but constructed memory is more common than is often believed.[7] One other peculiar human tendency that can lead to deeply held but flawed views taking hold is our remarkable ability to dispense with logic in our thinking. The late psychologist Stuart Sutherland describes numerous examples of this in his fascinating book *Irrationality* (Sutherland, 2007), such as the tendency of some to put off going to the doctor when they suspect they may have a serious illness in case they are proved right!

Trying to unpick what someone is convinced is true can be a fruitless task, and one that is normally best avoided unless there is a clear counterargument backed up with strong evidence. However, whilst it may be hard, there's always the prospect of 'converting' an individual who has formed a perception that evidence suggests is offbeat. Much more difficult is to challenge the thinking of someone who is determined to stick to his or her story, come what may.

Indeed, when both parties have a clear conviction that their version of events and supporting evidence are unshakable, then it's highly unlikely that mediation will end favouring the view of one over the other. In such circumstances, it may be preferable to simply acknowledge this and for each side to recognize that a lack of evidence means that their case (as it were) cannot be upheld. This is the classic 'agreeing to disagree' scenario.

False memory

We are capable of reconstructing our memories, are often subject to selective bias in our thinking and even compose images of what we see or read by 'filling in the gaps'.[8] With the onset of bad feelings and hardening views, a balanced perception of a situation is unlikely, whilst for many of us, external attribution – the tendency to attribute the failings of others to the individual but explain our own failings by factors outside of our control – distracts perceptions even more.

What's more, the real underlying reasons for dissatisfaction may often not be consciously recognized, even by those who see themselves as 'victims'.

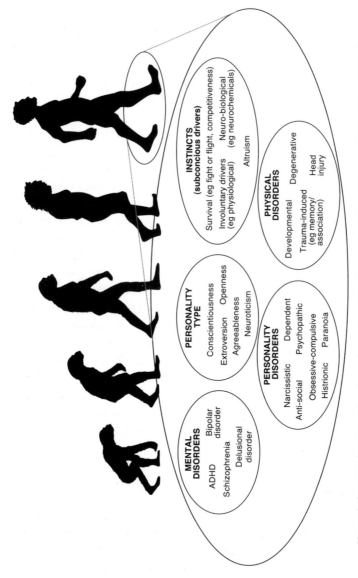

INSTINCTS (subconcious drivers)

Survival (eg fight or flight, competitiveness)

Involuntary drivers   Neuro-biological
(eg physiological)   (eg neurochemicals)

Altruism

PHYSICAL DISORDERS

Developmental   Degenerative

Trauma-induced   Head
(eg memory   injury
association)

PERSONALITY TYPE

Conscientiousness

Extroversion   Openness

Agreeableness

Neuroticism

PERSONALITY DISORDERS

Narcissistic   Dependent

Anti-social   Psychopathic

Obsessive-compulsive

Histrionic   Paranoia

MENTAL DISORDERS

ADHD   Bipolar
disorder

Schizophrenia

Delusional
disorder

Human beings may have learnt how to create complex civilizations and societies, but many of the in-built variables that drive our thinking and reactions have changed little since prehistoric days, perhaps even becoming more complex

Figure 7.1 Neanderthal to narcissist

Personality disorders, trauma and fantasies, included in Figure 7.1, are amongst possible complicating factors that may remain unseen, as may the impact of an individual's value system or self-perception (eg, low self-esteem, being out of his or her depth, newly promoted or put into a new post, lacking support, lacking assertiveness, a sense of poor career achievement). In some cases, this may manifest itself as aggression. A task for a mediator is to help individuals identify what is causing their concern, without making assumptions or falling into the role of a therapist.

Combined with false memories, compulsive drives for 'justice' and the fertile ground for triggering fresh anger that an open dialogue provides, resisting instant responses to automatic thoughts and controlling quickly inflamed emotions will be difficult for many.

EMOTIONAL AND PSYCHOLOGICAL CHANGE

Individuals' psychological and emotional states can change very rapidly during mediation, often without notice. Given the intense nature of conflict-based discussion and what may often be a fast moving exchange of information, it shouldn't be surprising that cognitive processing clicks into overdrive during mediation – and any mediator who has witnessed this should be able to testify that the effects can be exhausting! Reactions may be difficult to predict at a particular moment, but over a longer period of time (non-neuro-typicals aside) common patterns of change may be more readily observed.

Of course psychology has a big part to play in mediation, not just to help a mediator's understanding of what thinking may be driving an individual, but also to be able to respond appropriately to his or her chosen 'game'. For example, impasse often occurs because neither party is willing to offer a concession first, seeing this as a self-exposing manoeuvre or one motivated by weakness. The need to remain on top may similarly be driven by a belief that this will automatically position an opponent as the weaker party.

Game strategy

To help determine which game strategy is being used by the disputing parties, the 'Dual Concern' model is useful (attributed to Pruitt and Kim, 2004). This identifies four key strategies:

1. Competing/contending.
2. Yielding.
3. Avoiding.
4. Problem solving.

Which strategy a party is most likely to adopt is suggested to be a function of their concern for achieving their own outcome and the concern they have for the other party reaching a satisfactory result.

In a situation in which a conflict is escalating, a 'competing' strategy might be expected. By contrast, a 'yielding' or 'solution-focused' approach may seek to find a solution that is acceptable to both parties; however, these will have less chance of succeeding if one of the opposing parties continues to pursue a competing or avoiding strategy.

In their pioneering 'brief therapy' approach to psychotherapy, Steve de Shazer and Insoo Kim Berg also found that using a solution-focused approach was much quicker for establishing the cause of a patient's illness.[9] It focuses on what an individual wants rather than what he or she doesn't want (eg, wanting 'to work with her, sleep properly, feel useful, feel supported' is far more productive than just stating 'I don't want to work with her...').

To help tease this out where it's not glaringly apparent, we suggest that individuals might be directly asked in private how committed they are to wanting a satisfactory outcome not just for themselves, but also for the other party. Their responses may be quite revealing!

Recognizing the spiritual factor

Kenneth Cloke, director of the Center for Dispute Resolution in Santa Monica, California, goes further by suggesting that those who experience conflict may not only emerge with changed mindsets, but will have also undertaken a spiritual 'journey'. He asserts that:

> our experience has been that conflict is overridingly spiritual, because every conflict presents us with a life choice, opportunity for transformation, and an invitation to transcendence... Each resolution is a kind of minor miracle, in which parties moved from impressed solutions, antagonism to collaboration, revenge to forgiveness, isolation to community. (Cloke, 2001)

Perhaps one major difference between animals and human beings is that we can choose to forgive, collaborate and move on, or to remain in isolation and consumed by a distorted expectation. Cloke argues that the choices available to us are essentially spiritual choices, and that a preferred course for mediation should be an open collaborative or compassionate approach. Unless there is associated emotion, there can be no conflict – merely disagreement, which in itself is not necessarily a bad thing. But by being ready to let down our guard, to offer a concession or admission of a misunderstanding or false accusation, we can experience the spiritual power of transformation.

This is a wonderfully positive way of looking at conflict, offering the opportunity for experiencing a powerful transforming affect. His reference to a spiritual dimension in conflict also helps us conceptualize the deep drive that allows us to forgive with authenticity or re-form a relationship with a former adversary, although Cloke is the first to admit that defining what is meant by 'spiritual' is by no means straightforward. Perhaps it's enough to say, as he puts it, that the 'spiritual' goes beyond 'logic, emotion, or physical sensation'.

Changing perspectives

Another useful psychological monitor to keep in play considers how individuals may develop their perspectives in a dispute as it develops. Possible changes might be detected in terms of how an individual perceives him or herself, sees the other party, and evaluates the relationship between them. This is a principle of the 'LENS model' described by Wilmot and Hocker (2010) in their popular study textbook, *Interpersonal Conflict*. The model poses three questions:

1. What is each individual's assessment of his or her own image/position in the conflict?
2. What is each individual's impression of the other party?
3. How does each individual frame the relationship between him or herself and the other party?

In response to the first question, individuals will most typically perceive themselves to be beyond reproach, having the moral high ground in a dispute. Greater variation is likely to exist in response to the second, although a limited number of perspectives are still likely to be seen. In examining international conflict, Christopher Mitchell (1991) summarized these perspectives into a number of categories; we believe the following four are especially relevant in the workplace:

1. 'Black top' – they view their opponent as a true enemy, even evil.
2. 'Pro us' – in reality, they don't want to pick a fight with us, however they are being manipulated by others (eg, by a trade union representative).
3. 'Unified enemy' – universally branding members of a particular group in the same way (eg, 'everyone in that department is the same').
4. 'Intruder' – what they do or say is alien to reasonable behaviour amongst colleagues.

How an individual answers the third question (framing their relationship) may be more difficult for an observer to discern, although careful stakeholder analysis might point out possibilities. For example, in a dispute between a head of department and a subordinate, the junior party may put great stress on the line of authority present in the relationship, which he or she may see as having potential to prejudice his or her future career prospects, whereas a senior manager responsible for a large department may perceive that each individual's career opportunity is largely self-created.

In another scenario, a colleague may believe that he has a good friendship with another, who conversely sees him as being no more than a colleague. As such examples show, there can be a world of difference in how different parties may interpret their relationship, and in turn this can have a significant bearing on the way a conflict has deepened and in how it may best be resolved.

Changing goals

Individual's goals can change during the course of mediation, making it especially difficult to project manage a dialogue. In their 'TRIP' model, Wilmot and Hocker (2010) distinguish four types of goals:

1. Topical – relating to issues or positions.
2. Relational – focusing on how each party wishes to relate in future (eg, having put the dispute behind or having minimal contact).
3. Identity – the need to preserve dignity or save face.
4. Process – considering the approach taken for resolving the dispute.

The first three of these are particularly susceptible to change. What's more, goals that may have had only limited importance initially may become more critical as a dialogue proceeds; for example the need to save face. But where a conflict may only be resolved with a compromise, knowing which goals each individual is not prepared to surrender may help a mediator prioritize the possible negotiating trades that they might propose.

RECOGNIZING WHEN AN ALTERNATIVE INTERVENTION IS APPROPRIATE

A further difficulty may be recognizing when an intervention other than mediation is more appropriate, unless this is already happening. For example, it may become clear that referral to a coach, counsellor, medical/welfare officer or occupational health specialist is most appropriate. Mediators must resist the temptation to delay suggesting referrals, even though they might be persuaded that this is in the best interests of those involved in the dispute.

This may be especially hard for both externally recruited mediators and those who perform a role internally as an important part of their job specification. In both cases, referral might be considered as an act of failure on their part rather than strength for suggesting the most appropriate action. To help counter this risk, the role description for a mediator (whether internal or externally sourced) should encourage appropriate referral. The ethical code that mediators subscribe to and the supervision they receive may serve to support the same end.

SELF-CARE FOR IN-HOUSE MEDIATORS AND COACHES

Mediation and conflict coaching can be emotionally exhausting. Both the intensity of concentration required and the often fractious nature of the relationship dynamic between disputing parties call for strong perseverance and patience. Mediation sessions can run over many hours, often without any break, with sessions sometimes taking up to 12 hours or even more, whilst a very extensive number of points can be raised in a short time and at a fast pace. During this time, mediators may themselves be shouted at, put under pressure to broker a resolution and even be ignored.

Unsurprisingly, mediators need to be of strong mettle, not easily consumed by others' negative energy. They must take time for self-care. We strongly recommend that intermediaries take time to protect themselves from the negative stresses that may all too easily attach to their roles. This may involve recognizing when it's appropriate to suggest a break during a deeply intense conversation, detaching from undertaking all other work tasks when engaged in mediation, and allowing time for relaxation after completing sessions.

We recommend planning to do nothing else on any day set aside for mediation – and ideally, allowing time for relaxation both before and after the event. Of course, this may not always be possible, but simple de-stressing activities need not be time-consuming and are most important when aiming to switch off after an anger-filled day.

Supervisors might work with coaches and mediators to ensure that they take self-care seriously. For their part, those who engage internal intermediaries can take steps to stop over-burdening them at any one time, and consider the demands that may be being put upon individuals in other areas of their work when making matching proposals.

WHEN MEDIATION ENDS WITHOUT A RESOLUTION: LITIGATION

If an individual believes that he or she has a valid basis for taking legal action against an organization and if earlier attempts to resolve his or her concerns through ADR have been unsuccessful, litigation may be inevitable.

As we mentioned earlier, a desire to take an organization to task in court may have been a long-standing objective for some, driven by an expectation that those who they perceive as having acted wrongfully will be rebuked, giving the satisfaction of achieving a 'victory', as well as potentially benefiting from financial compensation as a part of the prize. As Socrates might put it, 'There is nothing quite so satisfying as being able to condemn someone else with full certitude and passion, thereby also to bask in the reflected glory of one's own superiority!'[10]

Litigation is rarely satisfactory either for a plaintiff or a defendant, costing significant time and money. If an organization believes that it has acted fairly in its treatment of a grievance and its attempts to resolve a dispute, its position will change when litigation is involved, from one in which an open mind is kept about which of the two disputing parties are 'in the right' to one in which defending the organization's own interests takes priority. This doesn't mean that organizations should abdicate their duty of care for their staff, or that they should stop valuing them as both employees and as individuals.

THE HOPE AND THE CHALLENGE OF MEDIATION

Very often litigation isn't needed. Just the mere act of involving a third party in an ongoing discussion can force fresh thinking and encourage a new commitment to work towards a resolution. Recent research at Northwestern University suggests that the arrival of a newcomer in a group means that each party has to work harder to understand the other's perspectives in order to convince the new person that their own has greater validity (Phillips *et al,* 2009).

When both parties are ready to participate in dialogue and can recognize common ground, mediation has a reasonable chance of succeeding. However, there may be further factors that quickly get in the way of productive discussion: a false understanding of what mediation seeks to achieve (despite what may already have been explained) and a speedy turnaround from any willingness to listen and understand the other party's perspective, retreating back into an entrenched position. Resistance, changing interpretations of what has been agreed and moving goalposts are all parts and parcel of mediation and realities that mediators must be equipped to address.

Mediation offers other challenges too, not all of them originated by the parties to the dispute. These include ensuring that time is used efficiently, moving a discussion forward to a new point once a conclusion has been reached on a particular issue, and limiting the risk of individuals backsliding to an earlier position from which progress had been made.

Meanwhile, mediators must be sufficiently self-aware to check that they don't stray from their objective and neutral position unless this is called for (for example, if an evaluative mediation approach is being followed). These are all important considerations for the practice of mediation, and ones that we'll discuss in more depth in the next chapter.

Summary

Stakeholder analysis aims to ensure that everyone who has an interest in the outcome of a dispute that has been escalated is involved, to appreciate their differing perspectives and how these may change as the dispute deepens, including psychological and emotional change. These stakeholders are not only those parties who are in dispute (the 'inner circle'), but their colleagues and a range of lobbyists and influencers from both within and outside the organization.

Engaging the 'inner circle' involves setting their expectations of what mediation aims to achieve and giving assurances about the confidentiality and conduct of the dialogue. Clear ground rules that the parties can agree to may be referred to during mediation if discussion moves off track. Similarly, time taken in planning mediation and agreeing clear criteria for when mediation should end should increase the prospect of a dialogue proceeding smoothly.

Mediators owe it to themselves to ensure that the frequently exhausting and exasperating course of a dialogue doesn't affect their own calmness, whilst owing those in dispute and their organization the good practice and professional courtesy to suggest when an alternative intervention to that which they can offer may become appropriate.

Notes

1. The term 'psychological contract' refers to the beliefs and informal modus operandi that drive an employee's relationship with his or her employer.
2. Notice the distinction here between the concepts of 'importance' and 'influence'. Influence refers to the power that a stakeholder may wield in bringing about a particular outcome in a dispute (eg, having the authority to take decisions on whether to expose the organization to potential litigation). 'Importance' relates to stakeholders' own interests in the outcome of the dispute or the way in which they or their work area may be directly impacted by it.

3. Many organizations allow individuals acting as supporters or representatives to be present in some grievance and DR conversations. This may be especially appropriate where one of the parties may be vulnerable, eg, someone who has been diagnosed with a mental health disorder.

4. Increases in discrimination-related disputes may be related to changed employment legislation in some countries. For example, the Australian Human Rights and Equal Opportunity Commission points to new age discrimination laws as a primary cause of increased age discrimination complaints in 2004–05. See: Yen, M (24 January 2006) 'Discrimination a mature woe', *Human Resources Leader.*

5. See, for example, the increase in employment-related cases in Australian disability and discrimination tribunals ('Growth in worker complaints', *Human Resources Leader,* 6 February 2007), and the increase in disability discrimination cases coming to UK employment tribunals in the year ending March 2009 (*Employment Tribunal and EAT Statistics,* September 2009, Tribunals Service).

6. Extensive data about our tendency for implicit social bias (ie, feelings, cognitions and making evaluations about others unconsciously) is collated as part of 'Project Implicit', an online, ongoing public laboratory, coordinated by researchers at Harvard University, the University of Washington, and the University of Virginia. A selection of research findings can be accessed via the project website, www.projectimplicit.net, which also offers visitors the opportunity to participate in a range of tests.

7. Common theories of false memory and constructed memory are described in Bjorklund, F D (2000) *False-Memory Creation in Children and Adults: Theory, research, and implications,* Lawrence Erlbaum.

8. Michael O'Shea offers a wonderful example of how we 'fill in the words' when we read, in O'Shea, M (2005) *The Brain – A very short introduction,* Oxford University Press, pp 4–10.

9. See, for example: De Shazer S, Dolan, Y and Korman, H (2007) *More than Miracles: The state of the art of solution-focused brief therapy,* Haworth Press, and Berg, I K (2005) *Brief Coaching for Lasting Solutions,* W W Norton & Co.

10. This quote is taken from the eponymous column 'Dear Socrates' appearing in *Philosophy Now,* Issue 74, July/August 2009, p 52.

8

The practice of dispute resolution: critical encounters

So much for the theory; now we turn to the reality of managing a dispute that is in full flow. This chapter considers a range of common, and not so common, scenarios that may come up during the course of mediation, and suggests a range of techniques that might be used when facing them. Whilst not occurring according to a particular pattern, any and very often many of these may need to be faced during the course of mediation.

INTRODUCING THE CONFLICT-BUSTING 'MICRO-TOOL'

In describing the range of interventions suggested in this chapter, Appendix 1 and elsewhere – question structures, tips, mnemonics and the like – we prefer to talk about the idea of a 'micro-tool'.[1]

Most micro-tools take the form of a sharp, quick, to-the-point dialogue, designed to help move individuals toward a particular point. For example, in response to someone who announces that they're 'really angry', a simple tool might consist of just a few brief phrases:

'I'm listening, please go on…'

'Tell me what has caused you to react like this.'

'What is it that you want to happen?'

Micro-tools help get to the heart of what people want rather than what they don't and may be used in virtually any scenario: formal or informal, brief or extended, and encouraging a manager or mediator to focus on listening and allow a complainant to sound out.

FIRST PRINCIPLES OF MEDIATION

Mediation 'best practice'

A number of principles and techniques might be found to be more effective than others; these might fairly be described as being 'best practice'. Amongst the most pertinent are:

- A mediator's primary role isn't to establish facts, but to help views to be aired and qualified: a mediator *isn't* an investigator!
- In negotiation, a mediator's role is usually primarily one of facilitator, to help each party reach agreement. However, they can help individuals consider options and identify common ground between them.
- A mediator's role is as much about giving uninterrupted airtime to each party as providing structure and guidance to move the discussion forward.
- Mediators don't talk people out; they *listen* them out.
- A mediator isn't called upon to be liked at the expense of being objective and fair.
- Ultimately, a mediator's focus is always to help two individuals who are in dispute find a suitable rather than a necessarily 'perfect' way forward.

How long should mediation last?

It's difficult to be prescriptive about what time may be needed for mediation, since the range of issues and complexity of relationships will vary from case to case (as will the readiness of individuals to play their part). In general, initial sessions usually last around two to three hours, unless a full day (or multi-day) session has been reserved. We'd recommend a break of at least 30 minutes after a three-hour discussion, and a briefer break might be offered to participants during the mid-course of a morning or afternoon session.

Of course, flexibility should be allowed for discussion to continue beyond a planned break if both parties feel that progress is being made. Mondays or the first working day of a week should generally be avoided; conversely, Fridays are often suitable for mediation, ending with a natural weekend break for individuals to follow their experience, in preference to immediately returning to their work environment.

Signature presence

Writing about executive coaching, Mary Beth O'Neill states that all coaches have a signature presence that is unique to how they coach, whatever model or approach they use, just as their signature is unique to them (O'Neill, 2000). We might just as easily say that all managers and mediators have such a signature presence too that they may be able to exploit to advantage. By being authentic, a mediator may be better believed and trusted.

Where two mediators are involved, varying styles can work to advantage, offering different appeals to the individuals in the room. This of course assumes that mediators who've come together for the first time have already established a *modus operandi* between themselves, and are committed to working to complement each others' styles rather than acting in competition. To help create this mutual understanding, we've seen mediators sharing information about their preferred style and personality type, such as their Myers Briggs Type Indicator® or FIRO-B type.[2]

Mediators can often bring a human touch to their work. One excellent example is shown by the late British politician Mo Mowlam, who was instrumental in brokering the Good Friday Peace Agreement, which marked a turning point for ending the bitter political divisions in Northern Ireland. Her down-to-earth, frank and refreshingly human approach included her famously removing her wig during discussions, and later commenting to the then US President Bill Clinton that she was 'the new tea lady around here!' (BBC, 2000).

The risk of transference

A well-known in principles in policing is that police officers investigating the scene of a crime aren't immune from leaving their own mark, potentially spoiling evidence by transferring fingerprints, DNA, etc. In police parlance, 'every contact leaves a trace' – the foundation of Locard's Exchange Principle (Locard, 1951). Mediators can similarly cross-contaminate their communication with unintended meaning: every sentence has the potential to trigger different interpretations.

Such transference is a real risk in any relationship in which emotional responses and value systems may be triggered. The term, first coined by Sigmund Freud, refers to the redirecting of emotion from one person to another – for example, someone who felt victimized by a parent as a child might be inclined to react with strong feelings of anger or attack many years later, but perhaps in a different context and with a different person. *Transference* occurs all the time –

take the example of someone who has just lost 'their' car parking space to an opportunistic pusher-in being more inclined to act more aggressively when holding their place in the queue to park next time! Closer to the workforce, unconscious stereotyping is a common form of transference. For example, onsider the gender-specific message that the following statements can imply: 'Rose has coped extremely well with any challenges and has managed to meet all deadlines' as opposed to 'Rose has overcome all challenges and met deadlines.'

Since transference occurs unconsciously, it's very difficult for anyone to detect – and mediators can be as susceptible to transference as anyone else. However, psychoanalysts say that it's possible to become aware of your tendency toward counter-transference and so be mindful and able to regulate emotional communication that might otherwise go unnoticed.[3]

Environment, dress and avoidable barriers

Venue

Due care should be taken when choosing a suitable venue for mediation.

Neutral venues such as training rooms and hotel conference facilities might be preferred, whilst places that may have strong associations for an individual should be avoided. The simple act of holding a meeting away from individuals' normal working areas can help produce a more conducive environment for mediation.

We prefer venues that are inviting but don't encourage relaxation. Simple details such as the presence of a small vase of flowers on a table or the presence of a coffee pot may help settle nerves and help discussion begin on a healthy footing.

Discussions need to be held in private, ideally in a sound-proofed room with closed walls. Thin-panel divides and the kind of all-glass surrounds popular in the 'goldfish bowl' design of meeting rooms found in many open-plan offices are best avoided when possible. A constant awareness of being on public view can scarcely help individuals feel comfortable about exposing what may be very sensitive issues for them.

The water-cooler walk

The principle of walking away from the scene of an argument applies in informal conversations too, for example between a manager and a member of his or her team. The mere act of walking to the water cooler or coffee machine can help defuse some of the immediate intensity of emotion that might be felt by an individual. Moving to an area where he or she may be able to feel more relaxed and able to talk confidentially can serve a similarly useful purpose.

Colour

Whilst easily overlooked, the colour of clothing and room decor can play an important part in signalling meaning. For example, brown is often considered to be a 'grounding' or supportive colour, whilst blue can help foster trust and aid clear thinking. Turquoise is thought to have a soothing effect that can aid communication. Red, by contrast, can stimulate energetic frenzy, so is probably best avoided in clothing worn for mediation (and, where possible, as a background decor in the mediation venue).[4]

Similarly, checked or striped shirts, suits or blouses can be subconsciously interpreted as a subtle barrier or defence, as though a mediator is pulling down the shutters or presenting an image of impenetrable prison window bars!

COMMON ENCOUNTERS

Identifying underpinning issues

Remaining alert to the possibility of what an individual may not be directly saying is an essential competency for mediators and managers. The ability to 'listen between the words' requires strong emotional intelligence and can draw on learning from a wide range of sources, including insights from neuroscience, NLP interpretations of behaviour, and analyzing body language and speech patterns.

Questions that may help to tease out what's really on an individual's mind don't have to be directly challenging, eg, 'What are you thinking when...?' However, remember that probing questions will often need reasonable processing time for a responder to think through the answer. Further examples of these types of 'Socratic questions' and others for exploring lines of thinking are included in Appendix 1.

Encouraging reflection on the perspectives of others may also help produce fresh insights. For example, the *Imagine Role-play* involves posing a simple question: 'Imagine you're watching this. What would you be thinking at this point?' The *Thought Pattern Critique* template described in Appendix 2 might also help individuals reframe their current perspectives.

Acknowledging and managing outbursts

As mediation approaches, individuals are increasingly likely to feel that their moment to be heard is coming. Anxiety and anticipation may be mixed with excitement and an appetite for a fight. At the same time, the finite timetable for reaching a closure will impose a new form of pressure, something that will continue throughout mediation.

Emotional outbursts and angry clashes may often need time for expression. Allowing time for individuals to say what they really believe or feel they need to say may pave the way for less emotionally charged and single-perspective thinking, which in turn may provide clues for mediators and others to better appreciate an individual's reasoning. This also allows a mediator to invite openness where he or she suspects that feelings are being suppressed, by using a check-in question such as: 'What are you thinking/feeling?' or, 'Describe what you're thinking/feeling.' (The *No-send Letter*, *Channelling Anger* and *Volcano* templates included in Appendix 2 might be used when helping individuals deal with their emotions.)

Exchanges that help clear the air or bring important issues into the discussion ('naming the elephant in the room') are nearly always productive, and so a possible ground rule might be suggested that allows such exchanges to occur before a mediator intervenes, unless one or both say otherwise at the time. Generally, mediators should only curtail an exchange if it's not beneficial for both parties. An angry exchange of views may often be necessary to clear the air and allow individuals to state exactly how they feel. Of course either party may call time on a point that has already been made, or declare 'enough already', to coin a phrase.

Exchanges that erupt into unproductive and disrespectful brawls need to be interrupted and brought back to a calm and solemn reflection of the agreed terms. However, not only must a satisfactory basis for progressing the dialogue be sustained, but also an unambiguous understanding of the conditions to test when mediation should end must not be pushed aside.

Once the dust has settled after an exchange, it may be relevant to draw attention and offer observation, inviting the parties to describe what they've noticed. For example (to the first party): 'When you were talking – I wondered if you noticed that [the other party] flinched?' Reflection might be invited from both individuals, possibly prompting the receiver saying that he or she wasn't unsettled by the exchange.

For the longer term, an opportunity to express feelings may serve a useful purpose too. Lessons from the South African Truth and Reconciliation Commission, set up following the ending of apartheid, might be relevant for us here. This gave an open hearing to individuals and organizations that alleged past wrongdoing, while granting an amnesty for alleged persecutors who were forthcoming in giving evidence. Whilst controversial, and leaving many unsatisfied, many commentators agree that progress of democracy in South Africa since the Commission set about its work is nothing short of exceptional (Taylor, 2007).

Reconciliation can obviously help in healing relationships, and is in stark contrast to an effort aimed at 'smoothing over the cracks' that in reality ignores underlying emotions.

Responding to new information during mediation

Revelations, fresh insights and changed views may occasionally warrant another look at the ground rules agreed at the start of the dialogue, for example by asking: 'Do we need to revisit the rules we agreed?'

One particular type of new knowledge that requires special handling is what we call a 'bombshell'. Bombshells can occasionally be dropped during the course of mediation, driven by highly charged emotion or arising from a sudden moment of self-insight. We've come across situations where individuals have disclosed that they have a drug addiction, are supplementing their income by working as a prostitute or were having an affair with their line manager, to name just a few examples.

Of course, considerable sensitivity is needed when such issues are brought to light, allowing time and space for the impact of the revelation to settle for all present. A possible approach is to first affirm the individual's honesty and courage ('I really respect your honesty'), then check whether they are comfortable with continuing the line of discussion, and finally use a scaling approach to gauge their level of sensitivity to the subject (eg, 'How do you feel about talking about this?')

Conversely, it may be appropriate to ask both parties how the disclosure assists their understanding of the wider situation. For example: 'How do you now feel as a result of sharing this?', 'How does this new piece of information help your understanding of [the other person's] perspective?' or, 'How does this additional information affect your current thinking?' A mediator can then affirm what has been said, whilst remaining neutral, for example offering the comment: 'Shall we acknowledge these factors as contributing to reaching an acceptable outcome?' If a 'big issue' has been revealed (eg, a revelation of assault), it's important that a mediator checks that the individual is comfortable to talk about the matter and for it to be acknowledged as having potential significance for the discussion.

One critical exception to allowing the dialogue to take its course following a 'bombshell' revelation is where a criminal action has been admitted. To continue mediation following such a disclosure could expose any of those present in the discussion – including the mediator – to be called upon to testify in a court should the subject of a revelation later be prosecuted. To be required to disclose the contents of a dialogue would clearly be contrary to the ethical code guiding mediation. In most countries, information relating to a criminal offence or which indicates a danger of harm to any person may need to be revealed.

Quite apart from this, there may be a potential threat of harm to an individual implied by the admission (including to the 'confessor' themselves). Given such circumstances, it would clearly be irresponsible to allow the dialogue to continue: discussion must be closed out quickly and sensitively, and both the individual making the admission and the matter itself then referred on to the appropriate authority.

Disclosures need not be sensational to have a significant impact on others. Similarly, a readiness to talk candidly in a controlled and safe environment may enable each party to develop a changed understanding of the other person's perspective. In one example of this kind known to us, simply being able to state his discomfort at being managed by 'someone no older than his daughter' was sufficient to allow a way forward to be worked out between a long-serving employee and his new young boss. Being able to say what he wanted to say, and his manager's positive acceptance of his honesty, led to improved appreciation and mutual respect.

Handling 'heavy landings'

Bombshells can result in an uncomfortable, strained dynamic between individuals, as can the thinking that results when any new information comes to light or following a heated exchange.

A mediator's best response to such 'heavy landings' may simply be to allow a brief period of quiet for the dust to settle or to suggest a break or longer cooling-off period. However, the discussion that preceded the 'landing' may need to be further explored, with any new questions, issues or other loose ends that it generated addressed. Possible techniques and questions for addressing these include: 'Shall we summarize where we are?' and inviting each party to give a view: 'How does this affect... for the future?' and confirming that both parties' commitment to work toward an effective outcome remains an irrefutable principle. Further examples are included in the micro-tools in Appendix 1.

Deviations

Unexpected diversions during the course of mediation may occur for a wide variety of reasons. Amongst these are:

- bombshells and new information being revealed (as we've already discussed);
- advice being offered by a third party during a break in discussion, possibly causing an individual to want to backtrack and reopen points already covered in discussion;
- individuals becoming overly focused on what may appear to be a point of limited significance, occasionally as a way of avoiding uncomfortable situations or having to name the 'elephant in the room';
- moved goalposts;
- deliberate stalling, for which there's a host of tactics: refusing to participate actively in the discussion, constantly rebutting invitations to comment with

silence, continually repeating points that have already been made, raising questions that appear to be totally out of context, obviously making it clear that any 'agreement' being made is done so reluctantly, being very articulate in pointing out what is wrong with others or their proposals but without making positive counter-proposals, and many more!

Case study: Anonymous criticism

A failure to name an 'elephant in the room' that finally is revealed to an alleged subject of a grievance can cause offence that might be avoided through tactful management earlier, as in the case of a friendly but loud member of staff with a raucous laugh who was working in an open plan office.

The individual's phone conversations sounded like broadcasts, causing friction. Attempted hints about the distraction were offered by colleagues, but without success. The matter soon became an 'in-joke', but the member of staff didn't understand why he was being cold-shouldered.

The patience of others soon wore thin. One morning, one left an anonymous note on their colleague's desk, making it clear that his loudness wasn't welcome and that he should shut up. Angry and hurt, the member of staff went to his line manager to complain. The manager listened and agreed that it was wrong for anyone to leave such a note, but observed that they may have felt there was no other way to bring it to the individual's attention and didn't have the courage to speak about the matter.

The manager committed to try and find out who had written the note. He also apologized and said he should have intervened sooner but had not known how to go about it. The subject listened and reflected; he was now sufficiently content to avoid a witch-hunt, but said that what he did want was to get on with the team. He went on to announce to the team in a humorous way that he knew he was loud, as his wife often reminded him! He promised to try to speak more quietly in future. This endeared him to others in the team, who appreciated his attempts to lower the volume and respected his candour. Harmony was restored without the note-writer ever needing to be identified.

Sadly, incidents of this kind are all too common. A manager's awareness of a mounting team concern and sensitive but early intervention might often prevent unpleasant consequences when someone breaks the silence, as inevitably someone will. But so too can managers and responsible team members role-modelling the types of behaviour that doesn't keep one of their fellow members in the dark about how they are perceived.

A mediator's dilemma when dealing with a deviation is that by following the 'anything goes' rule, and in recognizing that what might appear to be trivial or irrelevant may in fact not be, requires that virtually any new matter that is raised needs to be given air-time. This may often be simply a matter of clarifying why an individual feels the matter is important and, if appropriate, asking the other party whether he or she is content for the matter to be discussed. Alternatively, reference may be made to an earlier agreed ground rule to 'park' issues that are peripheral to the main discussion.

Questions posed by mediators should aim to help individuals search out their own inner resources in considering their response. Questions should benefit the person they are directed to rather than the questioner. *Direct route* questions can help individuals achieve this more easily, whereas those that take them into talking about problems or a dead-end are commonly called *possible deviations*.[5] Examples are given in Appendix 1.

Discretion is needed when a discussion may be going off course. Mediators must resist the urge to intervene in what we like to call a 'loggerheads' moment, giving an abrupt opinion on what they see as being a futile argument. A calmly offered intervention is likely to win greater support, for example: 'If a group of your colleagues were to listen in to your discussion now, what might they say?'

Depending on a mediator's personal style, and when feeling sure that the participants respond well to this, a more direct approach can occasionally be appropriate – especially in more informal situations and where doses of humour may be appropriate. The down-to-earth humanity of Mo Mowlem allowed her to often use this style without losing the respect of those she was mediating.

In another example, Clive likes to recount an incident he witnessed whilst travelling on a bus one New Year's Eve on the Las Vegas Strip. Filled to capacity with a large number of passengers already full of holiday *joie de vivre*, an angry argument had broken out between two groups of school pupils in the centre aisle. The argument quickly became threatening, resulting in a tense silence breaking out amongst others on the bus.

At this point, the bus pulled to a stop and the driver came down the bus to firmly but cheerfully intervene: 'If you guys don't shut up in a minute, I'll tan your backsides with my slipper!' A charismatic, larger-than-life but immediately likeable character, her tongue-in-cheek threat helped the boys' quarrel to quickly dissipate, persuading one to even quip 'Sorry ma'am!' What had been a tense and unpleasant atmosphere for the passengers immediately collapsed into a mood of good humour, continuing for the rest of the journey!

Knowing when to interject with humour and when not to is a useful capability for a mediator to develop, but one that requires strong emotional intelligence and sensitivity. To be effective with such a tactic requires an air of authority, not just well chosen words. And of course, inappropriate intervention can easily worsen a situation and weaken respect for the mediator's role.

Removing sticky jams

If discussion meets an apparent deadlock, an attempt to unblock the jam should almost always be made. A useful first step is to identify whether the jam can be broken down into smaller parts, of which some might be more easily resolved than others. Once the smaller aspects of an issue have been addressed, it may be possible for the parties to recognize that resolving their wider quarrel may not be insurmountable, or at least that there may be greater scope for reaching a compromise.

Participants might need to be reminded that their 'ideal solution' may not be possible. Examining the underlying reasons for their positions and encouraging them to consider what they feel able to negotiate may help them accept that a compromise may be better than an impasse. The powerful 'consequences' question ('What are the consequences of continuing with this particular approach?') may play a valuable role in encouraging this thinking.

Questions that should encourage individuals to reflect on the causes of any logjam may help them to move towards a more open mind, for example: 'How do you wish to resolve this issue?' or, 'How do you see this as being feasible?'

The *meta* technique might also be brought into play to help individuals consider the 'bigger picture' of the jam they are in, whilst helping neutralize emotions. Taking a meta perspective (or to 'look from the outside in') allows the nature of the impasse and the contextual factors that may have contributed to it to be considered, and may provide clues for breaking the deadlock. This approach can be especially helpful when considering how a problem might be broken down into smaller parts.

Impasse

One of the most difficult challenges a mediator faces is when a discussion appears to break down completely or when impasse sets in. This can happen when both parties see no obvious way for resolving a point of disagreement, perhaps because they view the issues at stake as being non-negotiable, or feel that any compromise that might bridge the gap would be too much for either to accept.

Breakdowns can also occur when emotional outbursts become the norm or when both parties renege on their starting promise to work toward a solution. In some cases, individuals may claim that they've reached a point where they feel that they cannot work with the mediator. Sometimes, realizing that there needs to be a parting of the ways is the positive outcome, even though accepting this can be difficult for some.

However, it's normally appropriate to at least attempt to break an impasse and re-establish a constructive dialogue, although this may involve battling against limited time and strained levels of patience for the individuals concerned. Almost always, a brief break is appropriate before reconvening to sum up the situation and, where it's possible, a longer cooling-off period might be considered. After reconvening, the task of summing up might also serve to qualify whether the end of the road has really been reached. Provision might also be made to reopen a closed discussion if there's significant new thinking in the days following the onset of an impasse, although normally a definite conclusion will need to be reached promptly.

Tough conversations

'Tough conversations' are those that involve addressing points that may be unpalatable for individuals to accept. Examples include labelling behaviours, confronting undesirable options and moving discussion toward a point where each party has an opportunity to name 'the elephant in the room', (eg, by asking: 'Is there anything else you might want to consider here?' weighed by a deliberate pregnant pause; other possibilities can be found in Appendix 1).

Once a difficult conversation is under way, a mediator's main task is to listen and observe. Many of the challenges that we discuss elsewhere in this chapter may arise during such conversations – amongst these are heavy landings, emotional outbursts, and defensive responses from the other listening party.

Following a particularly difficult conversation, emotions should be given a little time to settle. An approach that might be used to help re-establish a more comfortable dynamic is to acknowledge the passion and commitment of the individuals in attempting to reach an outcome. Possible defusers and escalators are shown in Table 8.1.

Humour can also be important in defusing tension, but needs to be used with care to avoid making the mediator seem like someone who doesn't treat each party's interests seriously.

Brief, every-day conversation isn't always out of place in mediation either, especially when opening a conversation. If used, it's best to ensure that neutral conversation is maintained, for example asking, 'How was your journey here?' rather than 'How are you feeling right now?' However, we believe that incidental comments should generally be kept very brief, to avoid the risk of small-talk undermining the serious focus of the discussion.

Table 8.1 Defusers and escalators

Possible defusers	Escalators
Allowing time for emotions to dissipate	Focusing unnecessarily on the negative
Giving equal airtime	Allowing one person more airtime than another
Preventing interruptions	Over analysis of 'the problem'
Keep a 'future positive' perspective	Poorly chosen language
Remaining mindful of the need to maintain a 'sterile corridor'	Transference

Managing time

The pressure in DR to manage time effectively is especially acute, given the perception of some that time and energy devoted to getting two parties to talk is 'wasteful', and owing to the tendency of some parties to deliberately attempt to distract from the core issues. The first of these may often be a false perception, but one which we need to acknowledge.

The normal rules of time management apply. Be aware of the time available and the time that has passed; have a rough plan of how best to allocate the time to the various topics thought to be necessary to achieve a session's end (even if some flexibility may be needed as discussion proceeds); and carry out regular checks to ensure that tangible progress is being made.

The task of timekeeping may often be performed without comment by a mediator, but explicit reference to the time that has passed and is remaining is normally appropriate when summing up particular stages of a discussion or when questioning whether a possible deviation is making the best use of the available time.

Exhaustion and breaks

Exhaustion can be a factor, especially if an intense mediation dialogue extends over many hours at a time, as is often the case. Sleep deprivation can interrupt the normal functioning of the prefrontal cortex in suppressing aggression, making us more inclined to become hostile.[6] Mediation is very often especially tiring for those who feel they have the most to gain or to lose – in other words, the disagreeing individuals.

Tiredness can produce a range of unproductive behaviours, irrational thinking and a lack of clarity. In particular, it can prevent individuals from seeing when they've actually achieved an acceptable outcome that can lead to a closure. Where it seems that tiredness has set in but there's a desire to continue with the dialogue until a conclusion can be reached, a mediator may wish to suggest a break or check whether all parties feel they can continue to do justice to the conversation.

Cooling-off periods

Where possible, a cooling-off period is desirable before starting mediation. Giving individuals the opportunity to reflect on their situation, regain composure and refresh their energy levels will almost always pay dividends.

Where an important challenge or ultimatum is proposed (eg, whether or not an individual is ready to work within the proposed terms), we'd suggest that a period of at least one week should be allowed for reflection before those being challenged are asked to make their final statement on the matter. Allowing reflection time, and with it time for the subconscious to process information, can often produce fresh insights and inspiration. We've quite often encountered situations where two parties felt that they had reached an impasse, even agreeing to conclude discussion, but after further reflection, one or both parties had indeed had fresh inspiration and in more than a couple of cases had independently approached the other party, with both then agreeing to accept the new proposal.

Handling backsliding

One problem with cooling-off periods and breaks is that they can risk individuals rethinking points that had produced progress in the discussion, especially if they are being advised by a third party. Where this is the case, they may seek to revisit points on the basis that they've simply changed their mind or been told to do so. The validity of moves to reopen old ground needs to be seriously questioned, especially to challenge whether the reasons for wanting to revisit old ground are significant when weighed against the progress that has been achieved.

Ground rules may need to check against unproductive backtracking, and using a scaling approach can be helpful to clarify desires. Backsliding usually implies that individuals will have reduced their rating of progress. It's then for a mediator to uncover what has caused the backward step and to challenge whether the backtracking threatens losing what had been achieved, asking, for example, 'When you had made progress, what had made the difference?' and, 'What's brought you to where you are now?' (See some other suggestions in the 'micro-tools' in Appendix 1.)

Backtracking may be very frustrating for the other party, who may have felt encouraged by the progress that had been achieved. Frustration can in turn easily lead to a retrenchment of negative perceptions of the other party and so frustrate efforts to put the dialogue back onto a stable footing.

Pride and apology

Another human trait may often stand in the way of breaking tit-for-tat disputes: the great difficulty many of us have in saying 'sorry'. In most societies and organizations, humility is far less in evidence than politicking or mud throwing. Why is it so hard for many of us to resist the temptation to fight for what we believe is right? Except where a health or mental disorder may be at work, perhaps for some this involves a sense of shame for having 'failed' or made a mistake.

The nature of work itself encourages competition between individuals, for security, status and reward, or to achieve the highest sales revenues in a quarter. Some even venture that arrogance is a virtue or – as Gordon Gekko memorably proclaimed in Oliver Stone's 1987 movie *Wall Street* – 'greed is good'! Competition is of course not in itself unhealthy – far from it; what matters is the way competitive energy is harnessed and channelled, and preventing this spilling over into raw conflict.

Mediators may find that they occasionally need to help individuals back off with dignity, and to address the fears they may have; for example for a manager, a sense of losing control; for a subordinate, a fear that they've permanently damaged their reputation. A sudden awareness of a mistaken perspective can also be difficult for an individual to handle: in Japan and elsewhere in Asia, 'saving face' means a loss of credibility or respect from others. Admitting a mistake involves a measure of humility, but usually also involves finding a strategy for preserving self-dignity and reputation.

The fight instinct

In the thick of mediation, mediators may have to combat a primeval human instinct – a drive to fight. Dopamine, the hormone associated with pleasure, is released when we engage in physical aggression, although our drive to seek a fight is suppressed by the frontal cortex, which is better developed in homo sapiens than our hominid ancestors. (Dopamine is just one of the neurotransmitters that may be at work during the development of conflict. Testosterone (associated with aggression), oxytocin (linked with promoting trust) and serotonin (a mood regulator) are amongst the others.) This is the same satisfaction that many motorists gain when overtaking another driver at the cross-roads, or by passengers making it to the front of the queue when an aircraft boarding announcement is made.

Worryingly, as the philosopher John Gray suggests, our 'civilized' ability to restrain violence is very fragile and can quickly be lost (Gray, 2009). Whether we recognize it or not, it's in our nature to be combative, to relish scoring against an individual we may not like, or taking satisfaction from seeing someone fall after a punch we've thrown. Many of us actually enjoy going into bat with an opponent.

In a recent BBC documentary, former British MP Michael Portillo discovered the thrill of taking part in a simulated boxing match, after believing that he didn't have an aggressive bone in his body. So too, the novelist Amanda Craig recalls that she enjoyed the adrenalin rush associated with confronting an intruder in her home, whilst the Tinku festival in Bolivia encourages individuals to bottle up aggression and then take this out in an annual ritual fight (BBC, 2009).

A drive to 'put one over' on someone else can become all-consuming, taking over an individual's mind and soul. Those who hold power in organizations can be particularly susceptible to self-delusion and losing a sense of reality, a medical condition that has recently been dubbed 'hubris syndrome' (Boseley, 2009). We've seen many cases where a deeply troubled person has collated hundreds of pages of notes reflecting on their situation, and sadly all too many examples of distressed individuals who succumb to long periods of sickness owing to poor mental health.

Overt and covert goals

The goals of individuals coming to mediation may not always be clear, or at least they may be misaligned. Moreover, many may simply not know what they want to achieve. An individual who feels grievously wronged may quite easily be able to say what they would like to see happen, driven by anger or a quest for vengeance or compensation, without any sense of whether this may be a realistic possibility. A mediator may therefore have to work hard to establish what their underlying goals are. Offline coaching can be very useful in this regard.

More difficult to illicit are the covert goals that one or both parties aren't willing to declare. A common example is where an individual is intent on pursuing litigation and sees mediation as a 'necessary evil', resolving that they won't deviate from their entrenched position come what may. Individuals may view mediation as a game in which they may be able to manipulate others or otherwise be disruptive. Impassioned goals may remain covert, but will still be their strongest motive for pursuing a dispute.

A mediator's skill in probing behind expressed desired outcomes might expose an altogether different motivation. Even if this isn't said openly, putting the spotlight on an area of possible discomfort may allow a mediator to remark on the futility of some 'perfect endings', without directly labelling them as the ones implied by what's being said, leaving the individual to form his or her own opinion.

Recognizing and managing issues that may not be black or white

Disputes often come about because there's a difference of perspective on a particular topic, due to one or both parties forming a view based on weak information, or because they are being driven by a core belief. Common examples include:

- managers believing that they are helping an individual by offering them the benefit of their wisdom, whilst the person to whom they've offered 'help' perceives the offer as an interference or suggesting that he or she is not capable of doing the job;
- a highly work-driven manager giving more and more stretching work to others, believing that he or she is supporting their development, but who is actually seen as being 'bullying' by those who don't adopt the same workaholic attitude;
- a loud, abrupt manner is the normal style of a supervisor, encouraged by the organization's culture as a mark of 'strong leadership', though viewed as bullying by some on the factory floor;
- an individual perceives that their private space is being invaded, whilst an alleged harasser perceives that they have just taken one or two simple steps to break the ice with a new colleague.

Amongst these examples, deciding what level of contact may be reasonable without this having been communicated by the individual feeling harassed is not clear-cut. Similarly, necessary and appropriate moving of the goalposts by management might be seen as manipulation by staff. Not all perceptions of bullying may appear as a malicious pattern of behaviour designed to break another individual's spirit.

Similarly, one person may not recognize another person's belief that they have made clear that they do not welcome their overtures of friendship. A lack of sensitivity or ability to read the signs may be at fault, for example because an individual has an undiagnosed autistic spectrum condition. Even when both sides know all the facts, there may still not be a 'right' answer. Each person's viewpoint may be equally valid, or not for another person to judge.

Disagreement may arise over what constitutes unacceptable behaviour and what doesn't (eg, what constitutes 'bullying' as opposed to 'strong manage-ment', or whether or not a particular decision to appoint a man to a new post in favour of an equally qualified woman was 'sexist'). Organizations can help themselves by ensuring that the definitions adopted for such behaviours are unambiguous. Even so, what one person perceives as being bullying or harassment (for example) may differ from another's perception.

Negotiation and compromise

Negotiation involves making trade-offs: commitments that can be met or 'traded', some of which are non-negotiable and some that may be subject to compromise. In DR, negotiation shouldn't be about squeezing the other party or harming them emotionally or otherwise, even though wanting to put the other down may be a common motivation for disputing individuals. Whilst negotiation skills may be important in mediating, it's important to recognize that a mediator isn't a negotiator – this role is reserved for the disagreeing parties.

The concept of 'negotiation' can have an unfortunate meaning for some people, perhaps based on their experience of achieving a good price in buying a new car or bartering at a market stall – that it aims to obtain the best price or prize, pushing the other party as much as possible. Carried over into DR, this connotation can easily perpetuate a perceived need for individuals to win over an opponent to feel satisfied.

However, the type of negotiation which will achieve the best prospect of a lasting peace should more appropriately start with two presuppositions for each party to consider: what they really see as being an acceptable outcome and what the other side may need to trade in order to achieve this. For negotiation to succeed, it's essential that both parties can recognize that agreeing reasonable trade-offs can realistically bridge a gulf in demands. Both parties must also see that there's a valuable part for negotiation to play.

Possible questions to tease out negotiable trades include: 'What are you prepared to compromise?', 'What sacrifices are you willing to make to achieve an acceptable end?' Possible questions to explore individuals' trading points include: 'What are you prepared to give up?', 'What is it worth to you to achieve this?' Appendix 1 suggests some other possibilities.

A mediator should be at pains to avoid interrupting individuals who are expressing a point of view, even if it's taking them time to articulate how they feel. Apart from frustrating an opportunity for individuals to say their piece and possibly to offer information relevant for the discussion, to interrupt in this way might be seen as being rude and patronizing. As we've already mentioned, one exception where intervention is permissible is where an individual is unreason-ably verbally attacking another or threatening violence.

Questions for managers and mediators

Questions may be put to a mediator during the course of mediation, and it's therefore as well to anticipate possible queries that may be raised. Some of the more common questions, and some possible responses, are shown in Table 8.2.

Table 8.2   Common questions and possible responses

Question	Possible Response
'What do you think we should (do), based on your experience [observation]?'	Don't become drawn in to offering advice. Simply remind the parties of the principle that mediators must remain non-directional in their approach.
	Turn-around – 'How do you think I might answer this?'
'Who do you think is right?'	A clear trap to avoid falling into. Simply remind both parties that you are impartial and not in a position to judge.
'Will you decide for us?'	Offer a brief reminder of your role, which restricts you from taking up this invitation.
	Help the parties refocus on choosing a process for reaching their own conclusion.
'Do you want us to stop?'	In some circumstances, this question may be asked at an appropriate point to close-out mediation. Ackowledge that it may be a suitable time for everyone to check back against the agreed criteria for close-out, whilst ensuring that the disputing parties decide whether these have been met.
'There's no hope for us to reach agreement, is there?'	Avoid answering directly 'yes' or 'no' to this question. It may be appropriate to summarize the status of the conversation as you see it, but pass back to both parties to confirm that your interpretation is correct.
	Discretion is needed to know whether a genuine impasse has been reached (after reasonable steps to find a breakthrough) or whether both parties are giving in, sometimes deliberately, at an early hurdle. In the latter case, ways forward might be suggested, backed by encouragement; in the former, both sides might be invited to check what has led them to form this view.

INTERVENTIONS RELEVANT FOR THE STAGE MEDIATION HAS REACHED

Opening

Opening may be an appropriate time to check whether each party is content with a guiding principle for the discussion that 'anything goes'.

Whilst coming into a joint session with at least a basic briefing, mediators are allowed to have a beginner's mind. They are able to ask questions to clarify what others may have felt uncomfortable raising for risk of belying their ignorance about 'the obvious', or something they feel they should know. The answers can be refreshing and lead to better understanding amongst the others in the room, not to mention the mediators themselves!

The act of acknowledging and affirming contributions is important throughout conflict brokering. Individuals should be encouraged to give more, and genuine recognition given to the fact that it may have been difficult for them to concede a point.

'Icebreakers', of the kind often used to warm up a new class of training delegates, should generally be avoided when starting a mediation session, unless they are appropriate and not seen to be trivial. Allowing reasonable time for discussion of ground rules is an exception, helping to detract initial attention from the detail of the dispute and allowing both parties time to settle.

Knowing when to end mediation, closing the process

It may be surprising to observe how frequently participants themselves recognize when mediation has reached its natural end point. In some cases, this is driven by available time, but very often comes from an acknowledgement that the main areas of concern have been covered as well as might reasonably be expected in the circumstances – whether or not the issues have been declared, and whether or not they've been addressed in the way either participant preferred.

When a sense that a natural end may have been reached isn't apparent between the parties themselves, a mediator may need to suggest that it may be appropriate to assess the stage the discussion has reached, eg, referring to criteria agreed earlier might allow a simple question to be posed: 'Are we at the point where we can start to draw conclusions?'

In closing, mediators should not communicate the subject content of the discussion to the individual who sponsored the mediation or others who weren't party to it, although they should feel free to offer comments on their impressions, eg, 'I believe this was a productive session.' If agreed by each party in mediation, it may also be relevant to mention any action points agreed in the discussion, as well as to summarize the main conclusions. However, as we've previously mentioned, the only documentary note that can be made after a dialogue ends is to record the fact that mediation occurred.

In reflecting and summarizing, a mediator should test the commitment of the parties to carry through what they've agreed by asking questions such as:

'When will you (carry out this agreed action point)?'

'What's the first step you will take after you leave this meeting today?'

'On a scale of 0 to 10, how committed are you to seeing this through?'

Participants might also be encouraged to allow general lessons learnt from their experience, that may help others in the organization, to be passed back, by asking:

'What has helped?'

'Can we share this [learning] with the organization?'

'Are there any useful insights you might want to pass on?'

'You've achieved a lot. Would you be content if we could share some of the general lessons learnt to help others…?'

'What else?'

Make sure that each individual is comfortable with any proposal made, and that they aren't just paying lip-service to appease the other party or the mediator, or simply to bring the discussion to an early close.

TWO EARS, ONE MOUTH

In this chapter we've spoken a lot about the use of questions, conversation structures and other interventions. However, it's all too easy to forget that a mediator is unlikely to be successful unless he or she is able to really tune in to what individuals are saying. As we like to say – it's good to talk, but even better to listen!

Summary

Micro-tools quickly get to the heart of what people want, and are useful for managers and in-house mediators alike. A wide range of techniques can help deal with the common challenges encountered during dispute resolution; techniques that are appropriate for the stage the mediation has reached, for breaking impasse, responding to questions put to mediators, handling hard landings and more. Many are included in Appendix 1.

Mediation has a better prospect of succeeding if it is carefully planned and attention is given to matters such as the venue for dialogue, dress and environment. Choosing a neutral venue can help defuse tension in an emerging dispute. For example, a manager walking with a disgruntled team member to the water cooler can help that individual step away from the immediate scene of his or her dispute – metaphorically as well as literally.

Not all issues can be described in 'black or white' terms – what appears to be reality for one person may differ completely from another's point of view, whilst trade-offs are often needed to help bridge the gap in what the disputing parties wish to achieve from mediation.

Notes

1. The concept of 'micro-tools' for coaching was inspired by Michael J Herth.
2. FIRO-B (Fundamental Interpersonal Relations Orientation), developed by William Schutz, examines the behaviours an individual displays in different relationship contexts (eg, personal, social). The Myers Briggs Type Indicator® helps individuals consider their preferences toward different dichotomies for a number of indicators of personality type (eg, a tendency to make decisions based on fact or feeling, needing other people as a source for energizing ideas). See: Schutz, W C (1958) *FIRO: A three dimensional theory of interpersonal behaviour,* Holt, Rinehart, & Winston, and Myers, I (1990) *Introduction to Type: A description of the theory and applications of the Myers-Briggs Type Indicator,* Center for Applications of Psychological Type.
3. See for example: Etchegoyen, H (2005) *The Fundamentals of Psychoanalytic Technique,* Karnac Books.
4. Exploration of the meaning of colours is offered in Gage, J (2000) *Colour and Meaning: Art, science and symbolism,* Thames & Hudson.
5. *Direct route* and *possible deviation* questions are concepts originating in solution-focused coaching (taught by Janine Waldman and Shaun Lincoln).
6. The effects of damage to the prefrontal cortex are illustrated by the story of Phineas Gage, a formerly placid railroad worker whose personality was dramatically changed following a freak accident in which an iron bolt was driven through his frontal lobes. See: Macmillan, M (2000) *An Odd Kind of Fame: Stories of Phineas Gage,* MIT Press.

9

Strategic planning and conflict management

A STRATEGY FOR MANAGING CONFLICT

The need for a strategy for managing conflict

Given the excessive time, cost and energy that unhealthy conflict consumes, it must make sense to give attention to reducing the potential for disputes occurring. However, all too often we find that no more than a bare-bone strategy and minimal training and support for minimizing and containing conflict are in place in the organizations that we talk to – that is, if they have a strategy at all.

Clearly more is needed than producing a grievance procedure, being able to appoint mediators on demand and including a module on handling workplace disputes in manager training – but putting in place effective measures to improve the way an organization deals with conflict needn't be burdensome. In the next three chapters, we'll examine how this can be done. We'll consider some simple processes that can be put in place, offering a template for implementing a CM strategy within your own organization.

Taking the CM scope 'umbrella' we introduced in Figure 2.1 as a basis (see page 30), our discussion in this chapter falls under three main headings:

1. Preventing/minimizing conflict.
2. Escalated dispute management.
3. Monitoring.

Preventing/minimizing conflict primarily concerns the role front-line managers can play in encouraging team relationships, allowing disagreements to be aired and unconstructive conflict to be recognized and contained at an early stage (with a majority being resolved within the critical 'Golden Hour'). Escalated dispute management focuses on the role of intermediaries in informal mediation, grievance investigation, ADR and litigation. Within this broad category, attention is given to sourcing options, as well as to building an in-house ADR capability. Monitoring considers not only keeping track of what happens in the aftermath of a closed dispute and containing the fall-out of disagreements that escalate into litigation and the public domain, but also at how the success or otherwise of an organization's CM strategy can be evaluated and how learning may be captured and disseminated for the benefit of others. Monitoring might be assigned as a responsibility for a CM champion (eg an HR manager), but involves consultation and communication with a broad sample of 'inner circle' participants in a dispute, line managers and other staff. All three key elements require genuine endorsement and support by an organization's top team.

First though, let's take a moment to define what we mean by 'strategy' when used in the context of managing conflict.

THE MEANING OF 'STRATEGY'

Put simply, a 'strategy' is a pre-planned approach aimed at achieving a particular end. At the level of corporate strategy, this will have potentially major ramifications for the future development of a business and its employees, not to mention fundamental matters such as the core nature of the organization's function.

At an individual level, 'strategy' might concern career progression, whilst a wide range of strategies may be seen at team, departmental, project and other operational levels (including an HR or people management strategy). A CM strategy may well form a part of a corporate strategy, but more typically will underpin a strategy for recruiting, supporting and developing people. Of course, this must support the organization's strategic direction and key objectives, as well as help define and be integrated with the policies, procedures and other mechanisms that shape the environments in which managers manage and staff members grow and operate.

Any strategy must exist for a purpose. In the case of CM, key objectives may be to 'minimize the occurrence and impact of unproductive conflict', and 'to channel constructive conflict effectively'. Deciding on an appropriate approach to achieve this ('the strategy') normally involves assessing what may already be in place to help achieve the desired end.

Key elements of conflict management strategy

This assessment might take account of the various mixes of elements that may influence relationships between teams and individuals, and examine how managers respond to the opportunities and challenges presented to them by their staff. These include mechanisms that an organization can set down as a way of regulating activity and behaviour, and those that seek to influence individuals via informal, non-prescribed means.

'Regulatory' mechanisms include:

- organization structures;
- role definitions;
- policies;
- processes;
- procedures;
- task definitions;
- lines of authority and reporting;
- reward systems;
- appraisal systems;
- codes of conduct (matters that should prompt disciplinary action).

Amongst possible influencing mechanisms are:

- leadership vision;
- codes of ethics;
- personal development/objectives plans/targets;
- team/departmental targets;
- training programmes, learning and development activities;
- recognition systems;
- management guidance/recommended best practice;
- management style;
- monitoring and feedback systems;
- informal routines and habitual ways of doing things.

Individuals who are responsible for defining and overseeing the implementation of a CM strategy may be able to exert influence in some if not all these areas, especially if they are a member of the organization's leadership team. Ultimately, such intervention is about changing the mix of beliefs, assumptions, ideas and opportunities for self-discretion and contribution that form a part of what the corporate strategy specialists Gerry Johnson and Kevan Scholes (1997) call the 'recipe' that produces an organization's culture.

For example, individuals must know when it's acceptable to raise a concern about another person, as well as to feel that by so doing they will not be branded a malcontent. To encourage widespread awareness that this is permissible, policy must be communicated, but management style, observation of the way others who raise objections are treated and having an expectation that the organization will respond to concerns appropriately all play their part. In turn, managers with the appropriate personal attitudes and skills must be recruited, trained and incentivized to be approachable and non-judgemental, whilst staff need to feel assured that they work for a 'listening organization' and one that 'walks the talk'.

CM strategy should also endeavour to take account of the power structures that may exist within an organization and underpin individual motivation, with a view to encouraging those who are politically driven to recognize the compatibility of their own objectives and those of the organization.

The lists of regulatory mechanisms and informal influences given above are by no means exhaustive. However, they offer a firm basis for considering how CM strategy can be made to work in practice.

KEY CONSIDERATIONS FOR CONFLICT MANAGEMENT STRATEGY

We turn now to consider a number of specific questions that any CM strategy might need to address.

What should the boundary interfaces for intermediaries be?

A dispute may involve intervention by more than one intermediary, albeit not normally at the same time. The baton for facilitating a resolution via ADR should typically have already passed from a front-line manager, possibly via an informal mediator, to an HR specialist and possibly one or more grievance investigators before passing into the hands of a mediator. A coach may also have supported individuals through a part or all of this process.

Moving from one intermediary to another should be quite straightforward, provided the boundaries that define each interface are clear: in other words, when the purpose of each intervention has been achieved (whether or not a dispute has been resolved). A coach should recognize when the limits of coaching are reached, whilst a mediator should know when it's appropriate to close-out his or her part in the dialogue and refer back to the customer sponsor. Less satisfactory exchanges may occur when boundaries aren't clear or when one intermediary forgets or ignores them.

Those responsible for overseeing an end-to-end DR process need to ensure that boundaries and contracts are made clear and, by obtaining feedback on how well process has been followed, make sure that they are adhered to and that the lessons learnt are passed back to the organization. (Judicious editing of what is presented may be necessary to protect the confidentiality of conversations with disputing parties.)

Similarly, it needs to be clear what the inputs and outputs of different interventions are intended to be, as well as which outputs can be made known to the next intermediary (this may not always be relevant or even desirable). This is especially true where a baton may pass back and forth between different intermediaries during a single dialogue, as illustrated in Figure 9.1.

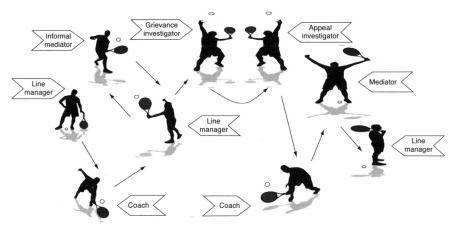

During the course of a dispute, a variety of intermediaries may take centre stage as a focal point for facilitating a resolution

Figure 9.1   Passing the ball

What should be put in place to prevent or minimize unhealthy conflict?

As we've already said, it may not be possible to prevent every dispute from occurring, but very often unhelpful disagreements can be avoided. The psychological contract that individuals have with their employer and manager is especially important in influencing how individuals deal with emerging disagreements. The more managers invest in building trust, the greater the opportunity there will be for discussing matters openly and constructively. Similarly, the degree of trust that individuals place in their manager for discussing concerns openly will make it easier for a manager to talk to them when a direct approach is necessary.

What's more, organizations that manage conflicts well are most likely to be those that have the happiest employees. Supportive and cooperative teams that genuinely share core values of mutual respect for alternative ideas, have esteem for colleagues and are open to sharing views will obviously be less likely hotbeds for conflict developing. With improved self-awareness and access to techniques that can be easily recalled and applied, both managers and the people they manage may be better able to recognize the first signs of conflict and have greater capacity to contain their reactions before their strong disagreement becomes apparent to others.

Perhaps the greatest payback from a CM strategy can be had in the relatively simple steps of training, building trust and helping individuals develop strong self-awareness, leadership and self-management skills. These steps should in turn help many to be better able to resist the urge to allow a cause of anger to fester and spiral into a bitter disagreement.

How should conflict management policy integrate with existing HR processes and codes?

We should say a word at this point about the need when implementing a CM strategy to review grievance procedures and any code of ethics or statement of core values that may have been adopted by the organization. The way in which grievance investigations are carried out – and the capabilities of those who conduct them – could also usefully be reviewed, especially since this is a further crucial factor in bringing disputes to a close. Equally, in some organizations, the investigation process is such that a grievance can be allowed to continue escalating through a series of internal appeals and re-investigations (we know of a record seven re-investigations of the same grievance!)

A simple check may be all that's required to ensure that established procedures are consistent with any planned new policies and guidance, especially concerning the interfaces between grievance investigation procedures and other stages in a DR process.

Consistency between the codes of ethical practice proposed for CM practitioners and any other organization codes should also be reviewed to avoid any possible contradiction. Consideration might also be given to the possibility of updating the organization's statement of its core values if these don't represent the behaviours required for minimizing conflict (eg, showing respect for colleagues who have different views). Of course, referral and consultation with the leadership team and others may be needed in such circumstances. This should aim to obtain their genuine commitment that the values will be 'lived and not laminated' (a phrase coined by Jackie when once observing the laminated statement of core values attached to the wall of a large organization's main office reception!).

Changes to procedures might best be communicated to managers as a part of their CM training, although other means of communication may be required when new procedures first go live. Similarly, the practical meaning and relevance of core values might be advised through general communication, cascaded by front-line managers and reflected in personal development objectives, role profiles, induction and other training.

Is a short-cut approach to conflict management worth the risk?

The premise of this chapter is that an organization will want to put in place a best practice approach for managing workplace conflict. In its most developed form, this implies a need for training all front-line managers, building a capability for offering a variety of forms of ADR and offering mediation or coaching to everyone whose disputes become formalized.

This may be an ideal; decisions on how much effort and expense can be invested in attempting to break disputes must be weighed against other priorities. Whilst not something we would recommend (and those who find themselves in this position might wish that things were otherwise), we appreciate that many organizations take risk decisions based on the cold hard numbers, having to face such questions as, 'What might be lost or saved if we let this particular dispute run its course?' and, 'Can we afford to lose?' A consideration of what risks might be acceptable may need to feature in a CM strategy.

If opting to take a risk, the full extent of the possible consequences in a 'worst case scenario' need to be thought through, as well as an attempt made to assess the likelihood that the risk event may occur and that the individual who may threaten litigation will actually follow through with the threat. Only by quantifying the risk in this way can an informed decision be taken on whether or not to accept it.

Possible consequences from not pursuing the escalation route include not being seen to have shown concern for staff, being penalized by a tribunal for not having attempted ADR, and being left with a damaged reputation. A dispute that isn't resolved when there may have been an opportunity to do so may cost much more if it moves on to litigation – and, depending on the nature of the case, risk significant damages if the organization is then found to be at fault, let alone possible harm to its public image.

A grievance investigator may uncover situations where an organization has been at fault and recommend compensation as a compromise in preference to being more heavily penalized in a public arena. Sometimes organizations need to confront the fact that there has been a failing on their part, and by being ready to acknowledge such weaknesses, some of the most valuable learning can result.

Unfortunately, valuable learning all too often disappears into the void of the corporate machine.

Decisions on some cases may be easier than others – for example, those for which only limited compensation may be payable if an employee wins his or her case. However, organizations that consistently fail to take reasonable steps to investigate staff grievances and attempt to find resolutions to disagreements may have to work extra hard to convince others that they're a fair employer. Our firm belief is that it's always right to investigate a complaint and strongly recommend assessing whether an attempt at some form of ADR has a prospect of succeeding.

A template for conflict management strategy

Those who are charged with 'owning' the development and implementation of a CM strategy are likely to be best placed to determine the scope, presentation and organization of documentation related to the Strategy, as they know the inter-relationships with other strategy and policies, house style, quality assurance procedures and the like. However, we suggest that the following might be considered as main headings:

1. Scope and purpose of the strategy.
2. Specific objectives.
3. Rationale/key success factors.
4. Policy and procedure:
   - preventing/minimizing conflict;
   - informal mechanisms supporting implementation;
   - implementation plan/responsibilities;
   - evaluation plan.

PLANNING IMPLEMENTATION

A shared responsibility?

By now, you might have formed a strong impression of what needs to be done to put a CM strategy into practice. Chances are, you'll recognize that a number of individuals may need to be involved in this process, either to help inform or be informed about different aspects of the strategy or to be actively involved in its implementation.

An HR or organization development director might be a normal sponsor for defining and implementing a strategy in larger organizations, although others may be appointed as care-takers or to drive through the actual implementation. Learning and development managers may naturally take up the task of developing, commissioning and scheduling CM training; leaders of coaching programmes may recruit, groom and moderate the professional practice of coaches, whilst procurement managers may play a central role in negotiating contracts with external suppliers.

Other important participants may include occupational health specialists, legal advisers and heads of department. Critically too, an organization's top team needs to subscribe to the plan's objectives and set direction so that it can be integrated with the priorities of corporate strategy.

Responsibilities for developing a conflict management capability may well be shared, however it will certainly help if specific people can be recognized as being the overall sponsor and project manager for the implementation. Whoever is charged with putting a CM strategy into practice, successful implementation ultimately relies upon the involvement of a wide group of people. Of course, front-line managers have no small part to play in this.

Regulatory change

Governments have a habit of amending employment regulation from time to time, so it's important for a nominated person to look out for any changes that may affect their planned policies or ones that have already been put in place. This may be a simple matter of maintaining online registration with appropriate government information feeds, scanning the pages of HR journals and confirming that others within their organization who monitor regulatory developments are aware of their interest and commit to passing on any relevant information that crosses their desks.

The need to maintain timely knowledge about developments in legislation is all the more important for organizations that employ staff across national boundaries, and especially at a time when many governments are contemplating or have already committed to significant new legislation. Local HR and/or legal knowledge may be necessary to keep abreast of developments in different parts of the world, implying a need for the leaders of CM implementation to establish and maintain good networks with their colleagues in all the countries in which their organization operates.

CM custodians operating within multinational organizations may also need to adapt their guidance on managing disputes to cater for varying practices in different countries. In some States in the United States, for example, it's permissible for individuals who are required to attend an employment tribunal to rehearse and be groomed in what they may say in response to questions they may face, taking guidance from legal counsel if desired. Conversely, in England and

Wales, a lawyer who offered such priming could possibly be charged with professional malpractice.

Influencing the 'recipe'

As we mentioned earlier in this chapter, a variety of regulatory and influencing mechanisms may be used to help establish desired practices for managing conflict. Such things as performance targets, reward systems and codes of conduct may be designed to enforce and incentivize compliance, as may role definitions, formal policies and procedures. Clearly, agreement with any others who may be responsible for managing such factors may be needed to incorporate the desired changes, whilst accounting for the broader objectives and priorities of the particular procedure or other control method.

Rules – or set ways of doing things – may go a long way towards ensuring that individuals act in the way they're meant to act, although to encourage voluntary change in behaviour another means of influence usually needs to be called upon. As we saw earlier, it's such things as the vision of leaders, having a genuine shared belief in company values, management style and informal routines and habits that are crucial for making a difference.

It would be a tall order to expect one person to bring about a change in any organization's 'cultural recipe' single-handedly. However, those responsible for overseeing CM can kick-start the process. Within even very large, hierarchical organizations, two overriding variables to bring to the fore are commitment and passion.

Commitment means not only seeing a task such as manager training through to completion, but continuing to be proactive in showing ongoing interest and support for those who have been trained. This may continue even after passing on responsibility for overseeing CM practice when moving into another role, offering continuing support for a new custodian and previous training delegates when required. In a comparable scenario, Jackie's experience goes even further: she still retains a level of contact and is occasionally approached by individuals who were groomed as coaches by her several years ago, even though she has long since moved on from having responsibility for upskilling coaches working for what is now her previous employer.

Such commitment may be driven by a genuine passion to influence positive change and one that is designed to benefit those who might otherwise have to manage or become embroiled in unconstructive disputes. Passion can be contagious, attracting interest and admiration from others, prompting them to decide to follow on from the example they observe: we believe that passion is a vital energizer for true leadership.

These two closely related drivers – passion and commitment – should motivate a CM programme leader to actively seek opportunities to promote the interests of the cause. This may include offering to speak at departmental meetings, co-facilitating CM training courses, and actively engaging with fellow HR protagonists.

Individual influence is important, but other approaches for influencing the 'recipe' may also be adopted. For example, informal networking amongst delegates might be encouraged following completion of a training course. Action learning sets, co-coaching and 'solution-focused circles' are amongst the activities that might be proposed for encouraging ongoing knowledge sharing.

In the case of a 'solution-focused circle', a small group of managers may resolve to meet periodically for perhaps just 30 minutes at a time, to jointly consider a current CM issue brought by one member of the group. Such meetings run according to a standard format:

1. The individual bringing the issue briefly states its nature and outlines the challenge he or she is facing.
2. Other members of the group then ask a question in turn to qualify their appreciation of the situation, whilst helping the problem owner to deepen his or her thinking about the situation.
3. Members of the group continue to ask questions in succession, but without offering comment (the sequence for asking questions is passed over to the next person in the 'circle' if an individual doesn't have a question to ask).
4. After 10 minutes or so, the round of questioning is brought to a close and the problem owner is then invited to take time away from the group to reflect on what has been discussed.
5. The remaining individuals then consider their own responses to what they have heard, identifying possible courses of action that may help the problem owner move forward.
6. After reconvening, the reflections are shared.

One advantage of the solution-focused circle concept is that all participants in a group are encouraged to carefully reflect on a live issue that they may themselves confront in future. As such, each is able to learn from the suggestions made by others as well as from their own thinking. (The solution-focused circle approach is included as a micro-tool in Appendix 1.)

Role-modelling can also play an important part in speeding up the process of recipe change. Even a small handful of advocates can begin to turn heads in a large organization by demonstrating and talking about the benefits of their new experiences of managing conflict. Front-line managers are often as well (if not better) placed as CM custodians to sell the benefits of taking CM training seriously, being more readily seen as being in touch with the day-to-day realities of managing 'difficult' staff.

Planning communication

In larger organizations especially, it's often difficult to succeed in getting messages heard when managers are continually being bombarded with directions and guidelines of all kinds. To make CM training mandatory may often be outside of the gift of a CM project leader, whilst e-mails detailing regulatory requirements may easily be overlooked in busy in-boxes. CM custodians therefore have their work cut out in raising awareness, and must take time to get communication 'right'.

Undoubtedly, well thought through communications should have a greater chance of registering with their intended audience than those that are quickly dashed off. The normal rules for good communication with which you may well be familiar apply:

- being brief;
- not including more than one message in a single communication;
- considering the interests of receivers and appealing to these;
- using simple language;
- choosing the most appropriate medium and the most suitable time to transmit a message.

Given the importance of messages being properly heard, it may make sense for leaders of CM projects to plan which should be sent at different stages as CM processes are rolled out and training programmes are launched.

Generally circulated communication such as e-mails are more likely to be given attention by readers if they're already engaged with the notion that effective CM matters. Again, groundwork prepared by a passionate CM project leader through their presentation briefings, involvement in training and relationship building with HR and other stakeholders should help pave the way for greater receptiveness when his or her occasional e-mails make their way across the company intranet.

Regulatory changes may also need to be communicated to front-line managers, depending on the nature of what has changed and a manager's need to know or to comply with the particular law.

Responding to feedback

Rapport building, mutually supportive liaison with stakeholders and effective communication are important elements for engaging others. However, communication shouldn't be seen as a one-off exercise designed to pass on information for others to act upon. CM project leaders who seriously want to build a strong CM capability need to be good listeners too.

Even during the early stage of rolling out a new CM function, opportunities for learning arise and opinions and observations may be proffered. By listening, and when appropriate acting, good practice can be established at an early stage. As a result, a pilot implementation may not have to be necessary before a full roll out is begun, provided that leaders of a CM implementation commit themselves to being receptive to what others have to say.

Moving from planning to taking action

We always recommend that organizations shouldn't take too long forming a 'perfect' plan before starting to realize the benefits of a new CM strategy. The disadvantage of procrastinating is clear: we've come across some organizations taking nearly three years just to recruit external specialists, during which time the world had slipped into recession, their management teams had experienced considerable comings and goings, and (for some) their entire business model has changed!

Quite apart from potentially missing opportunities to curtail costly disputes that take hold whilst the final touches are still being added to an implementation plan, for most organizations the world changes quickly, and with it corporate and people management strategies, stakeholder responsibilities and organizational structures. CM policy needs to be able to keep abreast of regular change and be able to adapt quickly in response.

Summary

Without a strategy for managing conflict, organizations are prey to the devastating consumption of energy, time and people resource that unproductive conflict produces. Usually integrated as a part of a wider strategy for managing people, CM strategy should harness both formal and informal mechanisms for influencing behaviours and beliefs.

Implementing a CM strategy is ultimately a shared responsibility, but direction setting and ongoing support are needed from HR or another champion, whilst simple but effective communication needs to be planned and carefully constructed.

10

Implementing a conflict management strategy

THE PRACTICALITY OF IMPLEMENTING A CONFLICT MANAGEMENT STRATEGY

Implementing a CM strategy shouldn't be an onerous task, especially if decisions about what needs to be put in place have been taken during planning. Several key areas are likely to require most focus, and these are our main concerns in this chapter:

- addressing the training and development needs of conflict managers;
- providing supervision for mediators; and
- resourcing the CM function.

ADDRESSING THE TRAINING AND DEVELOPMENT NEEDS OF CONFLICT MANAGERS

Key skills and attributes for managers of conflict

In Chapter 6 we listed effective listening, questioning and rapport building as forming part of a basic skills-set for anyone who has to manage disputes. Other prerequisites include diplomacy, objective thinking, management counselling and coaching. Equally important are a high level of emotional intelligence, the ability to build trust and to motivate staff. Some might say that these are all important qualities for managers to have anyway.

Less effective conflict managers are likely to include those who are quick to rush to assumptions or judgement, those who prefer a dictatorial management style and those whose main focus is pursuing their own political agenda. Worse still are those managers who abdicate responsibility for attempting to resolve any dispute involving a member of their team, seeing 'people problems' as a matter for HR or someone else to deal with.

Other pitfalls that may easily unseat the unwary include believing that a manager always has to solve a problem, putting off facing tough conversations and focusing on what can't be done (we like to refer to such managers as having 'the "buts" disease', since they are usually the first to list a series of objections to a new idea!). Newcomers to CM may be especially prone to verbal gaffes, assuming that their personal style and perspective will naturally fit with those of others, not being able to stop themselves from saying more than necessary, and so opening up the strong risk of undoing any useful progress that may have been made ('Let's go over this… again [or] in more detail' is one expression many find too hard to resist). A tendency to rush to fill a gap during a pregnant pause may similarly lead to backsliding in conversation, as may re-opening a previously closed discussion.

Novice mediators may find it hard to deliver a message without bringing their own emotions into play, such as unwittingly using a mediation dialogue as an opportunity to vent their own frustration with a matter that is bothering them. They may be too keen to tackle a large issue without first attempting to break it down into more manageable pieces, and they may focus too much on the nature of the problems being brought to the table rather than in helping participants to achieve a positive outcome.

A lack of authenticity in mediators may be obvious to others, either because they are overly-concerned with following the letter of a process or because they have a genuine bias toward one party's point of view. Such artificiality may be a common flaw amongst individuals who tend to think in black or white terms and those who over-emphasize their commitment to ensuring impartiality.

Nevertheless, light-touch management can be just as harmful as taking a heavy-handed or exaggerated approach. Issues of real concern to those who raise grievances that seem unimportant for a manager may all too easily be played down or trivialized. It's rarely wise to advise team members to 'Just forget it' or, 'Get real!' Managers who don't respond to brewing disputes in a timely way – during the 'Golden Hour' – may not only allow a conflict to exacerbate, but may also appear to dismiss the importance of an issue in the eyes of a team member who is told to 'Come back next week' or that their manager is 'Too busy right now'.

We've also regularly encountered managers who are anxious to complete everything at once, taking everything upon their shoulders and so quickly becoming ineffective in how they manage their time. Others prefer to immediately reach for their Staff Management Handbook, sticking to what they see as 'rules', but which are really intended as guidelines. Literal interpretation may also be problematic when responding to heated outbursts, taking what is said as premeditated and factual, rather than recognizing that some comments may be made out of desperation and that a cooling-off period is often what's really needed.

More seasoned conflict managers aren't exempt from falling into common traps. A 'one size fits all' mentality may easily take hold if a particular approach has been found to be successful on several occasions, rather than being open to new learning and seeing each person and situation as unique. The wider implications of a dispute may be overlooked, such as considering how other team members may be affected by what they overhear or perceive, or failing to spot when it's relevant to escalate.

Any representative of an organization may be susceptible to exposing it to potentially damaging publicity and litigation. Their actions can produce other unhelpful consequences too, such as committing to promises that can't easily be delivered and otherwise setting false expectations.

Training undoubtedly has one of the biggest roles to play in grooming the right skills in managers, but so too can the various means for explaining what responsibilities a manager is expected to take on board (in role definitions, personal objectives, performance targets and the like). Of course those who are responsible for recruiting new managers should also be sufficiently competent to assess whether potential recruits are made of the 'right stuff.'

Training and development for managers

Conflict management may well feature in an existing management training syllabus, if not being a focus for specific courses of its own. In assessing the current state of CM strategy, it's important not only to explore the content and learning approaches used by any such training, but also how it's positioned. In particular, the relative priority given to CM (if it's included as part of a more general management development programme), the scope of training provided and, possibly, the expectation that managers should undertake the training should all be assessed. Similarly, the need for any refresher training and early provision of training for individuals who've recently joined the organization or who've been recently promoted into roles in which they must manage staff for the first time should be identified as a part of this analysis.

Honest self-assessment (as well as potentially using 180° or 360° survey feedback) should result if managers are challenged to consider the ways in which their own style of management, assumptions and prejudices may impact on individuals' readiness to speak up when a disagreement arises. Coaching may provide strong support for classroom-based training in raising this awareness, and continuing reflective practice may be encouraged through action learning sets and other informal networking.

Self-assessment might include considering how managers' use of language and behaviour may serve as triggers for conflict for others. They should be aware of the harm that may result if they insist on continuing to broker a dispute alone when third-party intervention may be more appropriate. Managers should have the skills training for handling conflict between teams (including virtual teams) and organizations, as well as being able to intervene in disputes that involve individuals at different levels within an organization.

One common weakness in training that we've come across is a failure to put CM in context with the fundamental responsibilities of a front-line manager and to highlight its important for the organization. This may often be a consequence of training being revised only infrequently, or originally not being designed in a holistic context of a wider people management strategy.

Training should include not only a wide range of practical techniques for managing conflict 'in the moment' (including the types of micro-tools we encountered previously), but also equip managers to recognize the possible signs of an emerging dispute and to be able to channel this effectively. Training should also enable managers to distinguish between unconstructive and constructive conflict and show how they might optimize the latter. It should make clear what managers can do during the 'Golden Hour' for containing potentially disruptive and enduring disputes, as well as demonstrating how to manage disputes that have already taken hold, possibly in adversarial circumstances.

As with any form of learning and development activity, to be useful training must be relevant, practical and easily recalled. Learning approaches that encourage role-playing, shared experience and personal reflection are most likely to be successful, especially if managers can recognize the benefits of applying what they have learnt about when it's inappropriate to escalate a dispute that hasn't yet had any proper chance to be resolved locally. So too, they should know how to choose the third-party intervention that is most likely to be helpful.

All of this calls for dedicated training, probably involving at least one day of classroom sessions combined with activities that will encourage continuing learning and self-reflection. The very significant value that managers can contribute to their organization by managing conflict effectively should justify the resources devoted to what is a vital management responsibility and training need.

> ## Suggested scope of training for managers
>
> ■ Regulatory and business contexts: why conflict management matters.
> ■ Why conflicts begin.
> ■ Recognizing conflict triggers.
> ■ Containing conflict.
> ■ Micro-tools for managing conflict.
> ■ Managing the aftermath of a dispute.
> ■ Managing conflicts in teams.
> ■ Managing conflict between teams.
> ■ Attending employment tribunals.
> ■ Preventing conflict.

Preparing managers and others to face employment tribunals

Many who are called upon to give testimony at an employment tribunal or in court in support of an organization's defence may be doing so for the first time. The success or otherwise in defending a case may well rest on the performance of such individuals, and therefore organizations may want to give careful consideration to supporting their preparation for presenting evidence (though not of course to rehearse a specific dispute, unless local regulation permits this).

At a basic level, this may involve a simple briefing, led by an individual who is familiar with tribunal processes and so able to advise on what may happen, including the likely structure of a hearing and protocols for behaviour. An HR professional or legal adviser might be suitable for this role. In addition to briefings of this kind, awareness training in employment tribunal procedures might be considered. Several organizations offer such training (in the UK, the law practice McGrigors has produced a DVD including an enactment of a mock hearing; for more information, see www.mcgrigors.com).

Training and development for leaders

Those preparing for or who are already in positions of leadership may also require training to highlight the importance of effective CM in achieving corporate objectives. In particular, training may be relevant where a responsibility for implementing the people management strategy needed to support corporate strategy is shared between a number of individuals, as may often be the case.

Unlike with manager training, leadership training should put the focus on collaborative reflection and decision making rather than on the practicalities of containing and resolving live disputes. Training for leaders allows a focus on how to integrate conflict management strategy with the organization's needs and priorities, may prompt thinking about how the risk of reputation damage may be limited and identify how constructive conflict may most effectively be harnessed. A briefing followed by a facilitated workshop approach might be used to engage participation.

Suggested scope of training for leaders

- Organizational and regulatory contexts of conflict.
- Organizational impacts and responses through a conflict lifecycle.
- Defining and enabling appropriate channelling of constructive conflict.
- Developing others to become effective managers of conflict.
- Conflict and the 'new science of happiness'.
- Defining and implementing a CM strategy,
- Evaluating the effectiveness and impact of a conflict management strategy.

Training for informal mediators

Managers may occasionally be called upon to intervene in a dispute affecting individuals in another team. They may be approached in an attempt to avoid formal escalation of a disagreement, or because they are seen as being a 'friendly' trusted intermediary by the parties involved.

Informal mediation shouldn't be an onerous process, perhaps being restricted to a single, tightly time-bound meeting and possibly preceded by brief one-to-one discussions between the mediator and the disputing parties (and potentially with their managers too). Guidance provided by the organization may define the normal expected scope of informal mediation, including template ground rules that can be proposed to participants (those presented in Chapter 7 might be used as a possible example).

Managers who accept an invitation to take on an informal mediator role are likely to need a level of training and guidance beyond the scope of what might normally be provided in management training. The essential skills of mediation need to be taught, but guidance must also be offered on the potential pitfalls of the task, the boundaries that need to be observed during mediation, knowing when it's appropriate to decline the role, and when formal escalation should take over.

The training and support needs for informal mediation are not significantly different from those required of other mediators. Since many individuals may only occasionally be asked to play this role, organizations might wish to weigh the benefits of training a large number of managers for this role.

A possible compromise may be to include an introductory mediation element as part of the CM training provided to all managers, and to offer one-to-one mentoring for those who are asked to play this role on demand. In this case, mentoring may help refresh the essential elements of earlier training, review the guidelines for formal escalation, and address any specific issues brought by the individual being mentored.

Time invested in developing and supporting informal mediation skills may reap benefits beyond what may arise from specific disputes. Apart from better equipping managers to take on further informal mediation in future, they may add to a ready pool of potential recruits for training as (formal) in-house mediators, subject of course to their own interests and suitability.

Experience gained through informal mediation may be taken back into everyday management within a manager's own team, whilst encouraging efforts to resolve disputes informally may support a broader aim of building a 'happy company'. What's more, if successful, the costly process of grievous investigations, appeals and further attempts to resolve a deepening dispute will be avoided.

The very fact that two parties can consider a third party with mutual respect (ie, someone whom they trust to be fair) should in itself be a reason to allow informal mediation a chance to work. However, managers who are approached with a request to take on the role may wish to think carefully before immediately accepting, however flattering an invitation may be. By becoming involved, they may unwittingly aggravate what may already be a strained relationship, expose their organization to an increased threat of litigation, and potentially frustrate their own relationships with the disputing parties and their respective managers, or otherwise become involved in the dispute by not maintaining impartiality. Whilst the latter may be unlikely, informal mediators need to be able to set clear boundaries around what they are prepared to do, and resist attempts by the individuals involved to push beyond those boundaries or who make unreasonable demands on their time.

Key skills and attributes for mediators

We suggest that, when recruiting external suppliers and developing in-house mediators, they need to have, or develop, the list of skills in the *Person Specification* template in Appendix 2 (this template is also available as a PDF file for download from our website: www.managingconflictatwork.com).

For arbitrators, a similar skill-set might be looked for, along with the ability to:

- objectively appraise alternative explanations and pleas;
- exercise and rationalize judgements;
- intercede between disputing parties (when both parties remain separated);
- accurately communicate information between parties who are separated in time and space.

Similar skills might be expected to be shown by coaches as those required of mediators, including an ability to:

- quickly discern underpinning issues and to present these back in a way that causes an individual to reflect and gain insight;
- help individuals who may have a narrowly focused perspective to think objectively about the full context of their situation and to envisage possible future situations that may result from taking alternative courses of action;
- cover a range of topics within a tight timeframe, without comprising on taking time to listen and giving time for individuals to formulate responses;
- deal sensitively with emotional outburst;
- recognize when a boundary for coaching has been reached.

Knowledge of regulations may also be necessary for some mediators and arbitrators, particularly regulations relevant to specific disputes they may be engaged to mediate. In the case of evaluative mediation, knowledge of legal case precedents that may suggest how a judge or tribunal may rule on a case if it were escalated into litigation should also be demonstrated. All intermediaries, including coaches, will benefit from having a broad appreciation of the process and contributions made by different types of intervention under the umbrella of alternative dispute resolution.

Desirable personal qualities of anyone recruited into an intermediary role include being:

- thoughtful;
- non-judgemental;
- confident;
- self-controlled;
- non-aggressive;
- tolerant;
- empathetic;
- self-aware;
- calm and having a calming manner.

In short, the expectations of intermediaries are demanding and it is unrealistic to assume that each candidate's skill-set will be perfectly honed. Instead, there should be a commitment to ongoing professional development and supervision. For in-house intermediaries, this implies a need for an organizational commitment to their training, support and development.

Training, support and development for in-house mediators

Newly recruited in-house mediators might be expected to undertake the same CM training as is offered to managers, if they haven't already done so. Additional training to equip them to start operating as mediators should follow hot on its heels. We suggest that the course content includes the following topics.

Suggested scope of training for in-house mediators

- Appreciating the role of the mediator and purpose of different types of mediation/other approaches to ADR.
- Appreciating the contexts in which formal mediation is usually engaged, including both common and more unusual scenarios that might be presented.
- Contracting and convening mediation.
- Divorcing situation from emotion.
- Identifying personal influencers that may impact on others.
- Awareness of potential pitfalls in mediation, including matters that may risk individuals coming to harm or expose an organization to litigation.
- Being able to apply a wide range of mediation techniques, strategies and tools.
- Being able to defuse sensitive situations, though knowing when to allow time for individuals to outpour emotion and for angry exchanges to occur.
- Being able to break an impasse.
- Being able to manage distractions.
- Being able to work with other mediators and third parties.
- Recognizing when to interface with other intermediaries.
- Managing personal resources to best effect.
- Knowing when mediation should end.
- Being able to bring each party to a satisfactory agreement.
- Mediator supervision, ongoing support and 'buddying' with other organizations.

Such training should provide a foundation for the competency and knowledge requirements that new mediators may need to develop. We have suggested a list of these, together with desirable personal qualities in the mediator 'person specification' in Appendix 2.

Training should ideally accommodate a range of learning styles, emphasize developing awareness and mix a high level of interaction with extensive role-plays and demonstration. A phasing of training may be desirable, allowing an opportunity for inter-stage learning consolidation and time to shadow other mediators in live practice, if possible.

Planning for post-training support is especially important to ensure that skills and practice aren't only developed but also sustained. Second stage development topics and activities might be offered through networking with other organizations, supervisor guidance, and a range of activities that have proved to be effective in consolidating learning, including action learning sets, mediation circles and occasional master-class workshops.

Mediators might be encouraged to plan for their continuous professional development, maintain a log of the mediation practice that they've undertaken and even be required to complete a range of 'apprentice' or shadowing activities before graduating from training into the in-house mediator pool. A variety of external suppliers offer mediator training, although larger organizations may wish to consider sourcing in-house course design and delivery, especially if they plan to upskill a reasonably large pool of in-house mediators.

Deciding on this matter begs the question of how large a team of conflict specialists needs to be to handle demand for their services and to match the varying profiles of mediators, coaches and others that allow for suitable matching – with in-house members of the pool representing a range of departments, personalities, sex, ethnicity and locations, if appropriate. One possible response is to initially train a slightly greater number of individuals than are thought to be needed for handling the organization's needs, but not so many that their services are rarely called upon or so they can't be adequately supported.

A limited number of preferred suppliers might be engaged for handling a majority of externally sourced needs, though without precluding an option to call upon the services of others when required.

Case study: Home-grown mediation

A large public organization in London has recognized the benefit of bringing mediation in-house, training and equipping almost 80 mediators capable of working across the organization's operations and serving a staff base of more than 60,000. The potential of internal mediation to reduce costs, better support staff and combat the stress associated with dealing with grievances, and possibly attending employment tribunals, had been proposed in an audit inquiry, and had been observed being put into practice in a similar organization.

From the outset, the need was identified to not only train individuals selected as mediators to a high level, but also to ensure that they would be properly supported through regular contact and continuing professional development.

Mediators were selected through a rigorous selection process, involving written applications and interviews, designed to test that selected candidates were not only of the right mettle, but to ensure that they had the right motivation for wanting to take on the role. Many who came forward in response to an intranet advertisement knew little about the context for the new service, but were clear in their own beliefs about the valuable role mediation could play. Some brought complementary experience, such as coaching, and most had had informal mediation experience in day-to-day management, though personal attributes, commitment and appreciation of the intended role were set as being perquisite over relevant previous experience.

Foundation training emphasized practical intervention, exposing trainees to a wide range of tools and mediation techniques, and incorporated a written assignment. Candidates are assessed as passing or failing the training, as a part of a wider programme to achieve their accreditation as mentors.

The mediation capability is managed by the 'Practice support team at work' in liaison with other HR functions, which provides a centre of excellence in DR, oversees the recruitment, supervision and development of mediators, and matches mediators to internal clients. Tandem mediation is used and believed to be best practice.

Since its creation, the team has built up a strong record of successful case resolutions. Varied matters have been brought to mediation, including bullying and harassment, allegations of discrimination and unfair treatment. The team has also been effective in helping resolve differences of view that had led to a grievance, such as arbitrating on a difference of perception of what constitutes 'bullying' as opposed to 'strong management', and whether a manager's apparent reluctance to consider a team member's request for flexible working was in fact discriminatory.

Now with just over two years' experience, the team responds to numerous requests from HR managers for mediator intervention each week, and is now preparing to expand the scope of its work to include team mediation (which Jackie supported) and championing the use of mediation across the organization.

The team has also been proactive in obtaining recommendations for some learning from its mediators' experiences being incorporated into leadership training, and observes that reports of 'Golden Hour' DR are now coming to its attention.

TRAINING AND DEVELOPMENT FOR EVERYONE

The role that front-line managers, HR and other representatives of an organization can play in preventing or containing conflict is rightly a focus for this chapter. However, we shouldn't forget that those who become embroiled in a dispute are those who are likely to be closest to its causes, may be most aware of common conflict triggers for themselves, and are uniquely positioned to decide how they wish a dispute to end. Hence, in discussing conflict prevention, it's very relevant to consider what can reasonably be done to help individuals manage potential conflict triggers and to be able to exercise self-control when disagreements with other individuals (or with the organization) first arise.

Basic training that addresses these matters is relevant for anyone. The scope of such training might include awareness of when emotion rather than clear thinking is driving motivation, being able to think through the consequences of allowing a dispute to continue growing, and learning techniques for maintaining self-restraint. As we saw earlier, a common condition pre-empting angry exchanges and unease is unmanaged inner conflict. Individuals may be able to contain this for a significant period of time before their frustration builds to a point where strong and often seemingly irrational emotion takes over. Individuals may benefit from knowing how to vent their frustrations in a more controlled way, whilst improving their prospects for impressing their concerns on others.

Managers too play an important part in allowing inner conflicts to be worked through, by recognizing what demotivates individuals and acting to counter this. For example, if it's clear that an individual feels undervalued because his or her suggestions are constantly being rebuffed, a manager might seek to demonstrate that he or she has listened and, when practical, been ready to put forward proposals made by the individual.

The *Thought Pattern Critiquing*, *No-send Letter* and *Volcano* techniques described in Appendix 2 might be suggested as ways for controlling how emotion is channelled. However, an important caveat is that these are merely suggestions, and ones that might not be relevant where behavioural responses are prompted by underlying psychiatric disorders. Individuals shouldn't feel under pressure to avoid expressing how they feel or raising a complaint when appropriate because they perceive that the organization may criticize them for putting into practice what they've learnt. Rather, training should give reassurance that it's ok to come forward when a dispute is emerging without fear of being marked down for doing so.

Ideally, training of a similar scope to that given to managers would be provided for every individual. In practice, this may often not be possible. As an alternative, awareness briefings might be encouraged, perhaps incorporated into team meetings, supported by one-to-one coaching or other development support provided by an individual's line manager. If HR or Learning and Development professional-led 'road show' briefings aren't possible, managers may need to be shown how to deliver this basic level of training, in turn helping to consolidate their own learning. Similar content should also be included in company induction programmes.

Self-containment of conflict

The seeds of conflict may often take time to germinate and reach a point where a public expression of discontent becomes unavoidable, for example if a manager's ideas are continually ignored in meetings or when an individual becomes increasingly aware that his or her hard efforts make no difference to the way he or she is regarded by a manager. As we've mentioned, it's 'the curse of the strong' that ultimately results in the greatest harm for an originator, not untypically predicating a breakdown in their mental health (Cantopher, 2003).

The composite frustrations that lead to such crises can rarely be aired easily without fear of being further side-lined, especially if the topic of complaint is applied against a group of senior colleagues and thought difficult to prove with a one-person defence. When a matter can't be borne any further, the intensity of the complaint can come as a surprise to the organization (eg, when an accusation of systematic sexual discrimination is made known), to the colleagues who are the subject of the grievance (eg, for undermining self-esteem as a result of incessant teasing) and to the complainants themselves (eg, in coming to realize that they don't have quite the thick skin they believed they had).

For individuals who feel victimized, knowing that they have open access to a listening ear – someone in whom they can confide without fear of launching an inevitable formal complaint – can be sufficient for them to determine a different tack. Such counsel may also possibly allow individuals to feel that they've been able to say how they feel to a representative of the organization (although a coach may often be a preferred point of contact for such conversations and not able to play this role). Managers especially often find themselves in an isolated position, without an obvious 'professional friend' to turn to.

By initiating such a dialogue, an opportunity is created for progress to be monitored and necessary intervention to be recommended before the matter overcomes the individual's capability to cope. However, for such intervention to work, individuals bringing a complaint must be able to recognize when they're fighting a losing battle by continuing to try to deal with their frustrations alone. This requires honest self-appraisal and (for many) an ability to resist the temptation to allow personal pride to stand in the way of seeking counsel.

Even before considering talking through an issue, individuals can help themselves by recognizing the early indicators of tension and taking steps to contain its effects. A certain level of stress may be needed to motivate and excite us, but too much pushes us beyond a point at which we continue to operate effectively.

Potential indicators of excessive stress include feeling constantly frustrated, unable to relax, being short-tempered and anxious. Repeated physical symptoms such as indigestion, headaches, tiredness and an abnormal appetite may signal the same. People who manage stress well:

- recognize and control mounting pressures;
- practise regular relaxation;
- sleep, eat and exercise well;
- react to stress in a constructive rather than uncontrolled or emotional way;
- use mental and physical tension-busters when they feel under pressure;
- regularly ask themselves, 'What's the worst that can happen?';
- have a good work–life balance;
- remain assertive;
- have good support networks;
- are organized;
- think positively.

A coach may work with an individual to help identify what serves as stress indicators for them, along with working through alternatives to succumbing to unhealthy pressures.

SUPERVISION FOR IN-HOUSE MEDIATORS

Supervision has been widely accepted as being essential for protecting both client and practitioner interests in a variety of fields, notably in what might be called the 'helping professions', such as psychotherapy and coaching. Various definitions of what supervision is have been proposed, of which our favourite is one offered by Nancy Kline (1998) in her wonderful book, *Time To Think*:

'Supervision is an opportunity to bring someone back to their own mind, to show them how good they can be.'

The role involves providing professional support to help a practitioner prepare for conversations with clients, as well as to help ensure that no individual comes to harm, including practitioners themselves. The process involves considering an individual's continuing professional development and encourages them to routinely engage in reflective practice, develop self-insight and build their capability through training and live practice. Of course this needs to respect all parties' confidentiality and so need not identify individuals by name or refer to specific details as opposed to a generalized scenario.

We believe that there is a place for supervision of CM practitioners, and suggest that this is a matter that should be given careful attention when implementing a CM strategy. Supervisors should be interested in achieving positive outcomes for the disputes that concern their mediator clients, as well as helping mediators to develop their professional practice.

As with the sourcing of intermediaries, supervisors may either be recruited from outside of an organization or grown internally. Similar skill-sets and personal characteristics to those described above apply to supervisors, recognizing that they may also act as mentors and coaches in their own right.

Supervisors shouldn't be considered to be 'above' the individual they are supervising or empowered to direct them. Rather, their role should be to offer the benefit of their experience and the ability to take a *meta view* of an intermediary's current needs.

RESOURCING THE CONFLICT MANAGEMENT FUNCTION

Disputes that escalate outside of the local management domain may make significant calls on specialist human resources, whose time may come at a high price. Strategy needs to ensure that these are only called upon when relevant and, when they are, that they are used effectively. In short, this means that the right people are called upon to perform the right tasks at the right time.

Involving appropriately skilled third parties and choosing the intervention that offers the best prospect for concluding a dispute satisfactorily and quickly may save significant time, money and energy. It therefore makes sense to put in place rigorous criteria for choosing who and what should be brought into play when a dispute becomes formalized. Since in our definition a 'third party' may include internal staff, this also involves considering how to build and resource an in-house CM capability.

Sourcing options

It may not always be easy to recognize when an intervention other than mediation is more appropriate, such as a referral to a coach, counsellor, medical/welfare officer or occupational health specialist.

Intermediaries must resist the temptation to delay suggesting referrals, even though they might be persuaded that it is in the best interests of those involved in the dispute. This can be especially hard for externally recruited mediators or those who perform a role internally as an important part of their job specification. In both cases, they might see referral as an act of failure on their part rather than a strength for suggesting the most appropriate action.

In the case of externally recruited mediators, there may be an additional motivation to maximize their revenue from an assignment, as well as to position themselves for future work by being seen as having led a 'successful' resolution. Both issues raise questions about the recruitment and the role description of mediators (whether internal or externally sourced), as well as the ethical code that they adhere to and the supervision that they receive.

Three options are available for sourcing a conflict management function:

1. outsourcing;
2. building an in-house capability; and
3. a combination of the two.

Outsourcing involves selecting and engaging suitable suppliers; building an in-house capability also typically involves a recruitment and engagement process, but is additionally likely to involve training and ongoing support for those who take on this role. Combining the two approaches requires thinking about which criteria might normally guide selection choices when considering how to resource mediation for a particular dispute. A range of factors may favour a choice of approach; see Table 10.1.

Table 10.1   Sourcing options compared

Outsourcing	**In-sourcing**	**Mixed sourcing**
Intermediaries may be perceived as being more independent than in-house mediators	Familiarity with the organization may be an advantage, though not in all circumstances	In co-mediation, any potential commercial interests of external mediators may be kept in check, whilst the dialogue may still benefit from the advantages that outsourcing can offer

External mediators practice their profession more-or-less continually

Mediation offers a professional development option for interested individuals

External experience and internal knowledge may provide complementary benefit

Mediators can bring insights and drawn on experiences from mediating in diverse environments and within different organizations

Using in-house resources may often be less expensive than outsourcing

Disputing parties may perceive that their organization is doing all that it reasonably can to find a resolution by dedicating appropriate resources in the DR process

Using external mediators doesn't require in-house specialists to take time away from other duties

Mediation skills may be applied in a range of ways that offer benefit to the business (eg, in commercial negotiation, project management, coaching)

Organizations don't need to sustain ongoing support and development for in-house mediators, when there are few if any disputes for them to broker

Outsourcing offers a high degree of flexibility in the choice of mediator personality, skills, experience, and reach (in terms of the numbers of intermediaries who may need to be engaged at any one time to meet demand and their geographical bases)

Mediators should be fully familiar with an organization's grievance procedures, ADR guidelines, etc

Internal resources may undertake preliminary private discussions with each of the disputing parties, precluding the need (and expense) for external parties to do this

Mediators are less likely to be known to the disputing parties and the paths of each may be unlikely to cross again (eg, in a future manager-to-subordinate role)

Commercial and other potential vested interests are much less likely to affect a mediator's motivation

A hybrid approach may maximize organizational learning

Mediators may be more experienced in facilitating disputes between senior managers, and both be comfortable operating at this level as well as being more readily accepted by the disputing parties than might a peer level or more junior in-house intermediary

Mediators may be more likely to suggest backing away from a mediation engagement if they don't feel that they are suitably matched for the task

> The personalities and mediation styles of mediators are likely to be known, assisting with matching decisions (although of course, the personalities and styles of external intermediaries who are regularly called upon will become known over time). Awareness of local politics, organization-speak and culture may be an advantage

These highlight a number of important matters for consideration: for example, the question of suitable matching of personalities. Individuals are likely to share a better chemistry with some people than with others and this of course applies to relationships between the parties involved in the dispute, including intermediaries. It may therefore be an advantage to be able to propose a diverse range of candidate profiles for mediation – to match 'horses for courses'.

Matching isn't an exact science, especially since there will not be an opportunity for the chemistry of a relationship to be tested before a mediator is engaged. Similarly, the disputing parties may have different ideas about their preferred candidate, and so a decision may need to be taken on their behalf that attempts to compromise their preferences, perhaps through co-mediation. Nevertheless, mediator selection can usually be made against broad categories – male or female, age and experience, ethnicity, level of the intermediary within the organization (if drawn from the in-house pool), loud and outgoing or calm and measured, and the like.

Whether a decision is taken to in-source, outsource or mix the two may depend on the specific nature of a dispute, as well as the more general preferences of an organization. We don't believe that a 'one size fits all' approach is appropriate, and therefore recommend that organizations should be ready to call upon known and trusted external resources when required, but may also want to consider building up an in-house capability. The following questions might help in making their decision:

- Does the nature of the dispute suggest a need for particular specialist intervention (eg, if discriminatory bias is alleged)?
- Are the disputing parties known to potential mediators with whom they might be matched, or otherwise be likely to come into regular contact with them in future?

- What type of intervention (or mix of interventions) is most likely to be appropriate for the dispute (coaching, arbitration, evaluative mediation, etc)?
- What sourcing preferences (if any) have been stated by either of the disputing parties?
- What budget can be made available for attempting resolution?
- What is the likely cost for the organization of not attempting resolution?
- What is the nature of the working relationship/levels of the individuals involved?
- Where are the disputing parties and potential intermediaries physically located?
- Should co-mediation be favoured over the involvement of a single intermediary?
- What are the likely business impacts for taking in-house mediators away from their other activities?
- How might the disputing parties perceive the relative independence of an in-house intermediary versus an external one?
- How ready are the disputing parties likely to be to work with an external versus an in-house intermediary?

There may not be right or wrong answers to these questions, not least when dealing with unknowns. However, when considered together, a reasoned judgement on which seems the most appropriate sourcing option should emerge.

Selecting and contracting intermediaries

Given our previous discussion, it shouldn't be a surprise that effective recruitment is essential for getting the right people engaged for dispute resolution. Whilst there are also differences, a range of similar criteria apply for selecting mediators irrespective of whether they are sourced internally or externally. In the case of the latter, greater attention may be given to available experience rather than the potential to develop as mediators, and of course commercial terms and conditions must be negotiated.

Seeking suppliers

A search for possible suppliers might involve scanning personnel services directories, tracking down professional body membership lists, liaising with other organizations to gain referrals, carrying out online searches and tendering/advertising for expressions of interest.[1]

In spite of requiring mediator-by-mediator contracting, lone operating specialists should be given fair consideration when selecting external suppliers, especially since most operate without the 'sell-on' targets that may be expected of employees of larger practices.

Prospecting for would-be internal mediators may take the form of advertising requirements to managers, allowing them the discretion to pass the information on to relevant members of their teams as they see fit, as well as presenting themselves as possible candidates if they so wish. Since recruits may not necessarily have had any prior mediation experience, it's important that they are given some idea of what may be expected of them should they be selected for the role.

We've found that including a simple one-page role profile alongside an advertisement or information distributed to managers can greatly assist with filling in any gaps in knowledge, and serve to sell the benefits of enlisting as a mediator as well as making clear the commitment and personal qualities expected of applicants. A possible role profile ('person specification') template is included in Appendix 2.

In larger organizations, one further advantage of cascading an advertisement is that the potentially high volume of applications may be avoided had the advertisement been published more generally, restricting applications to individuals who managers feel may be suitable for the role and those whose involvement would be consistent with their own career objectives. Involving managers in this way also helps to ensure that they are ready to give permission for individuals to take time out for training and mediation tasks, although this commitment must be confirmed before individuals are recruited into the in-house mediator pool.

Recruitment

Recruitment involves sifting through the applications of potential candidates and interviewing those who are shortlisted. Formal presentations, reference checking and other contracting meetings may be necessary when recruiting external suppliers.

Recruitment should seek to probe for evidence to confirm that what individuals say is true, for example, by presenting candidates with scenarios they may need to address or using brief role-play exercises. Potential topics that might be explored during recruitment interviews, for external and in-house candidates, include the following.

For external suppliers:

- previous experience and track record;
- personal attributes;
- mediation (coaching, etc) style;
- responses to a variety of example challenges that may be faced in mediation;

- accreditations/membership of relevant professional bodies;
- previous training;
- evidence of commitment to continuous professional development;
- core values/commitment to a published ethical code;
- perceptions of own suitability for acting as a mediator in different circumstances (including types of mediation to which they don't feel themselves to be most suitable; eg, individuals who don't have an awareness of relevant legislation, case precedents and tribunal processes are unlikely to have appropriate experience to conduct evaluative mediation);
- knowledge of different types of interventions for DR, and opinions on the relative advantages and disadvantages of each according to the needs of different types of dispute;
- understanding of the particular requirements of the role for which they are presenting themselves (eg, the nature and challenges of conflict coaching when compared with other uses of coaching);
- awareness of techniques that may be used in mediation;
- suggested approach for structuring mediation;
- ability to identify when it's appropriate to close-out on their intervention, as well as being able to pass and receive the baton to and from others who are involved in a DR process;
- attitudes towards co-mediation, including working with other organizations and with other intermediaries within the customer organization.

For in-house recruits:

- motivation for applying for the role;
- personal attributes;
- how the role will support personal development or career objectives;
- what impact taking time out for training and mediation activity will have on other work (eg, how they will manage competing work priorities);
- previous experience (if any) with mediation or any involvement in managing conflict (which may include having been a party to a dispute themselves);
- appreciation of the personal attributes expected of the role, and evidence offered and observed that they possess these;
- appreciation of the skills required for performing the role, with evidence of any that they feel they can already offer;
- enthusiasm and passion for taking on the role;
- thoughts about potential challenges facing a mediator and what the reality of mediation involves.

Enthusiasm and passion are especially important if commitment is to be sustained beyond receiving training and being able to add mediation to an internal CV. A clear desire to take on the role is all the more critical if opportunities for actually practising mediation may be limited.

Selection also involves deciding whether to continue to re-engage mediators over time. This decision may be guided by the learning gained through experience, which may indicate mediators' suitability or otherwise for particular types of intervention. Whilst a track record of continually failing to achieve resolution might raise questions on whether the intermediaries themselves are responsible for this, the number of disputes that have been successfully settled and sustained shouldn't on its own be a reason for disqualifying or favouring using an intermediary in future engagements, useful though such information may be.

Engagement

Once selected, individuals need to be engaged. In the case of external resources, this may involve a process of relationship building, potentially over a significant period in which the supplier's services aren't called upon. While occasional face-to-face or at least verbal contact is desirable, such interaction may often be limited to brief telephone conversations, perhaps once every three months or so. Subscribing to supplier news mailings, if offered, and participating in any cross-organization networking activities that they host may help further build relationships.

In the case of in-house resources, a more concerted effort may be required over time to support, inform and maintain skills and motivation amongst newly selected mediators. Training is likely to be required to build the necessary skills and for new mediators to become familiar with the DR philosophy and procedures of the organization.

At an early stage of engagement, contracts need to be put in place with the individuals who are expected to act as intermediaries (or with their organizations). By 'contract', here we mean the actual operating agreement for a mediator or coach, both with the customer sponsor and with the individuals he or she will work with, rather than the commercial arrangement, which should already have been agreed. An example contract may be downloaded from the website that supports this book (www.managingconflictatwork.com), along with a wide range of other easily adapted templates. Mediators will, of course, undergo a similar contracting process with the parties involved in each dispute they engage with, as we discussed earlier.

Generally, we recommend engaging more than one external supplier under framework contracts that allow assignments to be undertaken at short notice. Engaging a mix of suppliers increases the base of experience and approaches to mediation, drawing on the specific skills and the wider resource pool offered by a mix of organizations.

As an example, looking to a legal practice may be most appropriate when sourcing evaluative mediation, whereas an individual or organization that specializes in conflict coaching may be more appropriate when sourcing coaching needs. There may also be a commercial advantage in suppliers knowing that they don't have an exclusive partnership with an organization, although buyers of mediation services should also remember that it's in their interests to maintain and build strong two-way relationships with their partners. This may justify a policy of restricting the number of external suppliers engaged, at least initially.

Whilst local procurement policy may dictate otherwise, in the absence of any fixed procedure we generally recommend against designating particular organizations as 'preferred suppliers', which can act as a barrier for engaging other specialists at short notice when required. We also recommend against engaging organizations on a retainer basis, at least until it's clear what the likely demand for their services may be. This implies a need to review commercial relationships periodically, perhaps annually. We suggest that this might usefully be built into the task of evaluating the effectiveness of a CM strategy.

Briefing contractors and suppliers

Similar codes of behaviour might be expected from individuals who aren't on the staff roll of an organization but who form a part of its extended team, such as suppliers, lone contractors and partners. The established cultures, rituals and political structures may be less of an influence for these, but many will want to conform to the organization's ways of operating so as to avoid jeopardizing the prospect of future engagement.

Whilst it may often not be appropriate or possible to offer training, individuals coming into an organization on this basis should be familiarized with the way in which conflicts should be addressed, given assurance that coming forward with a concern won't prejudice any future engagement with the organization, and made aware of the organization's disciplinary code. In some cases, contracts made with individuals and partners might be used to formalize commitments to adopt the organization's CM policy. Those involved in procurement might be encouraged to be mindful of this when negotiating agreements with suppliers.

Close working partners may even collaborate and 'buddy' with other managers, sharing knowledge of how they deal with conflict in their own organizations. Inviting external providers to any review workshops held for an internal DR team may also facilitate enhanced collaboration and sharing of experience.

Summary

Effective conflict management calls on front-line managers to have sharpened skills for spotting the early signs of emerging disputes, know how to contain mounting conflict and be ready to anticipate the various pitfalls that can unseat the unwary, as well as having well developed emotional intelligence.

Mediators who are called upon to intervene in escalated disputes need to be carefully selected, whether externally supplied or grown in an in-house mediators' pool, whilst their continuing development and supervision need to be properly supported. Mediators should pay attention to managing their own continuing learning, reflecting on their own experiences and those of others.

Note

1. In some countries, including all members of the EU, formal advertising and tendering is required for contracts over a particular value that public sector organizations seek to place.

11

Monitoring and evaluation

MONITORING

It might be easy to play down the need for monitoring, even if its value can be readily recognized. Once a dispute has been resolved, precious time and effort can quickly be turned elsewhere. But by neglecting this task, new problems may be overlooked and opportunities missed for preventing and minimizing unhealthy conflict in future. What's more, inefficient and ineffective aspects of current CM strategy may not come to light unless time is taken to reflect on past experiences. We therefore believe that monitoring the aftermath of individual disputes and routinely evaluating the performance of a CM strategy should be an integral part of managing and deserving of serious attention.

Monitoring the aftermath of a dispute

Disputes that don't reach a clear point of agreement may generate fall-out of their own, including those that proceed to litigation and circumstances in which one party emerges as being unsuccessful in defending his or her case.

Individuals who feel deflated, humiliated or seriously wronged in their attempts to seek justice may react in a variety of ways. Whether they are stunned and subdued or privately remain determined to inflict revenge on their aggressor, careful staff management will be required to help them recover motivation and feel reintegrated into the organization.

Even when it's practical, transferring individuals into other teams or relocating them to other offices should be considered with caution. The individual may not want to make the move; a forced or encouraged move could be construed as victimization or as a form of punishment. However, when a move is agreed or requested, it's wise to get the affected person's written consent, to prevent the possibility of him or her turning this against the organization in future.

Where a team member's allegation of unfair treatment by a manager has been upheld, a real risk for later reprisal may exist if the two remain in a direct reporting-line relationship. Alternatively, a manager may feel disempowered and unsure about how to manage the individual concerned. In such cases, any sense of victory felt by the team member following a court's decision may be short lived, once he or she has come to terms with the need to continue working for his or her manager on a daily basis. This is one such circumstance where particular effort might be made to help explore and (when appropriate) facilitate a transfer to separate the individuals concerned. Where this isn't possible (for example, as is often the case in small organizations), it may need to be made clear to the manager that any out-of-the-norm judgements made against the individual must be capable of being properly justified (for example, suddenly marking him or her down in an appraisal when he or she had previously been consistently identified as a star performer).

For both parties, having a third party who would listen to any fall-out concerns and help identify constructive ways for dealing with them may help limit continuing friction and minimize the prospect for uncontrolled outbursts. Offering access to a coach might be appropriate in such circumstances.

Individuals may feel more motivated to put into practice what they've committed themselves to through the discipline of reporting back on their progress, if only informally. A mediator might invite the individual to send them an e-mail once they have undertaken an action, or suggest: 'If you wish, you can feed back to me after three months.'

Communicating with stakeholders

Once stakeholders are engaged, it's important to ensure that they are kept aware of the decisions made during a DR process (including advising on the final outcome). Stakeholder expectations may need to be managed throughout the process, especially if individuals have high expectations of what might be achieved.

In managing conflict, it's important to gauge when to inform particular stakeholders, and what level of information to provide to them. Many aspects of what is discussed between the disputing parties must remain private.

Managing the fall-out from publicly escalated disputes

Despite what some aggrieved employees might wish, relatively few disputes that escalate to litigation receive publicity. The news media are generally only interested in reporting cases that represent interesting stories, rather than covering the type of run-of-the-mill disputes that form the vast majority of cases that come before tribunals. Cases that involve a 'big name', lead to record-beating compensation awards or concern organizations that have already established a high profile for having to defend allegations of discrimination, claims of serious abuse of power in a public office and the like, are most likely to receive attention.

Unless a case is likely to become newsworthy, relatively little effort should normally be required to contain the effects of potentially negative publicity. Nevertheless, the possibility of information entering the public domain and especially being widely broadcast within the organization, its supplier and customer networks can never be discounted. This is all the more the case now that news can be communicated in real time via a wide variety of outlets – from YouTube to social networking blogs – and doesn't require the resources of a large media organization to do so.

False information can easily be disseminated with striking speed, and be quickly taken as being truthful. The potential for damaging relationships built on trust and, at worst, to sour the reputation of an organization as a whole, are real. It's therefore important for organizations to monitor what may be said about cases that have entered the public domain, and to be ready to correct any misinformation.

Press officers and trusted IT technicians may need to be involved in this task (for example, we've encountered several situations in which IT specialists have been able to detect damaging e-mails being exchanged between two individuals across a company's e-mail system, allowing prompt corrective action to be taken). Irrespective of the likely potential for a dispute to attract publicity, managers and others who may be approached by a journalist may need guidance in what they could be tricked into saying. In the extreme situation where a case achieves a high profile, training in press handling techniques or appointing a media-savvy spokesperson to comment on the case on behalf of the organization may be needed to minimize the risk of others making potentially damaging gaffes.

EVALUATING CM STRATEGY

What to evaluate?

What should be evaluated when considering whether the current CM strategy is hitting the right notes? We suggest that the following might be taken as key lines for inquiry:

- What are the impacts of the CM strategy?
- Has greater impact been felt at earlier as well as later stages of a dispute's lifecycle (compared to previous experiences)?
- How effective has training for front-line managers been? To what extent has this translated into action?
- How effective are different types of ADR intervention proving to be and in which circumstances?
- Are the most effective sourcing arrangements in place?
- Does the supply of mediators, coaches and others match forecast demand?
- What useful insights have been gained from the practice of CM? How could these give wider benefit to the organization?
- Is the current CM strategy still relevant?

This list is not exhaustive, but includes the more common areas of interest that might be considered. Let's briefly consider each in turn.

What are the impacts of the conflict management strategy?

By considering the original drivers and objectives for a new CM strategy, it should normally not be too difficult to identify the types of indicators that suggest evidence of impact. For example, in assessing an objective for CM training to better equip front-line managers to handle emerging disputes, possible indicators of success might include a reduced number of disputes being escalated into formal complaints, higher levels of staff satisfaction and anecdotal observations of more confident and effective management being demonstrated when disputes do arise. Of course such indicators aren't proof on their own – improving staff satisfaction may result from a range of different factors. Some attempt therefore needs to be made to distinguish what has changed as a result of the actions taken to implement the strategy (which we'll discuss in a short while).

It should normally be possible to set down quite robust objectives when defining strategy, although these don't have to be specified in terms of achieving precisely measured results. Indeed, when it comes to investigating what has actually happened, some of the positive consequences that are revealed may be quite unexpected: even the most diligent strategists and planners don't always anticipate every eventuality.

Has greater impact been felt at earlier as well as later stages of a dispute's lifecycle (compared to previous experiences)?

This line of inquiry can also be explored by referring to any pre-defined objectives for improving on CM performance or simply by comparing against previously collected metrics (eg, the number of grievance investigations that escalate to appeal within a set period).

Evaluation might focus on changes that indicate a trend toward achieving the end goals of a strategy, even if any significant variations over time may take a while to be achieved. Evidence that managers are trying to resolve disputes locally, for example, might be a reason to be encouraged even if the number of cases referred for investigation hasn't fallen substantially since launching manager training. In this example, possible indicators of a changing mindset amongst managers might include an increase in the proportion of approaches made by managers seeking advice on how to manage difficult issues relative to those who want to pass on this responsibility at a much earlier stage; or reference to actions a manager has undertaken to attempt resolution by those who are embroiled in an escalated dispute, and managers showing an appetite for further CM training.

In general, CM strategy should aim to achieve a higher level of lasting resolution for conflicts that conclude at an earlier stage than those that escalate, as well as to produce a reduction in the overall number of unhealthy disputes that see the light of day. If successful, there should be fewer cases reaching escalation, although care may need to be taken in interpreting whether successful resolution of those that do should be measured in terms of comparing the current and past percentages of 'cases solved'. A reason for urging caution here is that those disputes that do escalate are likely to include a higher level of complexity or difficulty than might previously have been the case. If all is going to plan, front-line managers should be in direct control of what might be considered 'more normal' cases.

How effective has training for front-line managers been?

If benefits of the sort described above are being seen, then it might reasonably be assumed that whatever training has been rolled out has been worthwhile. In such cases, a sequence of events, represented in Donald Kirkpatrick's *Four levels* model for evaluating training (Kirkpatrick, 1998) – consolidation of learning, mindset or behavioural change and results for an organization – should typically be seen. In reality, what causes individuals to put what they learn into practice is not always this straightforward, whilst a wide range of factors can influence what are identified as business results.

Whether or not positive results have been achieved, this doesn't imply that the training approach that has been adopted is necessarily the most effective. Evaluation might seek to explore which aspects of training proved to be most useful from the perspectives of trainees and others and, where possible, to compare the experiences of individuals trained using one approach with another.

Attention might also be given to how training has been integrated with performance appraisal, objective setting and other forms of personal development activity, and to assess any significance of the time that has elapsed since individuals were initially trained. This latter point is particularly important as a measure of whether learnt approaches for managing conflict endure over the longer term.

How effective are different types of ADR intervention proving to be?

Not all types of ADR will suit every individual or case. However, where alternative interventions are regularly being used – either singularly or in combination – an attempt can be made to assess which are proving to be most successful in different circumstances.

Are the most effective sourcing arrangements in place?

Determining which CM arrangements are proving to be most effective for particular types of dispute or in specific circumstances isn't straightforward. Unlike with many other supplier or outsourced contracts, an equivalent of a service level agreement will rarely exist for mediators, coaches and arbitrators.

The generally confidential nature of their work precludes the opportunity to monitor the competence of their practice, whilst merely counting the number of disputes that individuals resolve relative to those that escalate or end unsatisfactorily is not too informative either. Certainly just counting engagements that don't lead to further escalation as a measure of success should be avoided – as we've seen, satisfactory resolution should mean a lasting resolution and the ability of both parties to move on from their past differences.

Similar difficulties attach to assessing the effectiveness of in-house mediation and coaching, although examining the prevalence of case outcomes over time may help make some sense of performance. What may more readily be evaluated are individuals' responses to different types of intervention and their stated preferences for internal and external sourcing. Participants' views may also be sought on whether or not any extensions to mediation proposed by a mediator (as well as early close-out) were thought to be appropriate, as a means of checking whether a mediator's commercial or managerial interests might be prompting the proposals they make.

Does the supply of mediators, coaches and others match forecast demand?

The expected demand for dispute resolution services and the ability to match the supply of suitably qualified specialists to meet this need should be routinely assessed.

Recent trends in demand, in-house mediator or coach turnover, perceptions of using in-house and external suppliers, and awareness of plans for organizational growth or contraction are all relevant inputs for forecasting; however, the influences of other factors need to be taken into consideration too. These include:

- the flexibility of external suppliers in responding to short-term requirements;
- the likely incidence of *de facto* complaints resulting from an expected organizational change or external stimulus; for example, the demand for employment tribunals in the UK increased by nearly 50 per cent in 2008–09, the year following the onset of the recession (EAT, 2009);
- the motivation and commitment of in-house mediators/coaches to continuous professional development (and the threat of losing current skill levels if individuals have insufficient exposure to live practice);
- in-house practitioners resigning their positions; and
- unexpected calls made on in-house practitioners (for example, secondments and postings to manage important new initiatives).

We believe that in general it's preferable to slightly over-plan supply for demand by maintaining framework agreements with a range of external suppliers and similarly keeping a slightly larger in-house pool of specialists than is thought to be necessary. This approach should give flexibility for matching suitable mediators and coaches to particular cases and prevent against the risk of prolonged unavailability of practitioners to intervene in a dispute when required.

What useful insights have been gained from the practice of conflict management?

Learning should be an important part of every evaluation study. Lessons learnt may be fed back by any stakeholder of CM, although those responsible for overseeing how effectively the process works will normally be in the best position to judge what is most likely to be useful to apply in future.

Is the current conflict management strategy still relevant?

An evaluation study that answers the types of questions explored above should allow for an informed decision to be taken on whether the existing strategy needs to be adapted in any way. However, consideration also needs to be given to the continuing relevance of a strategy within the context of wider corporate and people management strategies. This means that it makes sense to periodically review CM strategy and its alignment with current business priorities.

How to evaluate

We've already suggested a number of approaches that can be brought into play in evaluation – comparing current experience with previous performance or predefined objectives described in a CM strategy; control group comparisons (such as assessing the effectiveness of alternative training provided to different groups of managers); and looking for indicators of impact.

Each of these has their place in analysis, but evaluation also needs to explain why a particular conclusion has been reached (for example, why we can be confident that what appears to be the positive impact of a new process does in fact result from that process as opposed to other factors). To achieve this, we suggest that evaluation is approached in a similar way to a criminal investigation. The evaluator's task is to gather evidence to support an explanation and to be able to present an argument that holds water.

An approach that is especially helpful for presenting compelling arguments is the Pyramid Principle model, developed by Barbara Minto (2001) for McKinsey & Company. A simplified form of the approach is shown in Figure 11.1.

We also favour using a simple Impact Chain diagram to illustrate the cause-and-effect relationships between different outcomes of a CM strategy; see Figure 11.2.

Both the pyramid and impact chain diagrams lend themselves to simple executive reporting. In both cases, associated evidence for each pyramid element/point in a chain can be referenced and detailed in a separate document. Of course, this should also provide a rich source of representative stories to further describe the benefits and experiences revealed by the evaluation. Even isolated examples are useful: as one commentator has said, 'When an organization's leaders stand up and say "We had a really good year, meeting or exceeding our business goals", then I know that the [training] has been successful' (Tobin, 1998).

The quality of the data used in analysis obviously has a critical part to play if a compelling argument is to be built around it. Meaningful data can usually quite quickly be amassed through well-planned interviews and focus group workshops involving participants of previous disputes and other key stakeholders who may be well positioned to offer their observations. If mixed sourcing is

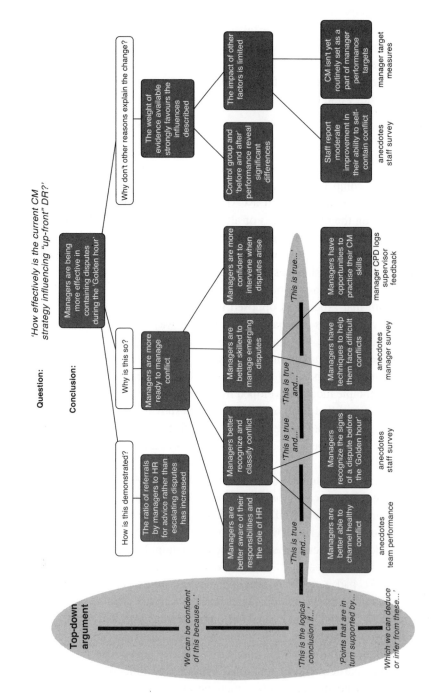

Question: 'How effectively is the current CM strategy influencing "up-front" DR?'

Conclusion: Managers are being more effective in containing disputes during the 'Golden hour'

Why don't other reasons explain the change?

The weight of evidence available strongly favours the influences described

The impact of other factors is limited

Control group and 'before and after' performance reveal significant differences

Staff report moderate improvement in their ability to self-contain conflict

anecdotes
staff survey

CM isn't yet routinely set as a part of manager performance targets

manager target measures

Why is this so?

Managers are more ready to manage conflict

Managers are more confident to intervene when disputes arise

Managers are better skilled to manage emerging disputes

Managers have techniques to help them face difficult conflicts

anecdotes
manager survey

Managers have opportunities to practise their CM skills

manager CPD logs
supervisor feedback

Managers better recognize and classify conflict

Managers recognize the signs of a dispute before the 'Golden hour'

anecdotes
staff survey

Managers are better able to channel healthy conflict

anecdotes
team performance

How is this demonstrated?

The ratio of referrals by managers to HR for advice rather than escalating disputes has increased

Managers are better aware of their responsibilities and the role of HR

Top-down argument

'We can be confident of this because...'

'This is the logical conclusion if...'

'Points that are in turn supported by...'

'Which we can deduce or infer from these...'

'This is true and...'

'This is true and...'

'This is true and...'

'This is true and...'

'This is true and...'

Figure 11.1 Pyramid argument

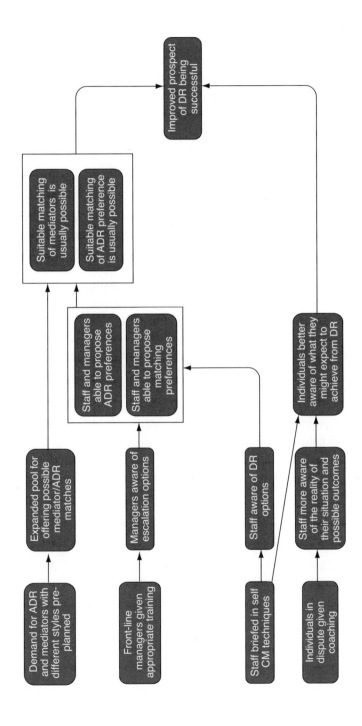

Figure 11.2 Impact chain

used, workshops or feedback dialogues may usefully include both external and internal practitioners, maximizing the opportunity for shared learning.

The same methods for collecting evidence might be used with sample groups of managers who have received CM training. We recommend live interaction with interviewees rather than questionnaire surveys, which don't offer the flexibility to probe to understand how an individual justifies his or her thinking. However, if a survey is the only practicable means for gathering feedback, consider using just two questions (an approach frequently used for assessing how customers value a company): 'How likely on a scale of 1 to10 are you to recommend [mediation]?' and, 'Why did you score as you did?'

It's the second question that should prove most revealing, giving a respondent total discretion to comment on any aspect of their experience, but inviting them to think about their response. This technique, based on the *Net Promoter's Score* developed by Fred Reichheld (2006) can be sufficiently powerful to extract a wide range of informative qualitative data than might otherwise be achieved using a lengthy questionnaire.

The *Pyramid Principle* approach can then be used to construct an argument. To be compelling, an argument needs to be able to stand against a counter argument – why things are the way we believe them to be rather than for some other reason. It's therefore necessary for an evaluator to play the devil's advocate in seeking out evidence and to ask the questions to prompt those whose views are sought to rationalize their thinking – 'what else?', 'why not…?', and 'why this?', being amongst them.

Hence, if a staff satisfaction survey suggests that fewer individuals are feeling aggrieved than in a previous period, evaluation needs to explore whether this is due to new styles of management, a revised rewards system, or other changes in the organization, as well as or instead of improved CM. Taken on their own, averaged ratings drawn from such surveys may not reveal a true picture.

COLLECTIVE LEARNING

For an organization, the biggest challenge following evaluation is knowing how to act on what has been learnt. For individuals who want to advocate changes, a bigger challenge may be persuading others that it's worth their while to take notice of new insights gained from an initiative outside of their direct sphere of influence.

In the first instance, agreement must be reached amongst the disputing parties that generalized learning can be reported back to the organization, perhaps in combination with learning arising from other conflict discussions, fairness at work feedback, recommendations to be fed back through training, and the like.

Ideally, such protocols should have been agreed in advance, and left to the discretion of mediators to cover when closing out a dialogue.

Alternatively, individuals may need to be separately consulted shortly after they have been involved in a part of the CM process. This may offer an advantage over incorporating feedback as a part of a dialogue itself, especially if the opportunity for contributing thoughts has to be squeezed into an already busy agenda and may come at the end of an intensely charged session when participants may lack the energy, will or intellectual capacity to give their feedback the attention it deserves.

No one should feel under pressure to complete feedback surveys or answer questions unless they are ready to do so, and any briefing for a mediator to complete evaluation as a part of his or her task should take the form of a guideline rather than being presented as an obligatory part of the process. Being able to judge the right time and place to gather input from participants is critical in ensuring that they give considered responses.

Occasionally, feedback will be volunteered without the need for invitation. In such cases, it's wise to be curious about particularly negative criticism. The motivation for being negatively critical may not be immediately obvious, whilst for feedback to be useful, general perceptions and idle comments need to be properly qualified by probing for the facts and reasoning that lie beyond mere impressions.

Outside of specific disputes, feedback can generally be more easily solicited and opinions may usually be more readily trusted at their face value. As we've already noted, brief interviews and focus group workshops are generally most effective for eliciting meaningful feedback following training courses, as well as for assessing the impacts of learning some time later.

Learning may result from specific observations but may also be gained from structured analysis (such as that supported by the *Pyramid Principle* approach). In either case, the context of what has been learnt and its relevance for taking possible action are important to recognize. For example, if any procedural weakness has been identified during the course of the process of resolving a dispute, this might need to be corrected to improve the effectiveness of future exercises. However, a validation that conflict coaching helps to limit false perceptions for those coming to mediation may simply need to be recorded as mounting evidence for what is already known.

An owner of CM practice who also takes responsibility of capturing and making sense of the relevance of learning should be able to implement changes to CM processes, guidelines and training material content without a need to refer to others. Implementing the lessons learnt then becomes a living process of continuous improvement. However, where it's appropriate to suggest to others that they may benefit from what has been learnt, the task of effecting change is clearly dependent on more than one person recognizing the benefit for taking action. Rather than risking a brush-off from a colleague for having the audacity to suggest that he or she might want to consider a change, it may be tempting just to ignore knowledge sharing altogether. Yet, properly framed and communicated at the appropriate time, a suggestion may be well received and help make a significant difference for another person, training programme or function in the organization.

THE STRATEGIC CONTEXT OF CONFLICT MANAGEMENT

Recent research points out the tangible advantages recognized by organizations that have taken strides to build 'happy' workforces rather than ones that are regularly locked in grievous disagreements. In their book, *What Happy Companies Know* (Baker, Greenberg and Hemingway, 2006), the authors cite evidence that high levels of employee satisfaction translate into greater profitability and productivity.

Amongst the studies they reference, a University of Pennsylvania survey of 3,000 organizations showed that a 10 per cent investment in people yielded more than twice the increase in productivity seen after a similar investment in capital improvements, whilst consistently higher profitability amongst organizations with strong levels of trust, integrity and compassion was revealed by a study conducted by University of Michigan Business School (Baker *et al*, 2006, pp 278–79). For Baker and his colleagues, a 'happy company' is one in which:

> individuals at all levels of authority exhibit a diversity of strengths, constructively work together towards a common goal, find significant meaning and satisfaction in producing and providing high-quality products and services for profit, and through those products and services make a positive difference in the lives of others. (Baker *et al*, 2006, pp 201–02)

Amongst other characteristics, they suggest that happy companies commonly display an energizing spirit, share all-round respect, use constructive language, build supportive relationships, foster a climate of appreciation and balance competitiveness and cooperation. The list continues, but it shouldn't be too difficult to notice that such qualities contrast starkly with those that create ripe conditions for dissent, described in Chapter 1.

Most of the available measures of value that have been reported to date about happy companies relate to commercially-focused organizations. However, it's reasonable to assume that significant benefits should also be observed by public and third sector organizations that adopt the same principles.

The antithesis of an organization whose employees are regularly locked in dispute may well be a 'happy company', and therefore a people management strategy that encourages individuals to feel highly motivated is a good ideal to strive for. Regulatory controls can never be enough to achieve this; invariably, a new recipe is required to bring about a genuine change in mindsets and behaviour.

This notion of developing a target culture is often considered to be a desirable outcome of many people-related strategies (think of the idea of creating a 'coaching culture' as an outcome of training managers in coaching skills, for example), although we believe that the concept of specific cultures is often overstretched. In this case however, 'culture' seems a totally appropriate concept to use – not an isolated 'happy' culture or 'anti-conflict' culture – but one that embraces all of the core values, common purpose and ways of working of an organization.

Conflict management should be a discreet strategic priority; however, the means for instilling change in the way conflicts are responded to across an organization must be a part of a holistic corporate and people management strategy. Ultimately, this should be a concern for all those who lead others. Perhaps this includes you?

Summary

Monitoring the outcomes of mediation and managing the aftermath of any dispute are important tasks to be taken seriously. The latter involves continuing engagement with the stakeholders who have a strong interest in the outcome of a specific dispute, and the former is relevant for the organization as a whole.

The results of evaluation provide collected learning to share for the benefit of others and for strengthening an organization's robustness to unhealthy conflict. Evaluation need not be time-consuming, but the end objectives for carrying out any assessment need to be clear from the outset.

Appendix 1

Conflict management micro-tools

In Chapter 8 we introduced the idea of a 'micro-tool' as being a sharp, quick, to-the-point dialogue, designed to be used in particular situations to help move individuals towards a particular point. Some of our preferred micro-tools are summarized here. Most of them are relevant for virtually any stage of a dispute, in both informal and more formal conversations.

The list of tools we've included doesn't pretend to be exhaustive (you may well want to supplement our suggestions with ones of your own, as well as adapting wording to fit with your own turns of phrase and the language used by others). Neither can we guarantee that applying any of our selections will always produce an intended outcome – unfortunately, real people and situations don't always conform to a perfect pattern! If these work for you or you find others that do, please let us know.

The basics

The seven rules of communication

(A charter for good conflict management practice):

1. Listen (*listen* individuals out rather than talk them out).
2. Empathize.
3. Adopt the appropriate attitude.
4. Be sincere.

5. Respect the dignity of others.
6. Build trust.
7. Show compassion.

Five 'WH' questions

1. 'What?'
2. 'Why?'
3. 'Where?'
4. 'When?'
5. 'Who?'

Socratic questions

(Encouraging others to reflect and find answers for themselves):

'What lies behind your thinking here?'

'What alternative explanations might be given for this?'

'What led you to start from this position?'

'What would be the result if…?'

'How can you be sure about this?'

'What seems to support your thinking?'

'How might this stand up in front of a jury?'

'What attracts you to this line of thinking?'

Direct routes and possible deviations

(Questions that aim to help individuals keep focus and ones that might lead them to stray from finding a resolution.)

Direct routes:

'How did you know that was right?'

'What might you have done differently?'

'What have you done before that helped you reach an understanding?'

'What did you contribute to the situation?'

'What did you learn from that experience?'

'How did you do that?'

'What went well?'

'What else?'

Possible deviations:

'Why did you do that?'

'What should you do next time?'

'What went wrong?'

'Is there anything else?'

'Is there anything you've tried before that led you to an answer?'

'What obstacles will you first need to overcome?'

'Why don't you put this into practice?'

'What's stopping you?'

Conversation management

JAM – 'Just a Minute'

(Or JAMMING – 'Just a micro managerial intervention negating grief'. For use in impromptu conversations or when time is limited):

'What's happening at the moment?'

'What do you want to happen?'

'What's been working?'

'What am I impressed with?' (Give affirmation, eg for the individual raising this.)

'What do you think you need to do now?'

'What is the first step you'll take?'

Structured mediation

1. Set the scene: ask each individual to give their view of the disagreement.

2. Identify desired outcomes: ask each person to say what they believe will bring the dispute to a satisfactory end.

3. Challenge any unrealistic expectations: suggest that these are weighed against the benefits of achieving an earlier and satisfactory (if not perfect) resolution.

4. Invite and (if appropriate) propose areas of common ground, then break down areas of difference. Give affirmation where there are areas of agreement.

5. Invite suggestions about how each individual believes each difference may be resolved, how he or she assesses the practicality of achieving his or her suggestions quickly and highlight common or similar proposals that both can work with.

6. Invite both parties to say whether any of their remaining differences may be met with a compromise or allowed to let lie in the interests of securing a peace. If either party believes that this isn't possible, question how they wish to take the matter forward, exploring options if appropriate.

7. Summarize agreements, commitments and actions. If appropriate, invite both parties to shake hands, and give encouragement and – *very important* – affirmation for the progress that has been made. Ask for commitment that any continuing difference will not be allowed to interfere with relationships with others. Ask if the individuals are content with the way the process has been handled and whether general feedback and learning may be passed on to others.

Objective and outcome setting

'Imagine looking back on this in two years time… What do you think it will look like then?'

'What do you want to do [gain from this]?'

'What do you want/need to happen/achieve?'

'What would be your ideal outcome?'

'What are your priorities looking forward?'

Confirming ground rules

'Do you both agree to respect/accept these ground rules?'

Reflecting and summarizing

(Mirroring language used by participants):
'You said that you would…' (use exact phraseology).

Re-checking the approach as the dialogue proceeds

'Are you finding this approach helpful?' (If the reply is positive, ask: 'What exactly are you finding useful?'; if negative, ask: 'What would you find useful?')

'What do you think is the best way for getting to the bottom of this?'

'Can we approach this in another way?'

Breaking sessions

(Teasing out whether both parties want to continue beyond the planned end of a conversation):

'Is this a good place to end your discussion [today]?'

'Can you place a mental marker of where you are so you can re-engage [tomorrow]?'

(When individuals may be tiring): 'Are you able to focus and do justice to this matter right now?'

Requesting feedback as learning for others

'What's helped [been useful]?'

'Can we share this [learning] with the organization?'

'Do you have any suggestions about how we might feed this back into the organization?'

Exploring meaning

Gathering information

'What are you thinking [when...]?'

'How do you believe this situation arose in the first place?'

'What's your view of how the grievance procedure works?'

'What options have you considered?'

'What have you achieved since we last spoke?'

Where greater clarity is needed on how strongly an individual believes something, using *scaling* can be very powerful (see below).

Exploring a thought chain or idea

'What might [the other party] feel like if this were to happen?'

'What lies behind your thinking?'

Clarifying understanding

(For the questioner and/or the person being questioned):

'I'm not sure I understand how you believe this explains your disagreement. Can you explain this for me?'

'[Your views] should help me appreciate your thinking…'.

'I've heard you say… Please correct me if I've misunderstood' (use the same phraseology as the person/people being spoken to).

'TED-PIE'

(Tell me, Explain to me, Describe to me – Previously, In detail and Exactly):

'Tell me what has brought you here [to this]…'.

'Explain to me what will be useful [what it is you want to achieve]', 'Explain to me how this has come about…'.

'Describe what you are thinking [feeling/experiencing]?', 'What if…? Describe how you'd feel in this case…'.

'Previously, before this began, what was going well?' 'Previously, how was your working relationship?' (Note the emphasis here is on what was *right*, not what's now wrong.)

'On a scale of 1 to 10, how do you feel about [this idea]?'

Channelling emotion

Helping an individual express emotion

'Did you see [name of person]'s reaction?'

'I noticed that when you said…, she appeared annoyed/upset.'

Labelling emotion

'Tell me your grounds for feeling like this?' (Reflect on the emotion.)

'What's the strongest feeling you're experiencing in [the dispute].'

Responding to aggression

'Please try not to shout. This doesn't help me.'

'I know you don't mean to [attack me]… we all have to let off steam at times; however, I'm feeling quite intimidated.'

Challenging assertions and behaviour

Framing challenges

(As invitations rather than as points of view):

'What are you thinking when…?' as opposed to, 'I feel there's something you're not saying.'

'I've noticed you've a dry sense of humour. However, I've also noticed that not everyone appreciates this. Can you bear this in mind?' might be better received than, 'I think your office banter can often overstep the mark and not everyone appreciates it.'

'How have you reached this conclusion? Can we discuss?' may be less aggressive than, 'Didn't you understand what I wanted?'

Challenging convictions

'How can you be sure about/know this?'

'What seems to back up your thinking?'

'What's your understanding of this situation? How did you reach this view?'

'What do you [think you] know?'

'What evidence is there to suggest otherwise?'

The 'consequences' question

'What would be the consequence of not addressing these issues?' (This question may serve as a wake-up call for some.)

Challenging behaviour

'What stops you doing this?'

'How would you feel if you were able to say sorry?'

'What would happen if you said sorry?'

Exploring and reframing perspectives

Considering others' viewpoints

'If a group of your colleagues were to listen in on your discussion now, what might they say?'

'If you were able to observe yourselves speaking at the moment, what observations do you think you might have?'

'What would an independent observer make of this current situation?'

'If we were to put this to [the other party], how do you think they might respond?'

Imagine role-play

'Imagine you're watching this… What would you be thinking at this point?'

'How might this stand up in front of a jury?'

Visioning

(Taking a future perspective):

The '10:10:10' question: 'What will this look like in 10 days? … 10 weeks? … 10 months?' (May help put an issue into perspective.)

'Imagine that you're working together and your differences have been resolved. What's the first charge you notice? What's happening? … What are the benefits for you? … For others? … For the organization?'

'If I were to talk to you in six weeks' time, what will be different when these issues are solved? … What will others notice?'

'How do you see your relationship in the future?' 'What would you be saying/doing/feeling?'

'What should you stop/start/continue doing?'

Considering alternatives

'What other ways could you look at/explain this?'

'What are the possible outcomes?'

'How might a devil's advocate respond to this viewpoint?'

Encouraging conversation

Selling the benefits of talking about a concern

'Would it help to talk to someone who's not involved in this?'

'Would it help if we went and found a quiet place for a coffee?'

'I'm not here to judge.' (Offers reassurance that to engage is safe.)

'It doesn't seem to me that you're making much headway sorting this out alone. Can we talk?' (Challenging the current situation.)

'Is there anything I can do that would make it easier for you to explain this?'

Negotiation

Identifying tradable concessions

'What are you prepared to give up [compromise] to achieve this?'

'What's it worth to you to achieve this?'

'How important is this for you [use scaling]?'

'What's the best way forward for reaching an agreement?'

Reaching agreement

Confirming each individual is comfortable with proposals made

'Do we have a common agreement on this?'

'Is there anything else you want to add, [name of each individual, asked in turn]?'

'On a scale… where are you now compared to when we started the session?' (If an individual's rating is higher than before, ask: 'What is it that's different that has got you to this?' If a score is lower, ask: 'What's made things fall back?')

Checking commitment

'When will you carry out [the agreed action point]?'

'What's the first step you will take after you leave this meeting today?'

'What can you control?'

Scaling

'On a scale of 1 to 10, where 1 means "not at all important", how committed are you to seeing this through?'

'What is working to get you to a 5?' (Build on what's working.)

'Would doing more of that enable you to move from a [5] to a [6]?' 'How committed are you to making this happen? … When will you do this?'

'Would you be willing to send me an e-mail/phone me when you've achieved [this]?'

'What will you do in the coming week?'

Handling deviations and backsliding

Directing and focusing attention on relevant topics

'What's best for us to focus on now?'

'How does this fit with what we've already discussed?'

'Let's please remind ourselves of the ground-rules we agreed to respect...'.

'Might we be moving away from the agreement we made earlier to be open with each other?'

Clarifying the reason for backsliding

'When you had made progress, you agreed that... [had rated progress since we started speaking on a scale at '7'] ... Where are you now? ... What has caused you to come to this point?'

Direct challenges to advice from third-parties

(For example, lobbyists):

'What are the consequences of continuing with this particular approach?' (The 'consequences' question can be especially powerful in focusing minds where serious consequences may result from a particular course of action.)

'What effect are external influences having on you reaching an agreement?'

'Might there be alternatives that would also work for you?'

Hard conversations

Confronting a difficult issue ('ILRAG')

Introductory statement ('There's a matter I need to discuss today. This may be uncomfortable...').

Labelling statement ('We've had several conversations about..., however this is still an issue').

Rationale: ('It's clear we need to try something else...').

Assertive statement ('I've decided that...').

Give opportunity for response ('Do you have any immediate comments or suggestions to make? ... Should we meet again?').

Cutting to the chase ('SAW')

SAW offers a simple approach for managers who need to label or confront a matter that is likely to be uncomfortable for a team member. This offers a dialogue structure for moving onto the difficult subject matter quickly:

Situation statement – summary of situation, eg, 'After we met last time, you agreed to support and work with me; this is repeatedly not happening. For example...'.

Action or assessment statement – giving supporting evidence (what needs to happen or what will happen, eg, 'This isn't a satisfactory way for us to continue to work together. In future, I cannot be exposed in the way you've left me until now. You can either choose to work with me or not, but I need to know either way').

Wrap up – clarify, ensure all is clear, wrap up the conversation, eg, 'Can we please agree a new way forward, so that we won't have to speak about this issue again?'

Breaking log jams and problem solving

Breaking down a problem

'Which of the options we've discussed already feels most manageable?'

'How might we break this down?'

'How do you see this as being feasible?' (Helps reflection on the causes of a logjam and in moving an individual towards having a more open mind.)

'Are we dealing with a puzzle here, where we have all the pieces for a solution but can't yet see how to put them together?'

The 'meta distancing' approach

(Helping individuals to consider the 'bigger picture' of the jam they are in, by inviting them to imagine that they could stand back from the detail of their situation and look from the outside in):

'Imagine that this situation is being depicted in a movie. How would you describe the scene as if you were watching it on screen?'

'Imagine that you are hovering in a helicopter over the situation you are in now... you may need to imagine that you are in the open! What can you observe from this distance?'

'Solution-focused circle'

This approach involves a small group of managers or mediators meeting periodically to jointly consider a current conflict management issue brought by one member of the group. Such meetings need take only a brief amount of time if they adopt the following format:

1. The individual bringing the issue briefly states its nature and outlines the challenge he or she is facing.

2. Other members of the group then ask a question in turn to qualify their appreciation of the situation, whilst helping the problem owner to deepen his or her thinking about the situation.

3. Members of the group continue to ask questions in succession, but without offering comment (the sequence for asking questions is passed over to the next person in the circle if an individual doesn't have a question to ask).

4. Each circle member gives an affirmation to the issue holder. This is important as this is where actions tend to spring forth. If an individual doesn't have an authentic affirmation, then this may just pass.

5. After 10 minutes or so, the round of questioning is brought to a close and the problem owner is then invited to take time away from the group to reflect on what has been discussed.

6. The remaining individuals then consider their own responses to what they have heard, identifying possible courses of action that may help the problem owner move forward.

7. The issue holder then feeds back to the group what he or she found useful and whether any actions came about. Did anything give the issue holder a fresh perspective?

8. After reconvening, the reflections are shared.

Responding to unexpected disclosures

Checking how a disclosure assists each party's understanding of the wider situation

'How do you now feel as a result of sharing this?'

'How does this new piece of information help your understanding of (the other person's) perspective/affect your current thinking?' (Remind individuals of their commitment to work toward an effective outcome.)

'Can you describe what you are thinking?'

Appendix 2

Templates

TEMPLATES FOR MANAGERS AND MEDIATORS

Stakeholder analysis

Both 'inner circle' and more peripheral stakeholders can have an important part to play in how a dispute is managed, as well as having differing needs to be kept informed about progress or be engaged with the process. The grid in Figure A2.1 on the next page helps a mediator keep track of these different players and their interests.

Mediator Person Specification

Summary

In-house mediators play a crucial role in attempting to resolve disputes between individuals and teams. Very often, a mediator's skilful intervention can allow disputing parties to settle their differences without a need for further escalation. By helping to facilitate an acceptable outcome for each party and through assisting individuals to gain insight and a fresh perspective on their situation, expensive and potentially damaging litigation or other public dispute resolution might be avoided, whilst increasing the prospect that the dispute won't recur between the two parties at a later time.

Competency and knowledge requirements

■ Excellent 'essential skills' (listening, questioning, engaging and building rapport).

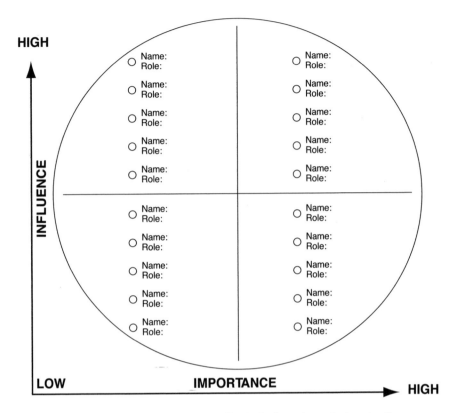

HIGH

INFLUENCE

Name:
Role:

Name:
Role:

Name:
Role:

Name:
Role:

Name:
Role:

Name:
Role:

Name:
Role:

Name:
Role:

Name:
Role:

Name:
Role:

Name:
Role:

Name:
Role:

Name:
Role:

Name:
Role:

Name:
Role:

Name:
Role:

Name:
Role:

Name:
Role:

Name:
Role:

Name:
Role:

LOW   **IMPORTANCE**   **HIGH**

Use the grid to identify stakeholders according to the importance for keeping them informed or engaged and their level of influence in supporting the outcome of the dispute. Colour coding may be used to identify each person or group marker (○), eg to distinguish active participants from those who have an immediate interest in the outcome, those who may need to be informed if the dispute escalates further, known/ unknown motivations and perspectives taken by each, etc. The choice of coding (if any is used) is discretionary.

A copy of this template, together with a worked example, may be downloaded from www.managingconflictatwork.com

Figure A2.1   Stakeholder analysis

- ▨ Well-developed emotional intelligence.
- ▨ Diplomacy.
- ▨ Excellent time management.
- ▨ Creative problem solving (eg, proposing possible ways for breaking a dead-lock).

Ability to:

- Maintain group control through adversity.
- Track multiple conversation threads and to see potential interactions between them.
- Conceive and present multiple scenarios (eg, alternative explanations).
- Confront potentially uncomfortable issues in a sensitive manner.
- Articulate points clearly.
- Lead and navigate a complex discussion.
- Quickly engage with and work in cooperation with a co-mediator.
- Defuse and redirect destructive behaviours and conversations, assertively but without undermining individuals' trust or integrity.
- Circumvent repetitive or unnecessarily overplayed discussion on a specific point.
- Achieve consensus.
- Achieve agreement and test commitment to follow through with pledges and actions agreed in conversations.
- Probe the reality of beliefs and claims.
- Close out a dialogue effectively and efficiently.
- Constructively challenge.
- Observe without evaluating.

Personal attributes

The person will be:

- Thoughtful.
- Non-judgemental.
- Confident.
- Self-controlled.
- Non-aggressive.
- Tolerant.
- Patient.
- Empathetic.
- Self-aware.
- Calm and having a calming manner.
- Gently relentless (positive attitude).

TEMPLATES FOR INDIVIDUALS WHO ARE IN CONFLICT

Thought pattern critique

The aim of this technique is to encourage individuals to consider whether they may want to reframe their certainty about a particular perspective or explanation, allowing themselves time to reflect on other possibilities and to assess how likely they consider these to be by 'sleeping on' their initial views. Typically (though not invariably), most individuals increase their ratings of possible alternatives after a break, being more likely to accept that their strongly held viewpoint might be open to question. The template for this technique is shown in Figure A2.2.

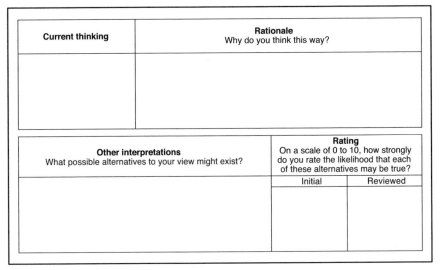

Start by writing down what your current interpretation of the situation is in the upper table (situations may include events, other people's positions, etc). Also write down the main reason(s) that have led you to hold this view. Next try to identify all possible alternative explanations that you can, noting these in the bottom table. Rate how likely you consider it is that each of these possibilities apply in this situation. Come back to what you've written after at least one day to see whether you feel you can revise your ratings.

A copy of this template, together with a worked example, may be downloaded from www.managingconflictatwork.com

Figure A2.2   Thought pattern critique

No-send Letter

As suggested by its name, a *No-send Letter* is simply a letter or e-mail that isn't sent to its intended recipient, but is written to allow the author to articulate what he or she would like to say and to help relieve angry emotions. In writing such a letter, an individual may actually consider sending it, but resolve to 'sleep on' the decision and to review what he or she has drafted at another time. This technique might seem to be artificial, but it can prove to be very effective for some (and especially those who like to write down how they feel and those who are inclined to act impulsively).

Channelling anger

The following conversation structure may help individuals confront an individual with whom they feel angry. Encourage them to take time to think through why it's reasonable to feel angry before broaching this with the other person. This may often mean delaying this 'clearing' process until later:

'I feel angry about...'.

'Because...'.

'What I would like is...'.

'For my part, I'll...'.

Volcano

Left unresolved, anger can build up within us until we feel we're ready to explode. When individuals can recognize this beginning to happen, the *volcano* approach should help them vent their anger in a positive way. A template is shown in Figure A2.3.

Other templates

A range of other templates can be downloaded from the website created to complement this book; see www.managingconflictatwork.com.

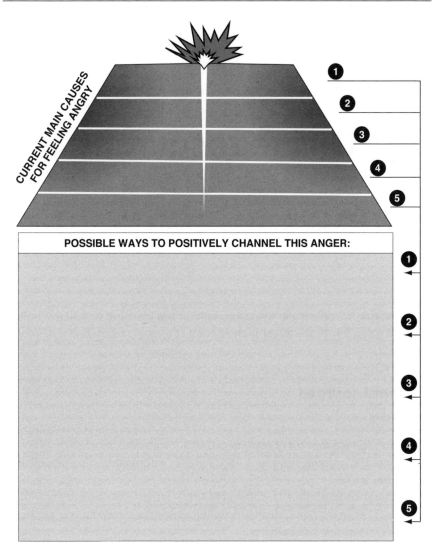

List the top five things that are causing you to feel angry at the moment in each of the 'strata' (rows) of the volcano. Next, consider and note in the lower box any ways in which you may be able to channel the anger you're feeling in a positive way (eg working out at the gym, writing a 'no-send letter', talking to a friend).

A copy of this template, together with a worked example, may be downloaded from www.managingconflictatwork.com

Figure A2.3   Volcano

Appendix 3

Online resources

A wide variety of valuable information, support and guidance is available online. Here are just a few of the many sources conflict managers may find it helpful to tap into.

National sources

Australia

Australian Human Resources Institute (AHRI) – www.ahri.com.au
   National HR institute, offering a wide range of information and news relating to workplace CM.
Institute of Arbitrators and Mediators (IAMA) – http://www.iama.org.au
   Network of ADR specialists (including workplace mediators), promotes standards, offers news and advice.
Victorian Association for Dispute Resolution Inc – www.vadr.asn.au
   Research and news source (for general DR, including workplace disputes).

Belgium

Centre Belge d'Arbitrage et de Médiation (CEPANI) – www.cepani.be
   Promotes the use of arbitration and mediation, offering research insights and news of recent developments in DR.

Canada

ADR Institute of Canada Inc – www.adrcanada.ca
Not-for-profit organization offering information and member contact information.

Human Resources and Skills Development Canada – www.hrsdc.gc.ca
Government department promoting healthy work relations. Offers news, information and resources.

France

Association Française d'Arbitrage (AFA) – www.afa-arbitrage.com
Association of mediators and arbitrators in France, providing regulatory news and information about ADR services.

Germany

Deutsche Institution für Schiedsgerichtsbarkeit (DIS) – www.dis-arb.de
Institute for arbitration, offering news, events, contacts and information about employment regulation.

Hong Kong

Hong Kong Institute of Arbitrators (HKIArb) – www.hkiarb.org.hk
Charitable organization created to promote ADR. Offers news, events and regulatory information.

India

Indian Institute of Arbitration and Mediation – www.arbitrationindia.com
Not-for-profit organization offering training, accreditation and member contact information.

Ireland, Republic of

Labour Relations Commission – www.lrc.ie
Conducts research and provides advice in addition to offering industrial relations and workplace conciliation and mediation services.

Mediators' Institute of Ireland – www.themii.ie
Professional association for mediators, offering training, research papers and advice on continuous professional development.

Japan

Japan Commercial Arbitration Association (JCAA) – www.jcaa.or.jp
   Institution and ADR portal (mainly relating to commercial arbitration). Offers advice and regulatory news.

Netherlands

Nederlands Arbitrage Instituut – www.nai-nl.org
   Not-for-profit organization established to promote ADR in business.

New Zealand

Arbitrators' and Mediators' Institute of New Zealand Inc – www.aminz.org.nz
   Promotes DR for organizations and in the wider public domain.
Department of Labour – www.dol.govt.nz
   Offers a wide range of information and advice concerning employment relations and law.
LEADR NZ – www.leadr.co.nz
   DR advice, articles, training and accreditation.

Philippines

Philippine Dispute Resolution Center Inc (PDRCI) – www.pdrci.org
   Support, advice and information (biased towards commercial mediation, although also covering workplace disputes).

Republic of South Africa

Arbitration Foundation of Southern Africa (AFSA) – www.arbitration.co.za
   Network of ADR specialists, mainly for sourcing mediators and arbitrators but also offering training and accreditation.
Commission for Conciliation, Mediation and Arbitration (CCMA) – www.ccma.org.za
   Information sheets, templates and training relating to industrial relations, conflict prevention and workplace DR.

Singapore

Singapore International Arbitration Centre (SIAC) – www.siac.org.sg
   Primarily serves commercial and international company interests, but provides news and information for workplace DR in Singapore.

UAE

Dubai International Arbitration Centre – www.diac.ae

Centre for arbitration in Dubai, primarily serving commercial dispute interests, but with a valuable journal tracking regulatory changes throughout the Middle East.

UK

Advice Services Alliance (ASA) – www.adrnow.org.uk

General information on types of ADR, benefits and mediation scheme profiles, not just workplace-related.

Advisory, Conciliation and Arbitration Service (ACAS) – www.acas.org.uk

Government-supported not-for-profit organization dedicated to DR in the workplace, mainly industrial relations and providing arbitration, conciliation and mediation services, but also offering training and advice for UK businesses.

Centre for Effective Dispute Resolution (CEDR) – www.cedr.co.uk

A not-for-profit centre of excellence for developing knowledge, skills and awareness of ADR and preventive conflict.

Mediation Northern Ireland – www.mediationnorthernireland.org

A mediation development agency based in Belfast, including training, strategic CM capacity building in organizations and reflective leadership.

United States

American Arbitration Association University – www.aaauonline.org

Education and resource centre of the American Arbitration Association (AAA), offering training, reference materials, regulatory information and more. A broad range of DR services are offered by the AAA (www.adr.org) and its international division, ICDR (www.adr.org/about_icdr).

Federal Mediation and Conciliation Service (FMCS) – www.fmcs.gov

Agency dedicated to maintaining and promoting peaceful labour-management. Offers a range of DR services, in addition to news, training and other resources.

General

Association for Conflict Resolution – www.acrnet.org

Washington DC based organization offering news and information concerning varied CM applications.

International Conflict Management Forum (ICMF) –
www.conflictmanagementforum.org

A volunteer-run forum created to promote knowledge sharing, learning and awareness amongst anyone who has an interest in managing conflict at work. Provides a variety of online resources, including a members' bulletin board.

International Institute for Conflict Prevention and Resolution – www.cpradr.org

Extensive resource base, offering news, podcasts, training and information (varied conflict applications).

Managing Conflict at Work – www.managingconflictatwork.com

Dedicated website created to complement this book. Provides a range of tools and templates for download (including many featured in the book), articles, podcasts and videos featuring Clive and Jackie's dulcet tones!

Mediate.com – www.mediate.com

Comprehensive source of information, news and articles relating to mediation in many different fields. International forum for mediators.

Journals and newsletters

Note: many of these are not restricted to workplace DR.

Asian Dispute Review – www.asiandr.com (news and general articles, ASEAN countries)

Conflict Resolution Quarterly – www.josseybass.com/WileyCDA/WileyTitle/productCd-CRQ.html (general CM applications, worldwide)

DIAC Journal – Arbitration in the Middle East – www.diac.ae/idias/journal (ADR and regulation in the Middle East, UAE and GCC states)

Employment Law Memo – www.lawmemo.com (information on employment law cases and NLRB decisions, United States)

Employment Today – www.employmenttoday.co.nz (HR and employment law, New Zealand)

European Arbitration – www.interarb.com/ea (editorial on European DR)

ICMF News – www.ecmf.co.uk/emnews.php (newsletter of the ICMF, workplace conflict emphasis, worldwide)

Recent Developments in Dispute Resolution – www.willamette.edu/wucl/journals/wlo/dis-res/ (news information service maintained by the Center for Dispute Resolution at Willamette University and College of Law, United States)

References

Chapter 1

AAA (2006) *Dispute-wise Business Management – Improving economic and non-economic outcomes in managing business conflicts*, AAA, New York

Argyris, C (1957) *Personality and Organization: The conflict between system and the individual*, Harper & Row, New York

Barnaba, C (2009), http://www.conniebarnaba.com/costofconflict.html

Business Wire (10 October 2006) Litigation as a growth industry

Cantopher, T (2003) *Depressive Illness: The curse of the strong (overcoming common problems)*, Sheldon Press, London

CEDR (May 2006) *Conflict is costing business £33 billion every year*, accessed at www.cedr.com

Europa (2000) Equal Treatment in Employment and Occupation, Directive 2000/78/EC of 27 November 2000, Establishing a general framework for equal treatment in employment and occupation, European Union, 2000, http://europa.eu/scadplus/leg/en/cha/c10823.htm

Europa (2009) Council Directive 94/45/EC, Official Journal of the European Communities, No L 254/64, 30 September 1994, http://ec.europa.eu/employment_social/labour_law/docs/directive94_45_en.pdf

Freeman, D and Freeman, J (October 2008) *Paranoia: The 21st century fear* Oxford University Press, Oxford

Gibbons, M (2007) *Better Dispute Resolution: A review of employment dispute resolution in Great Britain*, BERR, London

Haslam, I and Willmott, B (October 2004) *Managing Conflict At Work* CIPD, London

Human Security Center (2005) *The Human Security Report 2005 – War and peace in the 21st century*, University of British Columbia, Oxford University Press, New York

Ignacio, R (2004) *Wars of the 21st Century – New threats, new fears*, p 140, Ocean Press, New York

Indus Business Journal online (2009) US legal costs soar

Johnson, R A (1978) *Management, Systems and Society: An introduction*, Goodyear Publishing, Miamisburg, OH, pp 138–42

Lapid-Bogda, G (2004) *Bringing out the Best in Yourself at Work*, McGraw-Hill, Maidenhead

McAuliffe, K (2009) Are we still evolving?, *Discover*, March, pp 51–58

McGregor, D (1960) *The Human Side Of Enterprise*, McGraw-Hill, Maidenhead

Maslow, A (1943) A theory of human motivation, *Psychological Review*, **50** (4), pp 370–96

Monaghan, J and Just, P (2000) *Social and Cultural Anthropology: A very short introduction*, Oxford University Press, Oxford

Sandole, D J D (1980) Conflict management: elements of generic theory and practice, in D J D Sandole and I Sandole-Staroste (eds), *Conflict Management and Problem Solving: Interpersonal to international applications*, Frances Pinter, London

Sandole, D J D (June 2002) Virulent ethnocentrism: a major challenge for transformational conflict resolution and peacebuilding in the post-cold war era, *The Global Review of Ethnopolitics*, **1** (4), p 13

Sherwood, J J and Glidewell, J G (1973) *Planned Renegotiation: A norm-setting OD intervention*, adapted by Lapid-Bogda, G (2004) *Bringing out the Best in Yourself at Work, How to use the Enneagram system for success*, McGraw-Hill, Maidenhead

Thurston, C Q (2008) *Developing a Comprehensive Framework for Conflict Analysis: Sources, Situation, Attitudes, Group Maintenance, Escalation (SSAGE)*, The RAND Corporation, ISA, San Francisco, CA

Uppsala University (source data for 2004) *Uppsala Conflict Database*, Department of Peace and Conflict Research

Wang, E T, Kodama, G, Baldi, P and Moyzis, R K (2006) Global landscape of recent inferred Darwinian selection for homo sapiens, *Proceedings of the National Academy of Sciences of the United States of America*, **103** (1), pp 135–40

Chapter 2

Blake, R and Mouton, J (1964) *The Managerial Grid: The key to leadership excellence*, Gulf Publishing, Houston, TX

Kraybill, R (2009) *Style Matters: The Kraybill conflict style inventory*, Riverside e-Press, Bury St Edmunds

Thomas, K W and Kilmann, R H (1974–2009) *Thomas-Kilmann Conflict Mode Instrument*, CPP, Mountain View, CA

Chapter 3

Berg, I K (1992) *Working With The Problem Drinker: A solution focused approach*, W W Norton, London

Bush, B R A and Folger, J P (2004) *The Promise Of Mediation: The transformative approach to conflict*, Jossey-Bass, San Francisco, CA

Cloke, K (2001) *Mediating Dangerously: The frontiers of conflict resolution*, Jossey-Bass, San Francisco, CA, p 5

De Shazer, S, Dolan, Y and Korman, H (2007) *More than Miracles: The state of the art of solution-focused brief therapy* (Haworth Brief Therapy), Haworth Press, London

Epstein, B (accessed 2009), Amazon.com review of Cloke, K (2001) *Mediating Dangerously: The frontiers of conflict resolution*

Gilhooley, D (2009) Judicial mediation – a different approach to alternative dispute resolution?, *The Times Higher Education Supplement*, 10 July

Melchin, K R and Picard, C A (2009) *Transforming Conflict through Insight*, University of Toronto Press, Toronto

Nagao, A and Page, N R (2005) *Narrative Mediation: An exercise in question asking*, July, accessed at www.mediate.com

Peacock, F (November 2000) *Water the Flowers Not the Weeds*, Open Heart Publishing, London

Weinberg, O and Coyle, M (2003) *Transformative Approach to Mediation: Radical insight or pie in the sky?*, Canadian Forum on Civil Justice (clearinghouse), April 16,
http://cfcj-fcjc.org/clearinghouse/drpapers/2003-dra/weinberg.pdf

Chapter 4

American Psychiatric Association (2000) *The Diagnostic and Statistical Manual of Mental Disorders IV*, Text Revision, APA, New York

Freeman, D and Freeman, J (October 2008) *Paranoia: The 21st Century Fear*, Oxford University Press

Hay, J (2007) *Reflective Practice and Supervision for Coaches*, Open University Press, p 30

Human Resources Leader (2006) Bosses: The big bullies, 28 November

Krishnamurt, J (1929) Cited in Rosenberg, M (2003) *Non-Violent Communication: A language of life*, Puddledancer Press

NIMH-ECA (1982–84) study cited in
  http://ocd.stanford.edu/about/prevalence.html

Chapter 5

CBS (2009) *60 Minutes Podcast – Don Hewitt*, 23 August
Dönges, J (2009) You are what you say, *Scientific American Mind*, **20** (4)
Hersey, P, Blanchard, K and Johnson, D (2008) *Management of Organizational Behavior: Leading human resources* (9th edn), Pearson Education, Upper Saddle River, NJ
Keisch, B (1984) *The Facilitator: Descriptions, responsibility, selection criteria*, Xerox, New York
Kets De Vries, M (2006) *The Leadership Mystique – Leading behaviour in the human enterprise*, Prentice Hall, Harlow, pp 110–12
Krakovsky, M 2009) The load of lying, *Scientific American Mind*, **20** (4)
Rosenberg, M B (2003) *Non-violent Communication – A language of life* (2nd edn), PuddleDancer Press, Encinitas, CA

Chapter 6

Bandler, R and Grinder, J (1979) *Frogs into Princes: Neuro-Linguistic Programming*, Real People Press, Moab, Utah
Baron-Cohen, S (2003), *The Essential Difference: The truth about the male and female brain*, Basic Books, New York
BBC interview (September 1998) A *Very Singular Man – A film portrait of Ted Heath*
Kipling, R (1902) *Just So Stories*, Puffin, London
Saxe, R (2009) Rebecca Saxe: How we read each other's minds (September), TED, http://www.ted.com/talks/rebecca_saxe_how_brains_make_moral_judgments.html
Whitworth, L, Kimsey-House, H and Sandahl-Davies, P (1998) *Co-active Coaching – New skills for coaching people toward success in work and life*, Black Publishing, Palo Alto, CA

Chapter 7

Cloke, K (2001) *Mediating Dangerously: The frontiers of conflict resolution*, Jossey-Bass, San Francisco, CA, p 108
Mitchell, C R (1991) *The Structure of International Conflict*, Macmillan, Basingstoke, p 99

Phillips, K W, Liljenquist, K and Neale, M A (2009) Is the pain worth the gain? The advantages and liabilities of agreeing with socially distinct newcomers, *Personality and Social Psychology Bulletin*, **35**, pp 336–50

Pruitt, D and Kim, S H (2004) *Social Conflict: Escalation, stalemate, and settlement* (3rd edn), McGraw-Hill, Maidenhead

Skelton, C and Hall, E (2001) *The Development of Gender Roles in Young Children, Research findings*, Equal Opportunities Commission, London

Sutherland, S (2007) *Irrationality*, Pinter & Martin, London

Wilmot, W and Hocker, J (2010) *Interpersonal Conflict* (8th edn), McGraw-Hill, Maidenhead

Chapter 8

BBC (10 September 2000) *Life in Pictures: Mo Mowlam* http://news.bbc.co.uk/1/hi/in_pictures/4742349.stm, August 2005, *Mowlam 'Sidelined By Blair'*, http://news.bbc.co.uk/1/hi/uk_politics/918365.stm

BBC (April 2009) *Horizon: How Violent Are You?*

Boseley, S (2009) A doctor writes: politicians' pride is a medical disorder, *The Guardian*, 28 March

Gray, J (2009) *Gray's Anatomy: Selected writings*, Allen Lane, London

Locard, E (1951) *La Défense Contre Le Crime*, Payot, Paris

O'Neill, B (2000) *Executive Coaching with Backbone and Heart: A systems approach to engaging leaders with their challenges*, Jossey-Bass, San Francisco, CA

Taylor, J (2007) *Ubu and The Truth Commission*, University of Cape Town Press, Cape Town

Chapter 9

Johnson, G and Scholes, K (1997) *Exploring Corporate Strategy*, Prentice Hall, Harlow

Chapter 10

Cantopher, T (2003) *Depressive Illness: The curse of the strong (overcoming common problems)*, Sheldon Press, London

Kline, N (1998) *Time to Think: Listening to ignite the human mind*, Cassell, London

Chapter 11

Baker, D, Greenberg, C and Hemingway, C (2006) *What Happy Companies Know: How the new science of happiness can change your company for the better*, Prentice Hall, Harlow

EAT (2009) *Employment Tribunal and EAT Statistics (GB)*, Tribunals Service, September

Kirkpatrick, D L (1998) *Evaluating Training Programs, The four levels* (2nd edn), Berrett-Koehler Publishers, Berlin

Minto, B (2001) *The Pyramid Principle*, Prentice Hall, Harlow

Reichheld, R (2006) *The Ultimate Question*, Harvard Business School Press, Harvard, MA

Tobin, D R (1998) *The Fallacy of ROI Calculations*, Corporate Learning Strategies, London

Index

NB: page numbers in *italic* indicate figures or tables